Followership in Action

Cases and Commentaries

Followership in Action

Cases and Commentaries

Lead Editor

Rob Koonce
Creighton University, Omaha, NE, USA

Associate Editors

Michelle C. Bligh
Neoma Business School, Mont-Saint-Aignan, France

Melissa K. Carsten
Winthrop University, Rock Hill, SC, USA

Marc Hurwitz
University of Waterloo, Waterloo, Canada

United Kingdom – North America – Japan
India – Malaysia – China

Emerald Group Publishing Limited
Howard House, Wagon Lane, Bingley BD16 1WA, UK

First edition 2016

Reprints and permissions service
Contact: permissions@emeraldinsight.com

British Library Cataloguing in Publication Data
A catalogue record for this book is available from the British Library

ISBN: 978-1-78560-948-0

ISOQAR certified Management System, awarded to Emerald for adherence to Environmental standard ISO 14001:2004.

Certificate Number 1985
ISO 14001

INVESTOR IN PEOPLE

As one who has witnessed and experienced the power of followers whose actions have ranged from indifference, harm, or goodness, I commend this book because it reminds us we all must act—act with conviction and courage to ensure the betterment of our institutions and society as a whole.

– Edith Eva Eger, Clinical Psychologist, Auschwitz Survivor

Once your eyes are opened to "followership," you will see it everywhere. This very fine collection of case studies and thought provoking essays sheds new light on the role that followership plays in every field from business to the arts, as well as the importance of followership to an organization's (and a leader's) success.

– Robert Kelley, Carnegie Mellon University

This book has everything – memorable teaching stories, academic analysis, global contributions, every day examples, headline grabbing events and provocative dialogue-starting questions. There isn't anything like it yet in the field of Followership. What a great addition!

– Ira Chaleff, Author, The Courageous Follower: Standing Up To and For Our Leaders, and Intelligent Disobedience: Doing Right When What You're Told To Do Is Wrong

Followership in Action reflects the vital interplay between practice and theory and theory and practice. The editors of this volume and each of the book's contributors, skillfully and creatively address the opportunities, challenges, and ethics of what it means to be leader and follower – the critical importance of generative capacity, interrelationships, and authentic engagement. It is an important contribution to the field that should be read by many.

– Hallie Preskill, Managing Director, FSG

Followership in Action gives a long overdue voice to the "silent partners" in the leader-follower relationship. This collection of engaging cases and commentaries provides readers with a scholarly and practical introduction to the challenges facing followers in business, education, the military, the government, and other settings. Theoretical commentary and discussion questions equip students, faculty and practitioners to explore these issues in depth.

Followership in Action is truly a global treatment of followership, with contributors drawn from Europe, Asia, the United Kingdom and North America.

– Craig E. Johnson, Professor of Leadership Studies, George Fox University and Author, Meeting the Ethical Challenges of Leadership

Without Followership, there can't be Leadership! Drawn from business, education, the arts, government and the military, these crisp and compelling stories are a "must read" for all who want their workplace to be productive and their organization to be at the top of its game.

– Meena S. Wilson, Senior Enterprise Associate, Center for Creative Leadership India and Author, Developing Tomorrows' Leaders Today: Insights from Corporate India

Contents

List of Contributors

Rodger Adair	DeVry University, Mesa, AZ, USA
Tanuja Agarwala	Faculty of Management Studies, University of Delhi, Delhi, India
Sharon Armstead	Texas State University, Cedar Park, TX, USA
Paul Berg	U.S. Army Command and General Staff College, Fort Leavenworth, KS, USA
Thomas Bisschoff	College of Social Sciences, University of Birmingham, Birmingham, UK
B. Ariel Blair	Claremont Graduate University, Claremont, CA, USA
Michelle C. Bligh	Neoma Business School, Mont-Saint-Aignan, France
Melissa K. Carsten	Winthrop University, Rock Hill, SC, USA
Sandra Corlett	Newcastle Business School, Northumbria University, Newcastle upon Tyne, UK
Eric Downing	Pioneer Investments, Inc., Boston, MA, USA
Debra Finlayson	Vertical Bridge Corporate Consulting Inc., Vancouver, Canada
Andrew Francis	Hertfordshire Business School, University of Hertfordshire, Hatfield, UK
Heather Getha-Taylor	School of Public Affairs and Administration, University of Kansas, Lawrence, KS, USA

William S. Harvey	University of Exeter Business School, Exeter, UK
Marc Hurwitz	University of Waterloo, Waterloo, Canada
Eric K. Kaufman	Honors Residential College, Virginia Tech, Blacksburg, VA, USA
Susan Keim	Donnelly College, Kansas City, KS, USA
Kimberley A. Koonce	Ohio Christian University, Circleville, OH, USA
Rob Koonce	Creighton University, Omaha, NE, USA
Karlijn Kouwenhoven	Deloitte Consulting, Den Haag, The Netherlands
Suzanne Martin	transform., Birmingham, AL, USA
Rachael Morris	Newcastle Business School, Northumbria University, Newcastle upon Tyne, UK
Jennifer Moss Breen	Creighton University, Omaha, NE, USA
TamilSelvan Ramis	HELP University, Kuala Lumpur, Malaysia
Kae Reynolds	The Business School, University of Huddersfield, Huddersfield, UK
Rushton 'Rusty' Ricketson Sr	Luther Rice College and Seminary, Lithonia, GA, USA
Rhonda K. Rodgers	Claremont Graduate University, Claremont, CA, USA
Sonya Rogers	Columbia Southern University, Orange Beach, AL, USA
James H. Schindler	Columbia Southern University, Orange Beach, AL, USA
Steven Lee Smith	Co-Founder, The Human Business, Flagstaff, AZ
Eugene Y. J. Tee	HELP University, Kuala Lumpur, Malaysia

Douglas S. E. Teoh	University of Nottingham, Malaysia Campus, Semenyih, Malaysia
Ted Thomas	U.S. Army Command and General Staff College, Fort Leavenworth, KS, USA
Rens van Loon	Tilburg University, Tilburg, The Netherlands
W. David Winner	Regent University, Virginia Beach, VA, USA

Introduction

Research suggests that followers contribute an average of 80% to the success of organizations. Yet leading management scholars have argued for nearly a century that we too often assume the contributions of followers are an effect rather than a cause of that success. *Followership in Action* responds to this assumption by offering compelling cases and commentaries written from the diverse perspectives of more than 30 scholars and practitioners from Canada, France, India, Malaysia, the Netherlands, the United Kingdom, and the United States who lend support to the notion that followership is more than an outcome of leadership.

Although followership as a formal discipline is less than a century old, the applied organizational contexts of followership have existed since antiquity. As the study of followership further escalates into the global mainstream of leadership studies, the need accelerates for leaders to enable followers to be more productive for the cause. Through the use of story in case studies, scholarly post-commentaries, and discussion questions posed for furthering classroom and organizational dialogue, *Followership in Action* offers an excellent way to more proactively engage future leaders and followers in issues that they are likely to face in various organizational settings.

Followership in Action is a highly practical and scholarly book to which leadership scholars, practitioners, and students will actively turn to better understand and apply followership theory to everyday human resource development, management, and leadership contexts. It was written with administrators, coaches, consultants, executives, human resource professionals, academic professors, and support staff fully in mind. Its content will appeal to academia, corporations, non-profits, and other for profit enterprises.

Editorial Reflection

Several years ago, I vividly remember being first introduced to the term *organizational capacity*. I deeply resonated with the potential of the term and have since been captivated by its implications. Over the past decade, the relevance of the term has become increasingly noteworthy to me as the result of what I continue to see and experience in the world.

In the pursuit of my doctoral studies, my thoughts concerning organizational capacity turned to an organization's *relational capacity*. Well into the literature review for my dissertation, I literally stumbled across a journal article on verbal communication that specifically referenced the term *leader-follower* relations. It was a defining moment that extended well beyond what I was researching at the time. It altered the trajectory of my professional life.

I would be remiss not to mention a third term that stirred my passion for wanting to write this book. Appreciative Inquiry teaches that the *generative capacity* of an organization is limited by our appreciation for what is, imagining what might be, determining what should be, and creating what will be. This generativity, or lack thereof, begins with individuals who as active and passive participants influence relationships which, in turn, drive organizational processes.

ORGANIZATIONAL CAPACITY, RELATIONAL CAPACITY, AND GENERATIVE CAPACITY

Each of these provocative notions feed my interest in followership and leadership. In the complex and ever changing world in which we live, leading and following is at the heart of generative organizational processes. To accept something less than what an organization is capable of achieving is truly beyond me, yet as evidenced by the cases and commentaries in this book, organizations do it every day. An understanding of, and appreciation for, followership in the leadership literature can lead to more generative organizational processes. It was for this purpose that this book was written. This point also leads to a bigger question that was first entertained in writing the proposal for the book, that is, how can we teach these ideas to others? How can we more effectively integrate followership into our leadership curricula and workplace settings?

An initial response to that question came one day while using two of my favorite texts for teaching negotiation and conflict resolution. One of the texts is more scholarly, while the other is more practical. I have always been drawn by the ability to practically apply what I am teaching to others. I asked the question of what those two texts might look like if combined into a single text. That initial mental note ultimately led to the creation of *Followership in Action*.

Followership in Action was purposely written with three different audiences in mind: scholars, practitioners, and students. Each of the contributors to this groundbreaking volume on followership was made keenly aware of the editors' intentions to address these unique audiences while offering content to which each audience would relate. We believe that our desire has been firmly captured in the following pages by those who have constructed the cases and commentaries in this book. We thank each of the authors of this volume for their unique contribution. We also wish to thank Emerald Group Publishing for having the vision to pursue this project.

We now invite each reader to stand with us on the stairs of *Followership in Action* as it relates to the various topics of the book which include the arts, business, education, ethics, and government. We hope that you enjoy what this book offers and wish to hear how you are using it in your academic classroom or other corporate, for-profit, not-for-profit, or non-profit setting.

Rob Koonce
Lead Editor

Section I
Business

CHAPTER

1 All in "The Family": Leading and Following through Individual, Relational, and Collective Mindsets

Rob Koonce

Jon and KayAnn described their first experience in meeting Jim Madden, the CEO of AmTour, Inc., as something that had come straight out of a manual for how to build a positive relationship between a franchisor and franchisees. Jon and KayAnn were aspiring entrepreneurs and AmTour, Inc. seemed like the opportunity of a lifetime. Give up everything that you have financially, sign a multi-year contract, and off you go. Like so many franchisees before them, they were drawn by the opportunity to chase the dream of owning a business and franchising seemed so attractive. AmTour's professional marketing program offered just what they needed to attract clients and Jon and KayAnn were promised the independence that they desired to run the franchise as they saw fit. After hearing Jim Madden's initial sales pitch and meeting some of AmTour's key staff and successful franchisees, Jon and KayAnn were raring to go.

Many years later as I sat with Jon and KayAnn recounting the details of their former affiliation with AmTour, Inc., Jon recalled being hyperenergized by what he and KayAnn had experienced in their first year as franchise owners. He spoke openly about what the first convention had meant to him. It was all about hearing how other franchisees had successfully built million dollar enterprises and meeting newcomers like he and KayAnn. In the opening ceremony, Jon vividly recalled a popular post-grunge song from the late 1990s blasting in the background as one after another photo of happy franchise owners flashed before them. Jon said, "For whatever reason, I deeply connected to the lyrics of that song as I saw all of those happy faces. The entire experience seemed too good to be true. In that brief moment, I became fixated by the thought that we would be next! That thought never left me in our first year with AmTour, Inc. I truly felt like I was a part of something bigger than myself."

"At the end of its first year of operation, our franchise was celebrated as one of the most successful newcomers in the entire AmTour, Inc. franchise system." Jon added, "The night of the awards ceremony was one of the proudest moments of my life. When we returned home following that meeting, I remember being pumped to contribute, motivated to perform, and happy that we had become part of what CEO Jim Madden liked to commonly refer to as 'The AmTour Family'. The company was growing by leaps and bounds with vendors from all over the world who were rapidly becoming a part of the system. It just seemed that we could do no wrong, but the months that followed would begin to tell something more about 'the family'."

When I asked Jon to tell me a bit more, he paused to collect his thoughts. He continued, "Several years later, the whole experience is still so real. My wife and I had absolutely poured our souls into creating what we did over that prior year. Neither of us had ever worked that hard. It was so difficult, but so rewarding and something that you could never, never forget. With rare exception, we loved our clients and our clients loved us. I can truly say that. We took care of each other. Some were more collaborative than others, but we always tried to at least be collegial. In the end, some things worked better than others, but that experience left such a deep impression on me about the importance of relationships – not just having them, but how we approach them." [Jon paused to reflect]

"If there was ever an element of family buried within AmTour, Inc., it was expressed between the franchise owner and their clients. As I think about it, I could also say the same thing about the vendors with whom we worked the most. We fully supported each other and enjoyed what we were constantly attempting to create on behalf of our growing list of clients. If something went wrong, we corrected it while trusting each other in the process. I was always grateful for those jobs because our relationships with vendors were also tied to relationships that we had built over time with our clients. We protected those relationships by constantly delivering on what we had promised. Early on, we had to scramble to get potential customers to trust us with their work. As that trust grew, the collaboration ensued and clients began giving us bigger and bigger jobs as they also referred us to people that they knew. Our franchise benefited greatly through word of mouth. The best relationships that we developed with vendors and clients became more than a collaboration; they were cohesive." [Jon paused]

"I will never forget one job that we were doing for an association which represented an internationally renowned list of clients. Two days before this huge event for which they had entrusted an incredible amount of work to our franchise, the vendor with whom we had been doing more and more jobs delivered a final product to us that did not exactly come out as we had planned. Frantically, I called the vendor, described the problem, and told them that I needed this huge job to be reproduced and redelivered overnight. If we failed this one, we were toast with this client and in our business community because everything that we were doing for them was so tightly interconnected! Instead of pointing fingers at each other, they immediately swung into action and we pulled that event off without a hitch. Everyone raved about what we had produced. As we heard the raves, I stopped to ask myself what the result may have been if we had resorted to ranting about 'who did what' wrong. What we had pulled off was nearly impossible to do, but the importance of the relationship between our franchise and the vendor made it happen. As a result of that job, the client loved our franchise even more and we established an even deeper bond with the vendor and in our business community. What's wrong with that picture? Nothing. Without the ability to dialogue with vendors and clients about problems that we all occasionally faced, our best relationships and our best work never would have surfaced. It is really amazing when you stop to consider just how much dialogue matters to relationships. It demanded a different mindset than you typically see in business. That thought has never left me."

Jon continued, "What I just described is a far cry from what we experienced with Jim Madden and company. With all due respect, the AmTour staff were almost always courteous to us when we called to make occasional requests for marketing and other materials to help with the promotion of our franchise, but those calls were never based on something that I would describe as collaborative or cohesive. Those conversations were more about being collegial with one another; checking off boxes in a daily routine. Contrast that courtesy with one of the most tell-all times that we experienced with AmTour, Inc. One day about a year into our franchise, a senior administrator of AmTour, Inc. announced that they were planning to switch out accounting systems. That idea seemed innocent enough, but how AmTour carried out that process told so much of what we and other franchisees, vendors, and clients who were a part of the AmTour system would begin to learn about how "the family" really operated. In two months, AmTour was going to pull the plug on their existing accounting system that controlled virtually everything related to franchisees, vendors, customer accounts, you name it, and turn on a new system. When a group of franchise owners inquired what that meant for franchisees, we were all simply told not to worry. After all, everything had been carefully planned out by corporate (unfortunately without any input from franchise owners, vendors, or clients). The processing system for all orders, invoices, and payments for more than 200 franchisees and literally thousands of vendors and clients would be down for a maximum of 24 hours, and on the following day, voila!, the whole system would move forward (or so we were told)."

"What we did not know at the time was no parallel testing with the current system had been performed prior to this switchover that controlled the entire system. Again, we are talking about hundreds of franchisees and vendors and thousands of clients ranging from small mom and pop shop clients to massive, global organizations. We were all being told that some grand plan was in place. Yet, 48 hours after the old accounting system had been switched off, we were told they had discovered 'a small glitch' in the new system. In reality, the new system was not working. Once again, however, we were told that everything was under control. 'No problem', said Jim Madden and literally everyone with whom you were allowed to speak about the matter at corporate HQ. Give it a couple of days and everything will be just fine. Literally six weeks after this switchover occurred, dismayed franchise owners began to pressure CEO Madden for answers. Madden finally admitted that the problem had been a bit larger than AmTour had initially imagined. The problem with that six week period is that all franchisee accounts were down across the entire system, clients who had already paid their outstanding invoices weeks ago were increasingly upset by the overdue notices that they were being sent regarding 'unpaid bills', and vendors began calling franchisees wondering when they were going to be paid for work that had already been performed. During this same six week period, franchise owners were not being paid for completed jobs while senior administrators to include CEO Jim and all other corporate employees at AmTour's HQ miraculously never missed a beat with their own paychecks. To be frank, the entire system was in survival mode and no one at AmTour's HQ seemed to be truly concerned about it. In the meantime, our bills did not stop coming. It took them another two months to correct the error and we were left holding the bag. It made you wonder if these people really knew what they were doing and, yet, you suddenly realized just how much control that they had over your client's money, your vendor's money, and your own money. That doesn't even include the time that we had invested in establishing and maintaining all of our client and vendor relationships. What was important to us just seemed so unimportant to AmTour, Inc. and yet we had totally bought into this idea that we were part of this big happy family. What a mess!"

"We had sacrificed everything that we had to be a part of that system. Our dreams and hard work were wrapped up in a system which had been reduced to little more than a contractual arrangement that was increasingly difficult to support or imagine. The more that we examined the series of events that had occurred, the more that we and other franchise owners felt like we had all become part of a system that was closed, one-sided, and uninterested in receiving feedback from the rest of the system. After nearly being bankrupted emotionally and financially three months into that mind-numbing process, we finally cashed in our remaining chips and moved on."

Scholarly Commentary

> ... Reality is made up of circles but we see straight lines. Herein lies the beginnings of our limitation ... What we see depends on what we are prepared to see ... we need a language of interrelationships .... (p. 73)
>
> ... Hierarchy is antithetical to dialogue ... If one person is used to having his view prevail because he is the most senior person, then that privilege must be surrendered ... If one person is used to withholding his views because he is more junior, then that security of nondisclosure must also be surrendered .... (p. 288) (Peter M. Senge, *The Fifth Discipline*)

Leadership and followership are often viewed through a hierarchical lens in which leaders are superior and followers are inferior due to the respective professional roles played by each in the hierarchy. In stark contrast to this understanding, Burns (1978) suggests that leadership is relational, collective, and purposeful and acts toward goals that represent the values and motivations of leaders and followers alike (pp. 18–19). Burns also notes that leaders who attempt to control things do so out of an act of power, not leadership (p. 18). In retrospect, AmTour, Inc. could have learned a thing or two from Burns' suggestions.

Stemming from lessons learned from this case, the author defines leadership as a socially co-constructed and emergent process through which people in their respective roles individually, relationally, and collectively lead and follow other people through recurrent intra-agency and inter-agency interactions in the dynamic and purposeful pursuit of intertwining organizational goals and initiatives. As described in prior research, leadership is not about individuals; it is an expressed relationship between individuals (Hollander, 1992; Howell & Shamir, 2005; Shamir & Eilam, 2005). Leadership is not limited to formal relationships in an organizational hierarchy (Meindl, 1995; Schein, 2015); nor, as a relational (Uhl-Bien, 2006) or collective (Barnes & Kriger, 1987) reality, is it confined to a single organization. Leadership potentially extends to those with whom an organization has interdependencies (Adner, 2012; Edmondson, 2012; Hosking, 2007) such as suppliers, consumers, and others who in some way impact, or are affected by, an organization's activities. The intra-agency and inter-agency interdependencies of AmTour, Inc. perfectly illustrate these points (see Figure 1). The intra-agency and inter-agency dynamics of AmTour, Inc. include the hierarchy of its senior leaders, middle managers, and non-managerial staff, as well as the non-hierarchical relationships between hundreds of franchisees, a global network of vendors, and a countless list of clients who collectively comprise the various interdependencies of the AmTour franchising system.

As noted in Figure 2, four socially co-constructed patterns emerge from this interdependent framework which relate to the coordinated efforts and collective actions of the respective agencies and their constituents in the pursuit of intertwining goals and initiatives.

The coordinated efforts and collective actions of the four socially co-constructed patterns are respectively referred to as a *people orientation* and a *process orientation.* The people orientation refers to the coordination of individual, relational, and collective efforts and the process orientation refers to the collective actions of the respective agencies and their constituents in the individual, relational, and collective pursuit of intertwining goals and initiatives. The four socially co-constructed patterns include (a) a *contractual orientation* in which minimal to moderate emphasis is directed toward people and processes; (b) a *collegial orientation* in which minimal to moderate emphasis is directed toward people and moderate to maximal emphasis is directed toward processes; (c) a *collaborative orientation* in which moderate to maximal emphasis is directed toward people and minimal to moderate emphasis is directed toward processes; and (d) a *cohesive orientation* in which moderate to maximal emphasis is directed toward people and processes.

At any given time, all four socially co-constructed patterns are assumed to be present as represented by the coordinated efforts and collective actions of the respective agencies and their constituents. As described, not all socially co-constructed patterns in the model may have the same needs, for example, some organizational

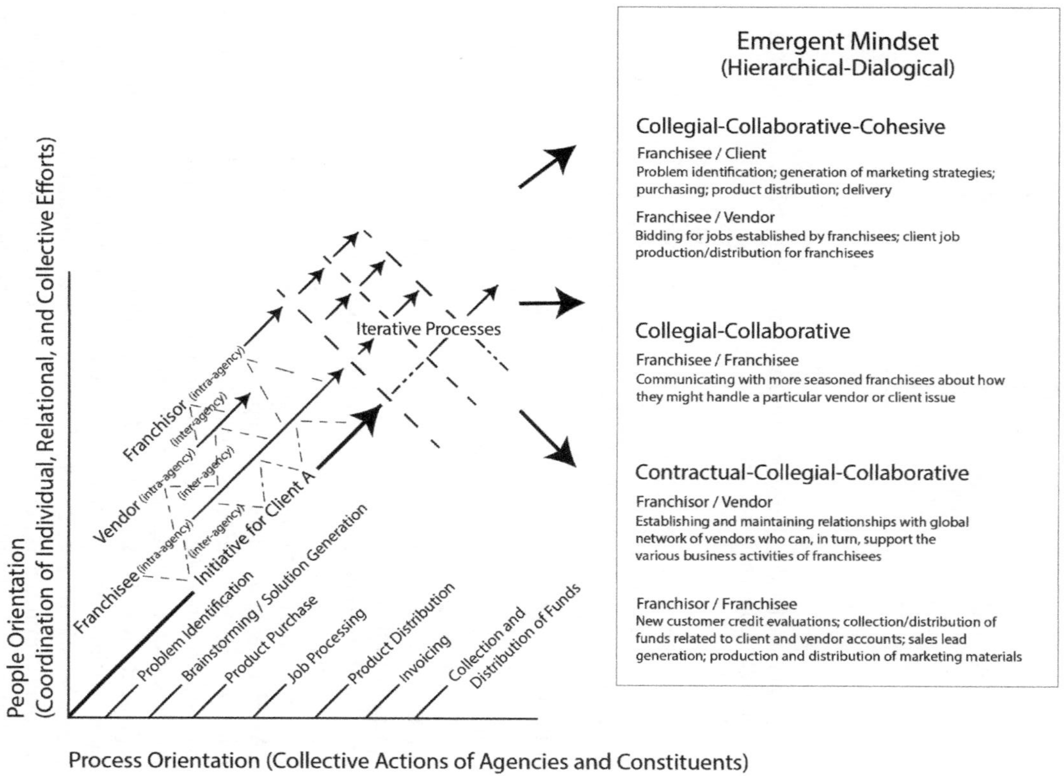

Figure 1. Graphical Representation of Intra-Agency and Inter-Agency Interdependencies within a Global Franchising System.

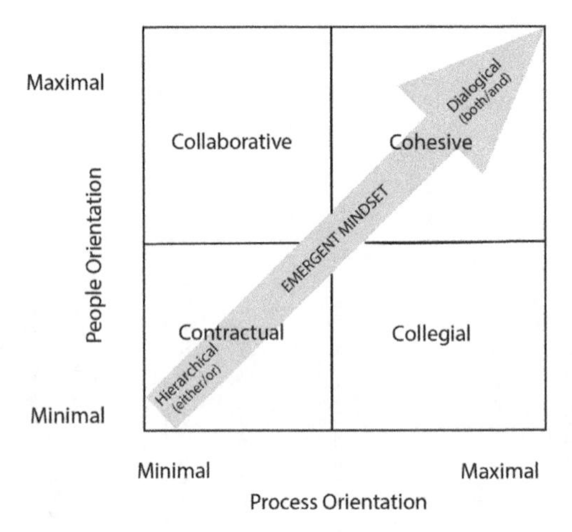

Figure 2. Emergent Mindset (Hierarchical-Dialogical) from which Each Socially Co-constructed Pattern Dynamically Flows.

initiatives may be more interdependent (Marchington & Vincent, 2004) and therefore more contingent upon rapport building and long-term considerations (Collins, 2001; Rogers, 1995), while others may be one-off dependencies in which a contractual or collegial orientation may seem more practical given the additional organizational resources that may be necessary for more collaborative (Bradbury-Huang, Lichtenstein, Carroll, & Senge, 2010; Isaacs, 1993) and cohesive orientations. Independent of these limitations, all agencies can potentially benefit from the model's considerations.

As also noted in Figure 2, each modeled orientation is further represented by an *emergent mindset* from which each socially co-constructed pattern of people and process dynamically flows. EACH emergent mindset is representative of either a *hierarchical mindset* or a *dialogical mindset.* A hierarchical mindset is symbolic of an *either/or* orientation (DeRue, 2011) for each socially co-constructed pattern, whereas a dialogical mindset is representative of a *both/and* orientation (Wheatley, 2006) for each socially co-constructed pattern. A hierarchical mindset is characteristic of a contractual or a collegial orientation, whereas a dialogical mindset is representative of a collaborative or a cohesive orientation. A hierarchical mindset is an individual (self), relational (e.g., dyadic), or collective (e.g., team or organizational) approach which leaders use to exercise authority and control over followers in the pursuit of inter-agency and intra-agency organizational goals and initiatives. In direct contrast, a dialogical mindset is an individual (self), relational (e.g., dyadic), or collective (e.g., team or organizational) approach which people use to lead and follow other people in the pursuit of goals and initiatives. As proposed, each socially co-constructed pattern (SCP) of leading and following can be represented by the following formula:

$$\text{SCP} = \text{people orientation} + \text{process orientation} + \text{emergent mindset}$$

Conclusion

In the pursuit of intertwining goals and initiatives, any socially co-constructed pattern of leadership or followership has the potential capacity from which to benefit or be hindered by the coordinated efforts, collective actions, and emergent mindsets of an agency and its constituents. Each coordinated effort, collective action, and emergent mindset begins with individuals in their respective roles as part of relational and collective groups. In the changing world in which we now live, socially co-constructing a new mindset often means shifting between members of a particular group as new teams evolve and different relational and collective mindsets emerge. Socially co-constructed mindsets are also dependent upon the fluidity and longevity of agency and constituent relationships; as well as past efforts, actions, and mindsets which further influence relationships within and between agency groups. These dynamics were all a part of AmTour, Inc., an agency which fully illustrates the emerging potential of individual, relational, and collective mindsets. Actively contributing to a family – as AmTour's CEO loved to refer to those who collectively comprised the inter-agency and intra-agency parts of the AmTour system – can be complicated; however, the outcomes that emerge from the inner dealings of those who contribute may benefit by first pausing to consider the deeper meaning behind the word – "family".

DISCUSSION QUESTIONS

1. Which of the socially co-constructed orientations mentioned in this case do you believe are more important to an organization in conducting its daily business? Do some businesses require more collaborative and cohesive orientations or does one size fit all? What information from the AmTour case can you use to support your response?

(*continued*)

2. As described in the AmTour case, are intra-agency or interagency interdependencies more important for a particular organization to pursue? Do you believe that these interdependencies benefit or harm organizations? How might social media be used to support your belief?
3. The AmTour case differentiates between individual, relational, and collective mindsets. Which of the mindsets do you believe has the greatest potential for impacting an organization? Explain your response.
4. Write an essay in which you describe leadership and followership that you have experienced in a professional setting. Who was involved? How would you describe the relationships between the various organizational members? Using the model developed in this case, how would you assess the relationships between people and processes in the organization? Into which categor(ies) of the model would you place each relationship? Do you believe that each relationship benefitted or hindered the organization? If you were to change anything about each relationship, what would it be and why? Please describe.

References

Adner, R. (2012). *The wide lens: A new strategy for innovation.* New York, NY: Penguin Group.

Barnes, L. B., & Kriger, M. P. (1987). The hidden side of organizational leadership. *The McKinsey Quarterly*, (Winter), 15–35. Retrieved from http://www.mckinsey.com

Bradbury-Huang, H., Lichtenstein, B., Carroll, J. S., & Senge, P. (2010). Relational space and learning experiments: The heart of sustainability collaborations. In W. A. Pasmore, A. B. (Rami) Shani, & R. W. Woodman (Eds.), *Research in organizational change and development* (Vol. 18, pp. 109–148). Bingley, UK: Emerald Group Publishing Limited. doi:10.1108/S0897-3016(2010)0000018008

Burns, J. M. (1978). *Leadership*. New York, NY: HarperCollins.

Collins, J. (2001). *Good to great: Why some companies make the leap ... and others don't.* New York, NY: HarperCollins.

DeRue, D. S. (2011). Adaptive leadership theory: Leading and following as a complex adaptive process. *Research in Organizational Behavior, 31*, 125–150. doi:10.1016/j.riob.2011.09.007

Edmondson, A. C. (2012). Teamwork on the fly. *Harvard Business Review, 90*, 72–80.

Hollander, E. P. (1992). Leadership, followership, self, and others. *The Leadership Quarterly, 3*, 43–54. doi:10.1016/1048-9843(92)90005-Z

Hosking, D. M. (2007). Not leaders, not followers: A postmodern discourse of leadership processes. In B. Shamir, R. Pillai, M. C. Bligh, & M. Uhl-Bien (Eds.), *Follower-centered perspectives on leadership* (pp. 243–263). Greenwich, CT: Information Age.

Howell, J. M., & Shamir, B. (2005). The role of followers in the charismatic leadership process: Relationships and their consequences. *Academy of Management Review*, *30*(1), 96–112. doi:10.5465/AMR.2005.15281435

Isaacs, W. N. (1993). Taking flight: Dialogue, collective thinking, and organizational learning. *Organizational Dynamics*, *22*(2), 24–39. doi:10.1016/0090-2616(93)90051-2

Marchington, M., & Vincent, S. (2004). Analysing the influence of institutional, organizational, and interpersonal forces in shaping inter-organizational relations. *Journal of Management Studies*, *41*(6), 1029–1056. doi:10.1111/j.1467-6486.2004.00465.x

Meindl, J. R. (1995). The romance of leadership as a follower-centric theory: A social constructionist approach. *The Leadership Quarterly*, *6*(3), 329–341. doi:10.1016/1048-9843(95)90012-8

Rogers, E. M. (1995). *Diffusion of innovations* (4th ed.). New York, NY: The Free Press.

Schein, E. H. (2015). Organizational psychology then and now: Some observations. *The Annual Review of Organizational Psychology and Organizational Behavior*, *2*, 1–19. doi:10.1146/annurev-orgpsyc-032414-111449

Shamir, B., & Eilam, G. (2005). "What's your story?": Toward a life story approach to authentic leadership. *Leadership Quarterly*, *16*, 395–417. doi:10.1016/j.leaqua.2005.03.005

Uhl-Bien, M. (2006). Relational leadership theory: Exploring the social processes of leadership and organizing. *The Leadership Quarterly*, *17*(6), 654–676. doi:10.1016/j.leaqua.2006.10.007

Wheatley, M. J. (2006). *Leadership and the new science: Discovering order in a chaotic world* (3rd ed.). San Francisco, CA: Berrett-Koehler.

CHAPTER

2 A Match Made of Mission

Susan Keim

Jason Young, Community Leadership Program (CLP) graduate and recently appointed executive director of L-NEAT, the local chapter of the nonprofit National Emergency Assistance Team (NEAT), was tasked with finding new volunteer board members for his complacent organization. He looked to CLP for new board members. Ella Starr, CLP director, joined the board not knowing the mission of L-NEAT. She could not refuse Young's charismatic recruitment effort. Starr believed in Young's leadership style as well as the passion and vibrancy he brought to the organization. Craig King, Deputy Fire Chief and CLP graduate, was also asked by Young to join the board. King agreed because he believed in the organization's mission of community disaster preparedness, fire safety, and fire prevention. King knew how important L-NEAT was in his community and he thought working with Young was a bonus.

With new board members in place to energize the board, Young began to grow the nonprofit through fundraisers and community outreach. Starr's connections helped Young use his community leadership network to revamp the annual golf tournament, add a wine tasting party at a local winery, and create a motorcycle ride which included an untapped resource of bikers. With new funds, Young worked with King to provide additional fire safety and health programs for the community.

Through Young's leadership, previous volunteers returned to help L-NEAT while the board of directors maintained an active presence in fiscal policy and program decisions. His predecessor practically begged to get enough board members for quorum; Young simply worried about what to do with too many volunteers. Starting an internship program, Young realized the value of using college students as interns and the potential of a renewing volunteer base. The old, established L-NEAT became a youthful and dynamic force for change.

The board was thrilled with the organization's growth and popularity in the community. When Young asked for assistance, Starr willingly helped out although she did not initiate volunteer activities. King eagerly worked with L-NEAT to promote fire safety. Board members regularly attended meetings, served on committees and participated in fundraisers, although little time was spent on board development. Staff capacity was expanded to handle more programs and activities. Increased visibility in the community brought more volunteers and funders to support the organization.

Many severe national disasters left NEAT in a financial deficit and organizational restructuring crept into the success of day to day activities. Responsibilities were regionally consolidated and soon local employees were working region-wide and reporting to other managers besides Young. With control now highly centralized, L-NEAT was caught in the middle. Inevitably, Young was wooed away by his alma mater, leaving the organization and the empire he created, just as it faced a major crisis.

Rose Hill, a registered nurse, was an inexperienced board member who became board chair, expecting to be guided by Young. Instead, she faced her first board leadership challenge of hiring a director without Young by her side. The NEAT reorganization gave Regional Director Robert Thomas authority to hire an outsider with limited nonprofit management experience over the local favorite which left L-NEAT board members grumbling. That newly hired director left after only six months, frustrating Hill's and Young's painstaking effort to introduce the new director to key stakeholders and orient her to the community. Once again, the board, with Hill as the board chair, was without an executive director. With added pressure from the regional office and less autonomy for L-NEAT, the board began the hiring process. When Thomas shifted responsibilities to the regional office, L-NEAT finally realized the board had quietly and unintentionally transitioned to an advisory committee. Local control of L-NEAT was being lost to regional management of NEAT.

In the parking lot and at other meetings, board members questioned the leadership of the Rose Hill and NEAT; however, they did not question their own actions or motivations at L-NEAT. No one thought about their personal values and reasons for joining the L-NEAT board or how those values would now affect the leadership of L-NEAT. It was all too easy to blame changes on NEAT and not consider what was happening at L-NEAT or with individual board members. Questions of board member motivation, whether board members were driven by the mission or the leader, did not arise. Instead, Thomas and NEAT stepped in to provide supervision and staff support which dictated new standard operating procedures to the struggling L-NEAT. Within a year after Young's departure, the recently reinvigorated agency languished.

Broken hearted by Young's departure, Starr could not bring herself to fight for L-NEAT. She tried a couple of times, but Hill and Thomas made it so difficult, she wondered if it was worth the effort. After all, she thought, it was really Young who drove the organization and she only joined the board because Young had asked. Without Young as the leader of L-NEAT, Starr decided to put her efforts toward other organizations where she believed in the mission. In doing so, Starr ignored email requests from L-NEAT and quietly disappeared from the board without actually resigning.

Craig King, was not about to give up on the L-NEAT presence in his community. When Young asked King to join the board, he agreed because he believed in the organization's mission. In L-NEAT, King found an organization which supported his work in the community. Without L-NEAT, he knew people would be homeless after emergencies. He believed in L-NEAT so much, King decided to throw the full support of his department behind keeping it viable.

Two years after Young's departure, only 2 of the other 18 board members whom he recruited remained active. Those were Hill and King. All other board members had either been recruited by Young's predecessor, or they had since resigned or disengaged. They were board members in name only. Despite Thomas's takeover efforts from the regional office, four active board members remained. They are collectively determined to keep L-NEAT alive in their community because they believed in the mission of the L-NEAT and the people the organization serves.

Scholarly Commentary

Active, engaged, and independent followers are critical to the success of organizations. Using community volunteers as a type of follower, this case study examines how follower motivation – mission-driven or leader-driven – contributes to the success or failure of an organization. Some followers engage in activities believing in an organization's mission while others engage because of the organization's leader (Keim, 2014). By examining follower motivation in the citizen engagement arena through nonprofit and civic organizations, the potential for a successful mission match between followers and nonprofit and civic organizations becomes more apparent.

Nonprofit and civic organizations utilize volunteers on projects, committees and boards to link followership and civic engagement through emerging follower motivation: mission-oriented and leader-oriented. The star followers (Kelley, 2008) and active followers (Chaleff, 2009) are more likely to be mission-driven while the sheep (Kelley, 2008) and bystanders (Kellerman, 2008) are more likely to be leader-driven. For organizations challenged with recruiting or retaining followers (volunteers), understanding that mission-driven followers become more involved and stay involved because of the organization's mission provides nonprofit and civic leaders with important mission match information to consider for volunteer recruitment and retention efforts (Brudney & Meijs, 2009). This could be a new approach to attract and keep volunteers over time.

The case study of L-NEAT investigates the motivation of two new volunteer board members who were brought on to energize a board that had become complacent. When Jason Young, the charismatic and forceful leader, convinced Ella Starr to join the board of directors, she said yes because she was asked by the leader. On paper, Starr was quite a catch for the board of directors with her community connections and proven ability to fundraise. Early on, Starr participated in events and activities when prompted by Young rather than promoting L-NEAT in the community. While Young did not confront her, Starr's lack of enthusiasm was probably a disappointment to Young who had observed Starr using her social network to engage in many other community activities. Rather, Starr appeared unwilling to use her vast social capital of trust and reciprocity, gained over time in the community, to benefit L-NEAT (Putnam, 2000). In this case, Starr is considered a leader-driven follower (Keim, 2014) who did not completely buy into the mission of L-NEAT. Use of her social network was limited and happened only when Young asked. When the leader departed the organization, Starr checked out. In the end, Starr was not an active, engaged, star follower (Chaleff, 2009; Kelley, 2008), rather she behaved more like a sheep (Kelley, 2008) or bystander (Kellerman, 2008).

A firefighter at heart, Craig King was willing to join the L-NEAT board and immediately became active in fire safety and emergency assistance programming. He used his position and social capital, on the board and as a fire captain, to reach out into the community for donations and involve the fire department in the community-wide smoke detector installation and replacement blitz. King was willing to use his social network for the benefit of L-NEAT and the community (Putnam, 2000). King's actions centered around his belief in the mission of the organization. Young did not have to ask King for assistance, King was internally motivated to promote the L-NEAT mission in any way he could. After Young left, King continued to work diligently for L-NEAT and is one of the few board members who continues to loyally serve the organization. King is considered a mission-driven follower (Keim, 2014) who firmly believes in the mission of L-NEAT. He continues to be an active, engaged, star follower (Chaleff, 2009; Kelley, 2008).

Starr and King demonstrate the stark difference in follower motivation between mission-driven and leader-driven followers. As Keim (2014) describes, mission-driven followers believe in the mission of the organization and are more likely to stay involved during leadership changes. To them, the leader is insignificant compared to the mission of the organization. Leaders come and go, but the mission and the organization remain. Leader-driven followers are more likely to become involved only because the leader asks. For them, the mission may not be as important as the leader who is involved with the organization. With the leader present, the followers can rally around supporting the leader. When the leader exits, the focus of the leader-driven followers disappears.

Had Young realized the difference between the mission-driven and leader-driven board members, he may have recruited volunteers differently, considered follower motivation and chosen different board members – those who were more mission-driven – to reach a better balance of mission-driven and leader-driven followers for the board of directors. As it turns out, there were many more leader-driven followers than mission-driven followers on the L-NEAT board. When the leader left, the majority of the board members also departed. Mission-driven followers would be more likely to stay and make a stronger stand against NEAT, preserving Young's hard work in growing the L-NEAT organization.

Young did not expect drastic national changes at NEAT and he most likely did not expect to leave L-NEAT, given he did not plan for long-term board leadership stability. Had more purposeful consideration been given to board leadership and organizational sustainability, Young and the board could have chosen a more experienced board member as chair of the board. Hill's board leadership inexperience coupled with Young's departure did not provide organizational sustainability or security for L-NEAT in the face of major organizational changes. Instead, Young and the board were riding a wave of popularity in the community and were focused on programming and fundraising without considering the future sustainability of L-NEAT.

Nonprofit and civic organizations, such as L-NEAT, are continuously charged with recruiting volunteers. Retaining those volunteers saves considerable staff time and precious funds (Hager & Brudney, 2004). As Keim (2014) indicates, organizations which rely heavily on volunteers could attract mission-driven followers by emphasizing the purpose and goals of the organization instead of relying on the difficult process of continually asking leader-driven followers for support. Volunteers who believe in the organization's mission and want to make it better may be more likely actively engaged in the organizations that they choose to support. Those mission-driven followers may also provide stability and continuity to nonprofit and civic organizations and their volunteer leadership.

The disconnect between volunteer follower motivation and the mission of the organization may result in failure, regardless of leader engagement within the organization (Brudney & Meijs, 2009; Hager & Brudney, 2004). Organizations able to perfect the match of mission and follower motivation will enhance overall follower motivation. This match between mission and follower motivation enables organizations to recruit volunteers who care about the mission of the organization and actively choose to volunteer, instead of those who say yes simply because the leader asks. This creates a more positive environment for engaged volunteers and saves costs in time and resources organizations use for recruiting and training volunteers.

In the case of Starr and King, Starr's leader-driven followership did little overall to enhance L-NEAT. As soon as the leader left the organization, Starr was not motivated to help L-NEAT in any way. On the other hand, King's mission-driven followership left a legacy for L-NEAT. King still believes in the mission of L-NEAT and continues to work to keep the organization alive in his community.

DISCUSSION QUESTIONS

1. Who are the main characters in this case study? What are their roles with L-NEAT? Describe what motivates each character. Which characters are considered stakeholders and why?
2. Explore the similarities and differences of Ella Starr and Craig King as board members and followers for L-NEAT. In what ways do their similarities and differences affect the overall successes and failures of L-NEAT?
3. Consider the role of board of directors and staff of L-NEAT in relation to the rising tension between L-NEAT and NEAT. What is occurring within L-NEAT to promote the disequilibrium?
4. Jason Young appears to be the L-NEAT hero. Examine his actions. To what extent did his actions contribute to

the successes or failures of the followers and the organization? To what extent did the actions of the followers contribute to Young's successes or failures?

5. Describe the different roles that mission-driven and leader-driven followers played at L-NEAT? How may their actions affect the outcome of this case study?
6. To create a more sustainable organization, what actions could have been taken by Young, the board chair, and the board of directors (followers) to protect the future of L-NEAT?

References

Brudney, J. L., & Meijs, L. (2009). It ain't natural: Toward a new (natural) resource conceptualization for volunteer management. *Nonprofit and Voluntary Sector Quarterly*, *38*, 564–581. doi:10.1177/0899764009333828

Chaleff, I. (2009). *The courageous follower* (3rd ed.). San Francisco, CA: Berrett-Koehler.

Hager, M. A., & Brudney, J. L. (2004, June). *Volunteer management practices and retention of volunteers*. Washington, DC: The Urban Institute. Retrieved from http://www.urban.org

Keim, S. (2014). Mission-driven followership and civic engagement: A different sustainable energy. *Journal of Leadership Education*, 4, 76–87. doi:10.12806/V13/I4/C9

Kellerman, B. (2008). *Followership*. Boston, MA: Harvard Business Press.

Kelley, R. E. (2008). Rethinking followership. In R. E. Riggio, I. Chaleff, & J. Lipman-Blumen (Eds.), *The art of followership: How great followers create great leaders and organizations* (pp. 5–15). San Francisco, CA: Jossey-Bass.

Putnam, R. D. (2000). *Bowling alone*. New York, NY: Simon and Schuster.

CHAPTER

3 Followers Alert a Leader

B. Ariel Blair

Maurice, an engineer in the Technology Transformation Business Unit (TTBU), is trying to decide what to do next. There is a problem in Sam's team, Technology Team A. Maurice and his colleagues are completely frustrated. They feel as though their team manager Sam is misleading David, the general manager, about team progress; their efforts to raise the issue through regular communication channels have been ignored. Maurice understands there is significant risk that the TTBU will not meet its commitments to TechCorp if the problem is not addressed quickly. He decides to talk with Amanda, the finance manager, who is viewed as a neutral member of the management team.

The TechCorp CEO created the TTBU business unit to convert pure research to consumer-ready products. TechCorp is a market leader in the industry and the TTBU team members are excited about their work (Figure 1).

There are three technology teams in the business unit. Each team is working on related, but separate technology. The teams are made up of approximately 10 people each. Members are highly skilled. Most are PhD scientists or engineers. The marketing team in the TTBU is responsible for taking the technology to market. They have marketing and intellectual property expertize. Many TTBU members have worked together in cross-functional teams for many years developing similar types of technology.

David is the general manager of the business unit. His staff includes: Sam, one of three technology team program managers; Amanda, the finance manager; Ben, the strategy manager; and Katy, the chief technology officer. David has had a long and distinguished career. He is known for a gruff exterior, but those who spend much

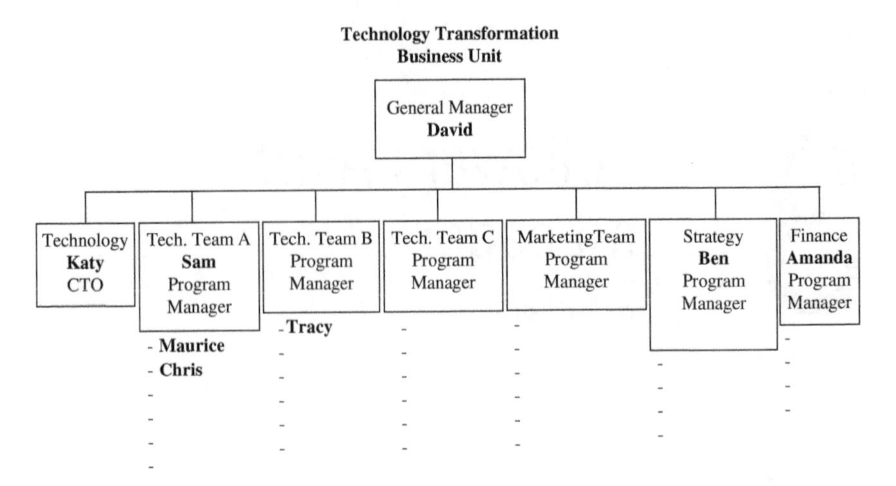

Figure 1. Organizational Chart.

time with him know that he cares about his teams. He puts himself on the line to protect them and to get the resources they need. People who have worked with him describe him as a strong leader. Ben describes an experience with David,

> David cares about his people. When I suggested there was a gender issue in the group, he talked with every woman and many of the men in the group and determined there were issues worth addressing. Not all leaders can have that type of personal conversation with most of the people in their organization. Each one of us is highly motivated, but because of David's confidence in us, we push just a little bit harder.

TTBU Culture and Environment

Because the business unit is focused on innovation, there are formal processes in place to encourage the sharing of thoughts and ideas. These forums range from very formal patent generation sessions to an online biweekly pulse survey to measure morale and allow comments. David explains the most informal TTBU forum,

> We have coffee talks every week when the group gathers to celebrate personal accomplishments and small milestones in the program teams. It is a time to get together and share good news. Because the work we do is so challenging, it is important to have small celebrations along the way.

The business unit is explicit in building a culture that supports innovation. In creating its culture, the business unit selected the metaphor of Pioneers moving into unfamiliar territory of the Western United States as a guiding image. For the TTBU, this metaphor signified the need for every member to contribute. This culture is consistent with the larger corporate culture which is one of minimal hierarchy and open door policies.

Because the culture of the TTBU is not hierarchical, technical disagreements tend to get resolved within each team. If the team cannot come to resolution, they sometimes ask Katy, the CTO, to participate. In general, David allows each program manager a great deal of autonomy only asking for updates on how they are progressing against an agreed upon work plan. He expects members of his team to let him know if they need his help. TTBU members know each other well and often socialize outside of work.

The Challenge

One day, Amanda stopped by Ben's desk and suggested they go for coffee. Amanda looked worried.

> I'm concerned. Tracy pulled me aside and said she has tried to raise concerns with David about the progress of Sam's team, but David won't listen. Tracy is not one to raise alarms and she understands the technology better than I do so I take her seriously. She thinks David will listen to me and wants me to talk with him.

Ben shared that he had a similar conversation with Maurice who was a member of technology team A. Ben and Amanda decided they would approach David with their concerns. David's response was not what they expected. Ben was caught off guard when David said, "I wish people would spend as much time worrying about doing their own jobs as they spend worrying about Sam doing his job." Ben understood why the team members were coming to him and to Amanda.

Ben reviewed the biweekly pulse survey since it often provided hints to understand concerns in the group. Ben later reflected, "I reviewed the pulse reports. There were comments expressing concern with meeting the schedule. We discounted them because most were from Chris who tends to be negative." The full extent of the problem came to light in a checkpoint meeting a few weeks after Amanda and Ben spoke with David. Sam was reporting on the progress of his team. He said, "We are on target to complete the discovery phase in six months." David asked, "You mean feasibility, right?" As Sam tried to gloss over the discrepancy in language, it became clear to everyone in the room that David understood what his followers had been telling him. Sam's team was more than a year behind on its program plan.

David is now faced with a dilemma. He has empowered his managers to run their programs. However, individuals in the organization have taken the initiative and spoken to him about a serious problem in one of the program teams. He now understands the problem clearly and has to decide how to intervene.

Scholarly Commentary

Followership literature is increasingly calling for researchers to combine the study of leadership and followership. Exploring the intersection allows us to see both sides of the coin, to see situations more holistically. Looking at just one side or the other is likely to result in oversimplified understanding of the full picture. This case highlights the relationship between leaders and followers as well as the complexity encountered when exploring both leader and follower roles. The case focuses on issues related to follower voice and dissent.

Leadership and Followership

By looking at how followers interact with and impact the leadership process (Uhl-Bien, Riggio, Lowe, & Carsten, 2014), the study of followership enables broader perspectives of the challenges faced in organizations. Followers have distinct ideas of what their roles should be. Carsten, Uhl-Bien, West, Patera, and McGregor (2010) construct followership into three categories: passive, active, and proactive. Passive followers believe they should implement a leader's orders without questioning. Similar to passive followers, active followers believe decision-making responsibility belongs to a leader. The final construction of followership is proactive. In the proactive construction, followers believe they should challenge and give advice (Carsten et al., 2010). These followers view themselves as active participants who will determine the success or failure of the organization. They see informing the leader of critical information as part of their responsibility. As is consistent with more active constructions of followership, followers with strong coproduction beliefs think they should collaborate with leaders, making suggestions and challenging leaders to improve outcomes (Carsten & Uhl-Bien, 2012; Carsten et al., 2010). It is likely that active and proactive follower beliefs align more easily with certain leadership styles.

The transformational leadership model (Bass & Riggio, 2006) is valuable for understanding leadership values that are likely to complement proactive followership roles. The characteristics of transformational leadership: knowing the individuals in the group well, inspiring them to do the best work possible, and seeking to deliver resources and clear organizational hurdles assume collaboration and follower autonomy. Transformational leadership is an intellectually appealing model. However, its appeal introduces the danger of analysis that idealizes leaders as is described by the romance of leadership (RoL) theory. In a review of RoL, Bligh, Kohles, and Pillai (2011) reveal patterns of bias and misattribution of outcomes to leaders in leadership research. To balance the focus, we need to analyze what followers think of leadership in order to understand the organizational system (Bligh et al., 2011).

Voice and Minority Dissent

In this case, the focus is on communication. One way that followers can demonstrate more active roles is through communicating, voicing dissenting views. When examining leadership, Gardner (1990) talks about the importance of two-way communication saying communication from a leader to followers is not sufficient. There must also be easy communication that incudes dissent from followers to leaders. The dissent of which Gardner is a proponent is described well in the voice construct. The definition of voice is that the ideas or opinions expressed in a work setting are intended to improve the functioning of the organization. Voice is pro-social, there is intention to improve the group or organization (Bashshur & Oc, 2015; Morrison, 2011). Voice is a tool used by more active followers to fulfill their role as co-producers of group outcomes.

Research on minority dissent clarifies the value of voice that originates from lower power group members who are members of an in-group. Because followers are lower status members, the minority dissent theory can help us understand follower influence within groups. When a dissenting idea is introduced by the majority or a leader, research demonstrates that there will be compliance instead of change. A dissenting message that is consistently communicated by a minority in-group member leads to change (Moscovici, 1980). Building on Moscovici's work, Nemeth's (1986) convergent-divergent theory asserts that what is important for influence is that ideas introduced by a lower status person are more likely to stimulate divergent thought and, as a result, improve decisions in the team. Persistent dissent by a lower status in-group member creates dissonance and leads the team to consider new and different ideas. The convergent-divergent theory helps us to understand that the value of minority dissent is that it incites attention to a broader range of ideas and results in better decisions and group outcomes (De Dreu & West, 2001; Nemeth, 1986). In addition, in a group where innovation is critical, the consideration of a broader range of ideas is important because when divergent ideas are more easily considered, the creativity necessary for innovation is more likely to occur (Csikszentmihalyi, 1997). In addition, Alvaro and Crano's (1997) leniency contract theory asserts that those ideas will result in delayed rather than immediate change (see also Crano & Seyranian, 2007). These theories suggest that divergent ideas are considered when an in-group follower disagrees with a high status team member and puts forth dissenting ideas.

An extension of the earlier research finds that reflexivity within a team combined with minority dissent is important to team effectiveness and innovation. Reflexivity was operationalized as team members participating in reviewing methods, discussing and modifying objectives, and evaluating how well they work together. When divergent ideas and participation in decision-making are present, there is a positive influence on innovation and effectiveness (De Dreu, 2002). These findings suggest that follower dissent or voice alone are not sufficient to improve outcomes.

An implication of De Dreu's research is that followers, at least those who believe in an active or proactive construction of followership, ought to be included in decision-making. A leader who invites divergent ideas without including followers to actively take part in how the work is done may lose the benefit of those ideas.

DISCUSSION QUESTIONS

1. In the technology team there were mechanisms designed to enable two-way leader follower communication and follower dissent. Were these mechanisms sufficient (Gardner, 1990)?
2. In what additional ways might follower concerns have been raised?
3. Was David's leadership effective? Why or why not?
4. Were Maurice, Tracy, and Chris effective followers?
5. Were Ben and Amanda leaders, followers, or both leaders and followers?
6. How could leadership or followership have been improved in the technology transfer business unit?

7. How can David respond to follower concerns without undermining the program manager?
8. Use minority dissent theory to explain the events in the case. How do you define the in-group? How did follower dissent influence the leader? Was the change immediate or delayed?
9. How would analysis of the case differ if you focused only on leadership or followership rather than combining both?
10. What policies or procedures does your organization have in place to allow followers to question decisions made by their leaders?

References

Alvaro, E. M., & Crano, W. D. (1997). Indirect minority influence: Evidence for leniency in source evaluation and counter argumentation. *Journal of Personality and Social Psychology*, *72*(5), 949–964. doi:10.1037/0022-3514.72.5.949

Bashshur, M. R., & Oc, B. (2015). When voice matters: A multilevel review of the impact of voice in organizations. *Journal of Management*, *41*, 1530–1554.

Bass, B. M., & Riggio, R. E. (2006). *Transformational leadership* (2nd ed.). Mahwah, NJ: Lawrence Erlbaum Associates.

Bligh, M., Kohles, J., & Pillai, R. (2011). Romancing leadership: Past, present, and future. *The Leadership Quarterly*, 22, 1058–1077. doi:10.1016/j.leaqua.2011.09.003

Carsten, M. K., & Uhl-Bien, M. (2012). Follower beliefs in the co-production of leadership: Examining upward communication and the moderating role of context. *Zeitschrift Für Psychologie*, *220*, 210–220. doi:10.1027/2151-2604/a000115

Carsten, M. K., Uhl-Bien, M., West, B. J., Patera, J. L., & McGregor, R. (2010). Exploring social constructions of followership: A qualitative study. *The Leadership Quarterly*, *21*, 543–562. doi:10.1016/j.leaqua.2010.03.015

Crano, W. D., & Seyranian, V. (2007). Majority and minority influence. *Social and Personality Psychology Compass*, *1*, 572–589. doi:10.1111/j.1751-9004.2007.00028.x

Csikszentmihalyi, M. (1997). *Creativity: Flow and the psychology of discovery and invention*. New York, NY: HarperCollins.

De Dreu, C. W. (2002). Team innovation and team effectiveness: The importance of minority dissent and reflexivity. *European Journal of Work and Organizational Psychology*, *11*(3), 285–298. doi:10.1080/13594320244000175

De Dreu, C. W., & West, M. A. (2001). Minority dissent and team innovation: The importance of participation in decision making. *Journal of Applied Psychology*, *86*, 1191–1201. doi:10.1037/0021-9010.86.6.1191

Gardner, J. W. (1990). *On leadership*. New York, NY: The Free Press.

Morrison, E. W. (2011). Employee voice behavior: Integration and directions for future research. *The Academy of Management Annals*, *5*(1), 373–412. doi:10.1080/19416520.2011.574506

Moscovici, S. (1980). Toward a theory of conversion behavior. In L. Berkowitz (Ed.), *Advances in experimental social psychology* (Vol. 13, pp. 209–239). New York, NY: Academic Press.

Nemeth, C. J. (1986). Differential contributions of majority and minority influence. *Psychological Review*, *93*, 23–32. doi:10.1037/0033-295X.93.1.23

Uhl-Bien, M., Riggio, R. E., Lowe, K. B., & Carsten, M. K. (2014). Followership theory: A review and research agenda. *The Leadership Quarterly*, *25*(1), 83–104. doi:10.1016/j.leaqua.2013.11.007

CHAPTER

4 The Acquired Executive

Marc Hurwitz

Terry was sitting at his desk in one of the executive offices overlooking Halifax Harbour. On clear days, you could see well out into the harbor, but today it was raining, as it often does during fall in Nova Scotia, Canada.

Usually, Terry's morning ritual consisted of preparing for a busy schedule of meetings with clients and staff, but the last few weeks had changed everything. Now, he was unsure if it was business-as-usual, or if he needed to change course.

The Business

Terry was Vice-President in charge of a profitable sales office of Maritime Life Insurance, managing annual revenues of over half a billion dollars with an ROI in excess of 20%. His main product responsibility was *trusteed insurance*: specialized insurance policies for multi-employer unions. Unlike most group insurance plans, the policy is the responsibility of the union, rather than the company for which an employee works. For example, in the construction trade, a union member may work for different contractors or on many different projects throughout the year. If the union did not negotiate and manage the insurance plan, an individual worker might never be considered a "full-time, permanent employee" entitled to on-going benefits such as life insurance, dental coverage, or long-term disability benefits in case of an injury. Due to the seasonality of work, having the union responsible also ensures continuity of insurance year-round.

In most trusteed plans, the union negotiates the benefits to which workers are entitled, and the insurance company is expected to support the union with advice on issues such as collective bargaining, legislation, and reciprocal agreements. Very few insurance companies offer these specialized services, and the number of potential clients is small. It is a profitable niche business for the few insurers who compete in it. Terry was one of the first sales representatives for the product in Canada. As the company for which he worked grew, so had his block of business and his career. Terry now ran the trusteed organization at Maritime Life including all the sales and support staff.

The Acquisition

Maritime Life Insurance had grown steadily since it was founded in 1922. In 1969, John Hancock Mutual Life Insurance out of the United States bought Maritime Life, but it was largely left to run itself.

In 2004, however, everything changed. Manulife Financial merged with John Hancock, acquiring Maritime Life along with it. Like Maritime Life, Manulife had a storied past. Founded in 1887, its first president was also Canada's first Prime Minster, Sir John. A. Macdonald. Despite this auspicious beginning, Manulife was a small to medium-sized insurer for the next 100 years. In 1994, it hired an aggressive, young CEO – Dominic D'Alessandro – who changed the course of the firm; over the next 10 years, Manulife went on a binge of new acquisitions that, with the addition of John Hancock, made it the largest insurer in Canada and, briefly, the fifth largest insurer in the world.

The culture at Manulife was unlike that at Maritime. Where the motto at Maritime had been, "Do what is right for the customer," the unofficial motto at Manulife was, "Be #1 or #2 in every market we serve, and earn an ROI of 17%." While staff, especially executives, had considerable latitude to act at Maritime, there were many more rules and procedures at Manulife, much more oversight, less spending authority for mid-level executives, and a greater attention to top- and bottom-line results. Finally, stretch goals were encouraged at Maritime with the understanding that failure was part of the process, while at Manulife, meeting goals was the behavioral norm and exceeding them was rewarded. In the five years preceding the acquisition, Maritime Life was considered one of "The Best 50 Employers in Canada" according to Canada's national daily newspaper, *The Globe & Mail*, while Manulife had never made a serious run at that list.

The Question

Although many of his Halifax peers were told they would be let go once integration efforts were completed, Manulife was impressed by the market dominance of Terry's team and its specialized skills. His professional attitude during the acquisition also played a part in the unusual decision to keep the sales office of Terry and his whole team in Halifax. The Canadian headquarters and Terry's new boss were in Waterloo, Ontario, over 1,000 miles away.

Terry recognized the need to "get with the program" of the new organization, and yet he found himself increasingly frustrated because he was out of the loop. Communication at the new company was guarded and rarely forthcoming compared to his old company, and the distance between his office and the parent company further exacerbated the problems with communication and connectedness. It felt awkward leading a sales office without understanding how or why decisions about products, services, or investments were being made and Terry's new boss, the Vice President of Group Benefits sales, had not clarified his priorities. Should Terry work more closely with regional sales offices across the country? Should he focus on top-line growth? Would it be valuable to introduce new products? Could he hire more sales staff? What level of information and updates should he provide to the VP? These were just some of the questions he was thinking about that morning.

As he sat in his office thinking about all the changes, Terry wrote down four ideas he had for dealing with his current situation. What he could not figure out was which one to use. Or was there a fifth possibility he had not thought of yet? Here is what he wrote:

1. *Book face time with my boss and ask about decisions directly.*
2. *Build an informal network at head office in Waterloo. Some of my old colleagues from Maritime Life are working there (at HQ) and they might give me advice on what was going on, and on how to change my approach to suit the new organization. I could pay them regular visits or send e-mails to get the latest news.*
3. *Prioritize building a strong rapport with my boss. Maybe I should find out what his favorite restaurant is and take him there for one-on-ones?*
4. *Stop worrying. I've made a strong impression. I know the marketplace better than anyone, so the fact that no strategic direction or framework had been communicated means that my boss has confidence in me.*

Scholarly Commentary

When circumstances change, that is the time to reassess the situation and determine what, if any, personal actions have to be taken to take advantage of opportunities or mitigate risk. After an acquisition, changes that might require a response can occur at any situational level:

- Intrapersonal factors such as job tasks and characteristics;
- Interpersonal relationships including the immediate team, peers, boss, or other senior leaders; and
- Organization-wide differences to corporate goals, culture, business-structure, and the like.

Problems arise when people involved in change under- or over-estimate the impact at a particular level, or assume that one factor compensates for issues with another factor. For example, the idea that work "speaks for itself" overestimates the importance of intrapersonal factors relative to interpersonal and organizational ones.

In this case, Terry was faced with a new manager, peers, corporate culture, informational flows and style, head office location, availability of peers, and corporate objectives. However, other aspects of his work remained the same. For example, with his team intact and being accountable for the same clients and products, Terry could reasonably assume that his leadership responsibilities would be similar to what he had experienced prior to the merger, while possibly requiring medium or longer-term adaptation to Manulife's corporate culture. In other words, his intrapersonal situation was largely unaffected, some interpersonal factors were different, and the organization had changed considerably.

Another perspective is that all jobs have technical accountabilities while also requiring leadership and followership skills (Hurwitz & Hurwitz, 2015). In this case, the technical aspects of Terry's job remained unchanged. Although some aspects of his leadership might need to adapt over time – for example, he might consider sharing less information with staff to conform more closely to Manulife culture – this was not an immediate concern. Rather, Terry's followership was the central issue.

What Is Followership?

The simplest way to describe followership is as what you do when you aren't leading. From a social constructionist perspective (Shamir, 2007), followership is the creation (whether real or imagined) of a role, or structural elements in relational interactions. In other words, there is an agreement that there are two separate roles when people engage with each other – leader and follower – with a specific assignment of responsibilities, tasks, and suitable behaviors to each role based on some implicit social schema. Hurwitz and Hurwitz (2015), however, define followership as pursuing the leader's goals, while leadership is about creating a framework for action by followers.

All of these definitions have one common element: leadership requires followership, and followership necessitates leadership (Lord & Maher, 1991). The two are an interdependent pair.

Both roles have value, and both deserve equal attention although academics, practitioners, and the general public often over-focus on leadership (Meindl, Ehrlich, & Dukerich, 1985). As well, followership is thought to be a secondary role with reduced performance expectations. Hoption, Christie, and Barling (2012) found that simply labeling someone as a "follower" was associated with lower levels of positive affect and fewer extra-role behaviors. Others, however, ascribe proactive characteristics to the role (Carsten, Uhl-Bien, West, Patera, & McGregor, 2010). In support of this latter view, everything from performance appraisals to organizational effectiveness can depend on non-task related factors such as organizational citizenship behaviors (Podsakoff, MacKenzie, Paine, & Bachrach, 2000). Sponsorship – the extent to which someone higher in the organization promotes an employee – is more due to followership than skills (Wayne, Liden, Graf, & Ferris, 1997; Wayne, Liden, Kraimer, & Graf, 1999), and leads to greater career satisfaction (Ng, Eby, Sorensen & Feldman, 2005).

The inability to recognize and adapt to a new situation is a leading cause of executive derailment (Van Velsor & Leslie, 1995), especially when that includes reporting to a new leader; career transition coaches note that up to 95% of their clients had a new boss within six months of being let go (Hurwitz & Hurwitz, 2015).

In this case, Terry has recognized that he needs to revisit his followership behaviors, but is struggling to determine:

1. How to build relationships with his leader and her peers;
2. The extent to which the new culture is relevant to his job;
3. What lines of communication would be most effective to stay informed;
4. And, the best way of accomplishing these three objectives.

In the framework of Motivating Language Theory (Sullivan, 1988; Mayfield, 2009), communication can be thought of as having three functions (Hurwitz & Hurwitz, 2015, p. 65):

1. *Building relationships and providing personal support*
2. *Developing organizational agility*
3. *Providing a framework for productivity.*

Sharbrough, Simmons, and Cantrill (2006) found that doing these three tasks well resulted in a 45% rise in perceived effectiveness. Clearly, each of Terry's questions maps to the same item in Motivating Language Theory: building relationships (items 1 in both cases); organizational agility, which can be equated with understanding the culture and sub-cultures (items 2); and staying informed, which is an antecedent to productivity (items 3). We discuss each of these in turn.

Building Relationships and Providing Personal Support

There are mixed opinions on the extent to which followers need to build relationships or provide support to their leader. For example, Uhl-Bien, Riggio, Lowe, and Carsten (2014) list behaviors they believe are required for a followership model including proactivity, initiative taking, obedience, and others, but neither relationship building nor personal support. At the other extreme, Watkins (2003) suggests that followers should "take 100% responsibility for making the relationship (with the boss) work." An intermediate view, leader-member exchange theory (LMX), is based on mutuality in the relationship, that is, that high quality relationships require both leaders and followers to engage with each other (Graen & Scandura, 1987). There is ample evidence supporting the importance of LMX to outcomes (Dulebohn, Bommer, Liden, Brouer, & Ferris, 2012; Gerstner & Day, 1997) and the difficulty of doing it when communications are infrequent (Kacmar, Witt, Zivnuska & Gully, 2003). Furthermore, there is nothing to suggest which role is more important for developing or maintaining an LMX relationship, although many believe that it is more due to leadership (Snodgrass, Hecht, & Ploutz-Snyder, 1998; Dulebohn et al., 2012). This gap in our understanding makes it hard to appeal to research in choosing Terry's best course of action.

There are models and frameworks that suggest possible courses of action. Hurwitz & Hurwitz (2015), for example, propose that relationship-building and personal support are equal, but distinct accountabilities of both parties. They call the appropriate skill for leaders "relationship framing" and for followers "relationship building." *Relationship framing* is about the leader creating a comfortable, professional, and equitable environment for each team member, while *relationship building* is about developing rapport, trust, and an understanding of how to work best with a leader and her peers.

Developing Organizational Agility

It is important to operate within the cultural norms of a group most of the time. However, while there might be a dominant culture in an organization, there are also sub-cultures that can survive and be effective over long periods, especially if people in a sub-culture are separated from the rest of the organization by some persistent factor such as geography, functional specialty, or even organizational level. Also, organizations differ in their tolerance for multiple cultures, or for the allowable cultural "gaps" between groups. Terry's problem, and one faced by many middle managers, is that he is part of many different groups, often with a unique subculture in each.

The ability to understand, appreciate, and display culturally appropriate behaviors, that is, organizational agility, has been called cultural intelligence (CQ). It is comprised of four skills (Earley & Ang, 2003): *motivation* to learn about a culture, *learning* the rules of a culture, *using* the rules appropriately, and *understanding* culture. Like general intelligence (IQ), people differ in their innate CQ, but specific skills can be developed to mitigate any personal gaps.

A Framework for Productivity

A main leadership responsibility is to create the frame within which followers can work, that is, setting up conditions, constraints, and support mechanisms that enable followers to pursue initiatives that work toward the goals of the team and the organization (Hurwitz & Hurwitz, 2015). For followers, however, taking on new initiatives – being proactive – can just as easily be destructive as constructive unless the initiatives are grounded in a deep understanding of what is useful, and what would be acceptable within that specific context. In other words, just as leaders have to create the frame, followers have to be informed about the frame and work within it.

In his pre-acquisition role, Terry had ready access to his leader and peers. What's more, the culture promoted communication between leaders and followers. Although the framework for action at Maritime Life allowed for considerable autonomy (a "loose" frame), there was also a complementary tolerance for risk-taking, stretch goals, and the mistakes that come with such behavior. By contrast, Manulife culture rewarded risk-mitigation, rigorous oversight (i.e., a more constrained frame), and reduced communication from leaders. The problem with guarded communication, however, is that followers have to find other means of understanding the relevant expectations, priorities, and success criteria. One remedy is to use a peer network to fill in the gaps. Another is to set aside additional time with the leader, but that can require having a personal relationship to get such "special" treatment. Physical separation is an issue with creating a strong leader-follower relationship, and with developing useful peer networks.

Overall, then, Terry was left to figure out how much adaptation was needed, the best way to do it, and what the consequences would be for his career, for his ability to carry out his own leadership responsibilities, and for his clients.

DISCUSSION QUESTIONS

1. Personal beliefs about what followership should be are called Implicit Followership Theories, or ILTs. What are your ILTs? Would you call a colleague a follower? Why or why not? Please explain.
2. What are the positives and negatives of each option Terry has proposed? Assess this from multiple perspectives including: career implications, chances of success, likely consequences, boss' reaction, and overall effectiveness. If you were in Terry's situation, what would you do?
3. Describe the cultural differences between Manulife and Maritime Life. What is the impact of culture on followership?
4. Terry has found himself cut-off from the pulse of the organization. The dominant culture above him has also changed. How accountable should Terry be for keeping himself informed and learning the new culture? To what extent is it the responsibility of his boss to bring Terry up to speed?
5. Does Terry have a high or low CQ? Which of the four components of CQ do you think Terry has? Support your answer with evidence from the case. What is the impact of your analysis and what should Terry do about it?
6. What constitutes strong followership? How might the definition depend on the culture of an organization?
7. Upward influence tactics and impression management are two ways in which followers can shape relationships with senior personnel, especially their manager. What is the connection between these tactics and strong followership? Should they be used and, if so, how should they be used?

References

Carsten, M. K., Uhl-Bien, M., West, B. J., Patera, J. L., & McGregor, R. (2010). Exploring the social constructions of followership: A qualitative study. *The Leadership Quarterly*, *21*, 543–562. doi:10.1016/j.leaqua.2010.03.015

Dulebohn, J. H., Bommer, W. H., Liden, R. C., Brouer, R. L., & Ferris, G. R. (2012). A meta-analysis of antecedents and consequences of leader-member exchange: Integrating the past with an eye toward the future. *Journal of Management*, *38*(3), 1715–1759. doi:10.1177/0149206311415280

Earley, P. C., & Ang, S. (2003). *Cultural intelligence: Individual interactions across cultures*. Stanford, CA: Stanford University Press.

Gerstner, C. R., & Day, D. V. (1997). Meta-analytic review of leader-member exchange theory: Correlates and construct issues. *Journal of Applied Psychology*, *82*(6), 827–844. Retrieved from http://www.apa.org

Graen, G., & Scandura, T. (1987). Toward a psychology of dyadic organizing. In B. Staw & L. L. Cumming (Eds.), *Research in organizational behavior* (vol. 9, pp. 175–208). Greenwich, CT: JAI.

Hoption, C., Christie, A., & Barling, J. (2012). Submitting to the follower label: Followership, positive affect, and extra-role behaviors. *Zeitschrift für Psychologie*, *220*(4), 221–230. doi:10.1027/2151-2604/a000116

Hurwitz, M., & Hurwitz, S. (2015). *Leadership is half the story: A fresh look at followership, leadership, and collaboration*. Toronto: University of Toronto Press.

Kacmar, K. M., Witt, L. A., Zivnuska, S., & Gully, S. M. (2003). The interactive effect of leader-member exchange and communication frequency on performance ratings. *Journal of Applied Psychology*, *88*(4), 764–772. doi:10.1037/0021-9010.88.4.764

Lord, R. G., & Maher, K. J. (1991). *Leadership and information processing: Linking perceptions and performance*. Cambridge, MA: Unwin Hyman.

Mayfield, J. (2009). Motivating language: A meaningful guide for leader communications. *Development and Learning in Organizations*, *23*(1), 9–11. doi:10.1108/14777280910924054

Meindl, J. R., Ehrlich, S. B., & Dukerich, J. M. (1985). The romance of leadership. *Administrative Science Quarterly*, *30*(1), 78–102. doi:10.2307/2392813

Ng, T. W. H., Eby, L. T., Sorensen, K. L., & Feldman, D. C. (2005). Predictors of objective and subjective career success: A meta-analysis. *Personnel Psychology*, *58*, 367–408. doi:10.1111/j.1744-6570.2005.00515.x

Podsakoff, P. M., MacKenzie, S. B., Paine, J. B., & Bachrach, D. G. (2000). Organizational citizenship behaviors: A critical review of the theoretical and empirical literature and suggestions for future research. *Journal of Management*, *26*(3), 513–563. doi:10.1177/014920630002600307

Shamir, B. (2007). From passive recipients to active co-producers: Followers' roles in the leadership process. In B. Shamir, R. Pillai, M. Bligh, & M. Uhl-Bien (Eds.), *Follower-centered perspectives on leadership: A tribute to the memory of James R. Meindl* (pp. ix–xxxix). Charlotte, NC: Information Age.

Sharbrough, W. C., Simmons, S. A., & Cantrill, D. A. (2006). Motivating language in industry: Its impact on job satisfaction and perceived supervisor effectiveness. *The Journal of Business Communication*, *43*(4), 322–343. doi:10.1177/0021943606291712

Snodgrass, S. E., Hecht, M. A., & Ploutz-Snyder, R. (1998). Interpersonal sensitivity: Expressivity or perceptivity? *Journal of Personality and Social Psychology*, *74*, 238–249. doi:10.1037//0022-3514.74.1.238

Sullivan, J. J. (1988). Three roles of language in motivation theory. *Academy of Management Review*, *13*(1), 104–115. doi:10.2307/258358

Uhl-Bien, M., Riggio, R. E., Lowe, K. B., & Carsten, M. K. (2014). Followership theory: A review and research agenda. *The Leadership Quarterly*, *25*, 83–104. doi:10.1016/j.leaqua.2013.11.007

Van Velsor, E., & Leslie, J. B. (1995). Why executives derail: Perspectives across time and culture. *Academy of Management Executive*, *9*(4), 62–72. doi:10.5465/ame.1995.9512032194

Watkins, M. (2003). *The first 90 days*. Boston, MA: Harvard Business School.

Wayne, S. J., Liden, R. C., Graf, I. K., & Ferris, G. R. (1997). The role of upward influence tactics in human resources decisions. *Personnel Psychology*, *50*, 979–1006. doi:10.1111/j.1744-6570.1997.tb01491.x

Wayne, S. J., Liden, R. C., Kraimer, M. L., & Graf, I. K. (1999). The role of human capital, motivation and supervisor sponsorship in predicting career success. *Journal of Organizational Behavior*, *20*, 577–595. doi:10.1002/(sici)1099-1379(199909)20:5<577::aid-job958>3.0.co;2-0

CHAPTER

5 Integrating Conflict and Releasing Creative Energy: A Case for Mary Parker Follett

Suzanne Martin

Isabel Rubio was re-energized from her sabbatical, marking her 15th year as Founder and Executive Director of the Hispanic Interest Coalition of Alabama (HICA), a 501(c) 3 with a statewide mission of serving and advocating for immigrants. In the last four years, HICA had grown from 3 staff members to 20, and tripled programs offerings. Within the last year, one-third of the staff was hired, 50% of whom had less than six months experience with HICA. New staff (0–4 years) outnumbered senior staff (8+ years) by 4:1, and Isabel was looking forward to an upcoming staff retreat where the focus would be on team building and collaboration. During Isabel's absence for her sabbatical, the Assistant Director Diana had enjoyed being in charge, having previously managed internal operations and quality control for eight years. Isabel initially believed that HICA managed well during her sabbatical. However, she became concerned when she learned that a relatively minor team conflict escalated during her absence and was not only impacting the team's productivity, but also threatening the morale of the entire organization.

Isabel reviewed the data collected by a consultant hired to facilitate the retreat and the team conflict emerged as a microcosm of HICA as a whole. The data showed that everyone loved the mission and believed they were making a difference. Staff admired her and the majority wanted direct access to her. One respondent said "... less layers instead of going through Diana." Staff described themselves as "family" and "team players," but it bothered her that several of the comments made teamwork sound like a long-term goal, not an existing reality. Most expressed the desire to collaborate across teams and to "seamlessly work together." They wanted more and improved communication with other team members, the "admin team," and between teams. In meetings, team leaders wanted to discuss ways to better collaborate, instead of "reporting on reports." They wanted group decision-making, more time for relationship building, and a deeper understanding of how they fit together. Staff who tried to collaborate across teams reported resistance from Diana. Some had problems with the reporting structure because it restricted information flow.

About a third complained about heavy workloads and number of services, citing "compassion fatigue" as a major problem. As a group, they wanted to streamline – do higher quality work with fewer programs and fewer clients. A few suggested developing a protocol to handle all the new ideas, concerned that too many of their ideas received too little thought prior to being implemented by leadership. Some wanted to be more strategic and results-oriented. Conversely, others wanted to be less risk averse, and more open to new ideas, programs, and processes suggesting a "why not" approach, instead of trying to explain away "why it won't work here." One staffer disliked something she referred to as the "risk calculus" at HICA, concerned that it was overly conservative. Risk calculus was the way HICA calculated risk taking. Some staff suggested new services like a credit union to meet emerging needs. Several wanted to address the bigger issue of systemic change by growing programs like the grassroots leadership effort. Additional comments, such as those regarding the collective response to the passage of Deferred Action for Childhood Arrivals (DACA) resonated with Isabel. Virtually overnight, dozens of new clients showed up. It was "all hands on deck," releasing higher levels of energy, interaction, and collaboration. It was "all for one and one for all" for weeks. When things slowed down, staff returned to their routines, silos, the chain of command, and interacted less across teams. Isabel wanted that same engagement, collaboration, and energy to be the norm. Did it take a crisis?

Isabel and Diana discussed the report. Isabel wanted to act on the requests for more communication, collaboration, new programs, and risk-taking. Diana preferred to focus on streamlining and slowing down. Isabel wanted to attend team leader meetings with Diana. Diana argued that Isabel hired, fired, and evaluated staff, but was not needed at the team level. "Senora, that would violate the chain of command," argued Diana. It might reinforce the good parent-bad parent dynamic with which they struggled. Isabel described her role as empowering others to respond to a changing environment. Diana saw hers as keeping staff in line to ensure timely reports and productivity. Isabel wanted self-leading teams, Diana argued that self-led teams were less accountable and could be less productive. Isabel viewed their differences as complementary, but today she wondered if they sent a mixed message, possibly fueling conflict within HICA?

Needing more than Diana's narrative, Isabel met with each member of the team in conflict. Gina, an idealistic attorney with vision, was the new team leader. Her style clashed with Diana's style to whom she reported. When Gina offered new ideas or questioned a policy Diana criticized her. To complicate matters, Layla, one of Gina's most experienced team members, was also Diana's cousin. Layla admitted that she reported Gina's hours, breaks, and process mistakes to Diana. Diana and Layla both thought that Gina was a weak leader who neither understood, nor valued, the procedures. Diana encouraged Layla to resist Gina's leadership and encourage others to do the same. As a result, team members took sides and work suffered. This conflict led to the resignation of HICA's first law intern, Laura, who found the organization and her team to be "unwelcoming." Laura shared her observations of bullying, sarcasm, passive aggression, and cliques that used language and culture to create an in-group out-group dynamic. Laura found it impossible to integrate. She loved the mission and Isabel, but doubted she would recommend any law student, graduate student, or permanent staff attorney to work at HICA unless the climate changed. She hinted that someone other than Diana should supervise team leaders.

Isabel cringed at the irony – the organization touted a mission of integration, yet the teams were described as "unwelcoming" and divided. Her intention to capitalize on the energy, creativity, and passion from the DACA days shifted to conflict mediation. She wanted to have an open discussion with all employees of HICA, but knew that it would threaten Diana. She had to tell Diana about the negative impact of her leadership style on the teams and work climate and address the issues noted with Gina and Layla. How could she do that without insulting or alienating Diana? HICA relied on Diana's operational expertize, losing her was not an option, but neither was doing nothing.

Scholarly Commentary

If Isabel Rubio could have engaged Mary Parker Follett, a management consulting pioneer from the 1920s, she would have received advice that was scholarly, practical, and hopeful. Follett's wisdom would have helped Isabel to reframe conflict and make it productive for HICA. Follett would have introduced her to integration, group process, and the concept of *power-with*. The path out of destructive conflict and into collaboration and productivity would involve developing followers into leaders, as well as creating a partnership between the staff and an *invisible leader*.

Follett defined conflict as the "appearance of difference" (Metcalf & Urwick, 1941, p. 30). Conflict at HICA was necessary, like friction essential to pulleys, violin strings, and polishing (p. 31). Conflict was the "essence of life," and led to "… invention, to the emergence of new values" (p. 36). Knowing "when to eliminate friction and when to try to capitalize on it" was the key (p. 31). Follett (1924) promoted *integration* as a process to make conflict fruitful, freeing both sides and increasing the power of the organization (p. 302). Conflict was not a battle between winners and losers. The outcome of integration was "unity, not uniformity" (p. 302) and variety was the path to unity. Follett (1918) was firm in her conviction that "differences must be integrated, not annihilated, nor absorbed" (p. 39). Metcalf and Urwick (1941) would have advised Isabel and Diana, the team in conflict, and the staff to "put their cards on the table, face the real issue, uncover the conflict, and bring the whole thing into the open" (p. 38). The challenge was to see one's opponent as a co-creator, a person with a valuable perspective (Follett, 1924, p. 174). Avoiding conflict would only create more dysfunction whereas integration would generate creativity and unity.

In 1924, Follett introduced *group process* as a way to approach the people and productivity issues in businesses, factories, and communities. Effective group process grew power in organizations, nourished individuals, and united the contributions of each person (p. xiii). This process would ensure that parts were "skillfully related to one another … functioning as a whole" (Metcalf & Urwick, 1941, p. 267). Creative power evolved through group activities and the interaction released the potential of all individuals (Follett, 1918, p. 3). Without group process, an individual's potential to contribute remained nothing more than potential, and this limitation cost the organization (p. 6). Effective group process required more than activity, it required everyone being "constructively active" (p. 28). Follett described effective group process in the context of a meeting. The purpose of a meeting was to develop a common idea through integrating everyone's input. Everyone contributed, not "shrinking from giving opinion, not dismissing one's experience …" (p. 26). Ultimately, group process freed "the energies of the human spirit" (Follett, 1924, p. 303). The primary function of a leader was to release all the human potential and integrate the conflicts and energies into a unified whole.

The structure of an organization and its orientation to power either supported or hindered group process. Metcalf and Urwick (1941) defined power as the combined capacities of a group (p. 248). HICA was structured like a "machinery of following" (p. 267) with power concentrated at the top and rigid chain of command. Follett described this as "power-over," when leaders exercise power over those below them. This kind of power was coercive and restricted communication and collaboration. The alternative was a "power-with" orientation within a more horizontal structure. Power-with was a "jointly developed power, a co-active, not coercive power" (p. 101). The leader shared power with, not over the people. A flatter structure would increase interaction and improve group process which would produce more power and ultimately, increase productivity. If HICA adapted its structure and shifted to a power-with mindset, they would create an opportunity to re-energize and re-engage staff, and experience the productivity of the DACA days.

Flatter organizations were progressive with "leadership in many places, not only in the president's chair" (Follett, 1949, p. 58) and Follett would have advised Isabel to train her followers to become leaders. Only a "second-rate executive" would suppress the leadership of followers or prefer staff who gave "unthinking obedience" (p. 56). Training released the energies of all staff, creating a readiness to lead whenever the situation arose. When the particular experience, knowledge, or abilities of a follower fit the needs of the moment, he or she would be prepared and empowered to function as the leader (Metcalf & Urwick, 1941, p. 277). Training everyone for leadership would grow power within HICA, not diminish Isabel's power.

Follett believed that leaders and followers engaged in followership. She described this as a "partnership of following" erasing the traditional dichotomy between followers and leaders (Metcalf & Urwick, 1941, p. 262). The essence of leadership was creating this partnership of joint responsibility for the organization. Follett would have suggested that leaders and followers at HICA were equal partners, sharing responsibility for both the internal aspects of the organization, such as culture and communication, as well as the outcomes. The real leader was not Isabel but an "invisible leader" – the common purpose. The common purpose of HICA was the source of power that held them together. The invisible leader should shape structure and strategy. The invisible leader was the integration of all conflicting ideas, desires, and energies within HICA. Follett would have argued that the charisma of the purpose was more magnetic and enduring than the charisma of a person. HICA would thrive to the extent that it organized around this common purpose and not around the charisma of

Isabel. The construct of the invisible leader was unique to Follett. She stated:

> Leaders and followers are both following the invisible leader – the common purpose. The best executives put this common purpose clearly before their group. While leadership depends on the depth of conviction and the power coming there from, there must also be the ability to share that conviction with others, the ability to make purpose articulate. And then that common purpose becomes the leader. And I believe that we are coming more and more to act, whatever our theories, on our faith in the power of this invisible leader. Loyalty to the invisible leader gives us the strongest possible bond of union, establishes a sympathy which is not a sentimental but a dynamic sympathy. (Metcalf & Urwick, 1941, p. 287)

Follett would have encouraged Isabel to lead by modeling how to follow the invisible leader, allowing the mission to guide all decisions including questions of structure and programming. She offered five practical steps to creating unity at HICA: (a) hold regular meetings, (b) engage in genuine discussion, (c) learn together, (d) find ways for everyone to take responsibility, and (e) establish regular communication between teams and with the community (Follett, 1918, p. 204). She would have reminded Isabel that following the invisible leader would lead them into conflict and difficult conversations. However, she would have urged her to welcome those conversations instead of being afraid, reflecting her belief that "fear of difference was dread of life itself" (Follett, 1924, p. 300). If they avoided controversy, they would also miss out on creating something new. Finally, if Isabel and her staff co-created a followership culture, she would spend less time micro-managing or mediating destructive conflicts and more time releasing creative energies through integration. Productivity and morale would be better than DACA days because they would last.

Additional Resources

Mary Parker Follett (1868–1933) was an early management scholar and practitioner with a substantial following in the business world. Her ideas are echoed in empowerment, horizontal structures, followership, and systems thinking as they are discussed in leadership theory and practice today. Ahead of her time, Drucker (1995) dubbed Follett the "prophet of management" (p. 1) for her forward thinking. Follett influenced the creation of the word *followership*. Merriam-Webster cites the first known use of *followership* circa 1928 (http://www.merriam-webster.com/). On March 8, 1928, Follett *presented* a paper, "Some Discrepancies in Leadership Theory and Practice" in which she used the term *followship* (vs. followership) in the text. The first printing of this paper was in 1930 in *Business Leadership*; it was reprinted again in 1941 in *Dynamic Administration: The Collected Papers of Mary Parker Follett* (Metcalf & Urwick, 1941). Crainer (2000) identified Follett's work among the first to highlight the role of followers in leadership 50 years prior to other scholars.

Although the word *followership* is not listed in all dictionaries, it has become part of the modern leadership lexicon (Chaleff, 1995; Hollander, 1978; Kelley, 1988; Rost, 1991). Hollander and Webb (1955) posited that leaders and followers were interdependent, the boundaries between the two were fluid, and sometimes, depending on system demands, their roles were reversible. Kelley (1992) depicted followers as valued partners or co-creators in the leadership process with very similar qualities and competencies. Both Burns (1978) and Greenleaf (1970, 1977) elevated the role of followers in leadership and reflected Follett's initial call to train followers to be leaders. Follett initiated the idea that followers were critical, but it took several decades for the scholarly community to catch up.

DISCUSSION QUESTIONS

1. Explore the connections in this case and commentary between power orientation and the organizational structure and culture. How does the power orientation and hierarchical structure contribute to the conflicts and organizational capacity of the Hispanic Interest Coalition of Alabama (HICA)? How would changing the power and structure impact the escalation of conflict in the organization?
2. What would it take for HICA to change from a power-over to a power-with orientation and practice?
3. What is the invisible leader and how could it lead HICA?
4. Identify the conditions and attitudes within HICA that would help develop a partnership of following the invisible leader?
5. What would it take for HICA staff to adopt an integrative approach to conflict? How could HICA benefit? What are the potential risks of integrating conflict?

(*continued*)

6. Given Follett's resistance to framing conflict as a win-lose proposition, how might she have advised Isabel to approach Diana in order to integrate their different approaches to leadership and chain of command?
7. Applying a Follettian framework, what steps would you take to address the escalating team conflict?

References

Burns, J. M. (1978). *Leadership*. New York, NY: Harper & Row.

Chaleff, I. (1995). *The courageous follower: Standing up to & for our leaders* (2nd ed.). San Francisco, CA: Berrett-Koehler.

Crainer, S. (2000). *The management century: A critical review of 20th century thought and practice*. San Francisco, CA: Jossey-Bass.

Drucker, P. F. (1995). Mary Parker Follett: Prophet of management. In P. Graham (Ed.), *Mary Parker Follett-Prophet of management: A celebration of writings from the 1920s* (pp. 1–10). Boston, MA: Harvard Business Press.

Follett, M. P. (1918). *The new state: Group organization, the solution of popular government*. New York, NY: Longmans, Green & Co.

Follett, M. P. (1924). *Creative experience*. New York, NY: Longmans, Green & Co.

Follett, M. P. (1949). The essentials of leadership. In L. Urwick (Ed.), *Freedom & co-ordination: Lectures in business organization* (Chapter 4). London: Management Publications Trust, Ltd.

Greenleaf, R. K. (1970). *The servant as leader*. Indianapolis, IN: The Robert K. Greenleaf Center.

Greenleaf, R. K. (1977). *Servant leadership: A journey into the nature of legitimate power and greatness*. New York, NY: Paulist Press.

Hollander, E. P. (1978). *Leadership dynamics*. New York, NY: Free Press.

Hollander, E. P., & Webb, W. B. (1955). Leadership, followership, and friendship: An analysis of peer nominations. *Journal of Abnormal and Social Psychology, 50*, 163–167.

Kelley, R. E. (1988). In praise of followers. *Harvard Business Review, 66*(6), 321–341.

Kelley, R. E. (1992). *The power of followership: How to create leaders people want to follow, and followers who lead themselves*. New York, NY: Doubleday.

Metcalf, H. C., & Urwick, L. (Eds.). (1941). *Dynamic administration: The collected papers of Mary Parker Follett*. New York, NY: Harper.

Rost, J. (1991). *Leadership for the 21st century*. Westport, CT: Praeger.

CHAPTER

6 Corporate President as Follower

Rushton 'Rusty' Ricketson Sr and
W. David Winner

As the son of a share-cropper, Jimmy Collins was well acquainted with hard work. Spending long days picking cotton in the sweltering Georgia heat was a normal way of life for the 10-year-old dreamer. As he sat on the front porch of their modest farm home, shirt and overalls drenched with sweat from a day's work in the fields, he looked on as the men and women filed past, many of whom were relatives, slowly making their way to their own homes for a meager meal and a night's rest only to awaken the next day to pursue the same monotonous, backbreaking chore. As he watched, a unique thought began to germinate in his mind. Jimmy realized that his desire for a successful and fulfilling life was never going to be realized by working in these fields. His dream was to have a job that required wearing pressed white shirts, neck ties, suit pants, and leather dress shoes. But that job might as well have been on the moon. How in the world was he possibly going to see his dream come true? He needed something to happen. He needed something to change.

The change occurred after World War II. Manufacturing jobs began to spring up in urban areas, and Jimmy's father decided to move the family to Atlanta. There, Jimmy was constantly looking for a role model, someone whom he could imitate that would lead him to become a success. As a member of the Civil Air Patrol Cadets in his school, Jimmy found one particular person who appeared to have everything he desired: confidence, a can-do attitude, and respect from other people. This person was his Cadet Commander. Jimmy made it a point to copy all the things that the commander did: how he talked, how he walked, even how he wore his cap. Upon wearing his cap in the same way as his model, Jimmy faced the ridicule of his fellow cadets for wanting to be like the commander. It was too much. Jimmy made a monumental decision that would impact the rest of his life and work from that point forward. Jimmy decided he would be ... himself. But who would that be?

A love for reading, instilled by his aunt and his maternal Grandmother, propelled him as a student to go beyond what was required. Throughout high school and college, he voraciously read books on leadership and becoming a leader only to discover that these writers could not come to any conclusion on a definition of leadership. One truth, however, resonated with the budding businessman. He understood that leaders were persons with followers, and followers were persons who had chosen a leader. This understanding became the fertile ground in which the seeds of followership principles would bear fruit. Assessing who he was, Jimmy came to the conclusion that bold, creative leaders needed bold, creative followers. That's who he would become: a creative follower.

The next several years took Jimmy through three demanding and difficult boss situations, so Jimmy decided to go to work for himself. As his own boss, Jimmy succeeded in establishing himself as a respected kitchen designs consultant. Being self-employed allowed him to learn much about his craft, but the adventure lost its appeal when he realized the limited growth potential of the business would not satisfy his long-term goals. That is that day that Jimmy Collins fired his boss. He fired himself to seek a boss with whom he could develop a loyal, respectful, and meaningful relationship. Jimmy set the following non-negotiable criteria for the new boss whom he was seeking:

1. I will not work for someone who is a lesser person than myself.
2. I will only work for someone I can respect, look up to, and learn from – someone who can help me become a better person.
3. I will only work for someone who is building or growing something.
4. I will only work for someone who will let me express myself, make decisions, and will value my input.

Jimmy needed to find a boss who would meet these criteria and allow him to become the creative follower he desired to be. The opportunity came through a previously established relationship.

Truett Cathy was a successful restaurant owner in the Atlanta area and had gained a stellar reputation for his Chick-fil-A chicken sandwich. Cathy had done business with Jimmy on the first franchise Chick-fil-A restaurant, and they developed a strong friendship and working relationship. Jimmy saw Truett as an outstanding businessman and a person of high moral character. Thus, criteria one and two had been met.

The Chick-fil-A sandwich had a strong following, and the growth potential was substantial. When Cathy decided to grow his own business, he invited Jimmy to join him in realizing his vision of a national restaurant chain. This invitation fulfilled criteria number three.

Still, Jimmy needed to think and pray with his wife about the offer because he was not sure if this relationship with Truett would fulfill criteria number four, being allowed to express himself and have his input valued. It seems that the previous consulting working relationship with Truett involved Jimmy simply listening to what Truett wanted to build and then designing it through different iterations of the same drawing. Truett was the idea guy, and Jimmy was simply the draftsman. Jimmy knew that such a relationship would never meet criteria four and that he would never be fulfilled in such a working relationship.

When the day came for him to give his answer, Jimmy went to Truett's office. Jimmy had been working on a set of plans that would serve as the prototype for placing Chick-fil-A restaurants in shopping malls, a radical idea in its day. Jimmy had worked on these plans with his own ideas. These plans were his designs.

Upon entering the office with plans in hand neatly rolled and secured with a rubber band, Truett asked Jimmy if he was going to work for him. Jimmy suggested that before he answered, they both needed to look at the plans he had drawn for the restaurant. Jimmy relates this conversation:

> As I was unrolling that rubber band, Truett asked me, "What do you think about what you have there?"
>
> I stopped and answered confidently. "This is it; this is a winner."
>
> I continued unrolling the rubber band, eager to share my new plan. When I was almost to the end of the roll, Truett spoke again. I stopped. He asked, "Are you sure?"
>
> I said, emphatically, "Yes!"
>
> He looked at the still-rolled-up plans and said, "Then that is what we will do."
>
> I looked down and the rubber band was not quite to the end of the roll. The significance of that moment was suddenly clear. (Collins, 2013, pp. 45–46)

The moment was life-changing. Criteria four had been met. Truett would trust Jimmy with the designs. He would be allowed to express himself and his input would be valued. Jimmy had found his boss, but he had also found a leader who had an attractive vision and, most importantly, a unifying purpose. Together they would work to establish the Chick-fil-A restaurant chain.

Because both men had a high degree of character and integrity, a mutual relationship of trust and loyalty developed. Jimmy would discover those things that Truett did not like to do and then fulfill them with excellence. This idea of second-mile service to others became a part of the organizational culture. As the company grew and expanded, Jimmy took on the role of company president. Yet, he still followed and instilled his creative followership principles throughout the company. Perhaps that is why, almost 15 years after Jimmy's retirement, when those who still work in the corporate offices of Chick-fil-A are faced with a difficult decision, they often ask, "What would Jimmy do?"

Scholarly Commentary

The experiences of Jimmy Collins align with much of the current and past studies on the relationship between leaders and followers. Ascribing to a process view of leadership (Lord, 2008; Northouse, 2013), Collins' emphasis on the necessity of a "unifying purpose" (Collins, 2013, p. 18) is consistent with the need for a common goal in many definitions of leadership (Northouse, 2013; Ricketson, 2014; Winston & Patterson, 2005). Northouse (2013) suggests:

> Leaders direct their energies toward individuals who are trying to achieve something together. By common, we mean that the leaders and followers have a mutual purpose. Attention to common goals gives leadership an ethical overtone because it stresses the need for leaders to work with followers to achieve selected goals. (p. 6)

Collins (2013) adds that the common goal is the necessary ingredient for followers to work with leaders. Additionally, Collins suggests that the leader's ability to communicate this unifying purpose is important to inspiring a shared vision (Kouzes & Posner, 2012).

Collins' list of the four non-negotiable traits of a leader to choose as a boss appears to ascribe to the ideas of implicit leadership theory (Junker & van Dick, 2014; Offermann, Kennedy Jr., & Wirtz, 1994). Nye (2002) supports the internal aspect of leadership expectations of followers. He contends followers have "well-defined, highly abstracted schemas about leadership" (p. 338). These schemas include characteristics and appropriate behaviors of the leader and become expectations for leadership. By having an idea of the person for whom you want to work, the follower is able to choose a leader with whom he or she shares similar goals, aspirations, and values. Some might argue that such a choice is not always possible when the primary objective is finding a job or when followers are engaged in large corporate environments in which personnel changes take place with little to no regard for the follower's desire.

Even so, when Collins' suggests that people choose their boss, he gives credibility to followers as more than merely workers who work for someone. Rather, he proposes that followers are persons who have skills, ideas, and energies that complement those of the leader (Howell & Mendez, 2008). As a result, a relationship is created in which leaders and followers are able to achieve much more than each individual could have accomplished alone (Hurwitz & Hurwitz, 2015). Collins' call to support these leaders embraces what Chaleff (2009) writes about courageous followers and the notion of providing honest feedback, being passionate, showing initiative, and influencing the culture resonate with Collins' life as a follower.

Loyalty and trust play a large part in Collins' ideas regarding the leader and follower relationship. Kouzes and Posner (2012) focus on trust as the cornerstone to all aspects of the leader-follower relationship, including being a significant predictor of employee satisfaction. The importance of trust as a beginning point for following others has been the topic of many studies (Dirks & Ferrin, 2002; Jung & Avolio, 2000). The details of these studies and the development of trust among leaders and followers are too broad in scope to be adequately covered in this short review. However, perhaps the importance of trust may be summed by Kouzes and Posner (2012) when they state, "Trust comes first; following comes second" (p. 222). Once trust has been attained, then loyalty can be exhibited. Chaleff (2009) suggests:

> The values statement evokes a circumscribed loyalty – to fairness, to quality, to honesty, to service, to a common purpose. Circumscribed loyalty to worthy values avoids the pitfalls of unlimited loyalty and may be an evolutionary step forward. Both leaders and followers are entering into a contract to pursue the common purpose within the context of their values. The loyalty of each is to the purpose and to helping each other stay true to that purpose. (p. 17)

One of Collin's keys to his role as a follower was his loyalty to founder, Truett Cathy. Collins' view of loyalty goes beyond fealty to a common purpose and evokes a relational component by emphasizing the human characteristics of trust, integrity, and honesty within both leader and follower. Collins was able to tap into the reciprocal influence (Yukl, 2013, p. 411) that trust and cooperation between leader and follower can create.

Leader vulnerability and transparency are subjects that have been explored at length (Avolio & Reichard, 2008). However, the idea of two-way or reciprocal loyalty between the leader and the follower is a specific construct that is not often addressed in the literature. Porth, McCall, and Bausch (1999) explore this construct as a Judeo-Christian spiritual theme within learning organizations, suggesting that spiritual teachings, such as valuing the human being, create organizational cultures that foster reciprocal loyalty and respect. Perhaps the idea of reciprocal loyalty might further be explained by Ricketson's (2014) concept of the Following-Leader as a follower with a strong spiritual/religious value system who understands that the best way to personal fulfillment is by operationalizing her or his spiritual values in response to others. Such responses constitute what many refer to as The Golden Rule: Do unto others as you would have them do unto you. Such a principle would be indicative of the manner by which Jimmy Collins influenced and led those around him.

DISCUSSION QUESTIONS

1. What do you think of Collins's idea of "choosing your boss?"
2. Collins had his list of four non-negotiables, what would yours be? Can you agree with his list of four? Which would you change and why?
3. According to Collins, trust and loyalty go together in creating a positive leader-follower relationship? Who has more responsibility in creating trust, the leader or the follower? How does the loyalty of a follower help build trust in the relationship?
4. How would you begin the process of building trust/ loyalty relationships between colleagues within your work context? Between you and your leader?
5. Collins went through a process where he had to decide to "be himself." Are you comfortable with yourself and directions your life is taking? What steps will you take, like Collins did, to change your career and pursue your purpose?
6. Collins was willing to "fire himself" to achieve his vision. What are you willing to stop doing to pursue your vision? Make a list of what to stop doing and what you need to start doing.

7. Leaders and followers can achieve more working together. Do you believe that this is a true statement? Explain your answer. How do leaders and followers work against each other? What are some important actions leaders can do to help followers feel valuable in their contribution?
8. How does an effective and/or courageous follower positively/negatively impact work relationships?
9. Collins maintains loyalty and trust support one another, but how far should loyalty extend? Is it OK to be unethical for the sake of loyalty? How can confronting unethical behavior be a form of loyalty?

References

Avolio, B., & Reichard, R. (2008). The rise of authentic followership. In R. E. Riggio, I. Chaleff, & J. Lipman-Blumen (Eds.), *The art of followership: How great followers create great leaders and organizations* (pp. 325–337). San Francisco, CA: Jossey-Bass.

Chaleff, I. (2009). *The courageous follower: Standing up to and for our leaders* (3rd ed.). San Francisco, CA: Berrett-Koehler.

Collins, J. (2013). *Creative followership: In the shadow of greatness.* Decatur, GA: Looking Glass Books.

Dirks, K. T., & Ferrin, D. L. (2002). Trust in leadership: Meta-analytic findings and implications for research and practice. *Journal of Applied Psychology, 87*(4), 611–628. doi:10.1037/0021-9010.87.4.611

Howell, J. P., & Mendez, M. J. (2008). Three perspectives on followership. In R. E. Riggio, I. Chaleff, & J. Lipman-Blumen (Eds.), *The art of followership: How great followers create great leaders and organizations* (pp. 25–40). San Francisco, CA: Jossey-Bass.

Hurwitz, M., & Hurwitz, S. (2015). *Leadership is half the story: A fresh look at followership, leadership, and collaboration.* Toronto: University of Toronto Press.

Jung, D. I., & Avolio, B. J. (2000). Opening the black box: An experimental investigation of the mediating effects of trust and value congruence on transformational and transactional leadership. *Journal of Organizational Behavior, 21*(8), 949–964. doi:10.1002/1099-13799200012021:8

Junker, N. M., & van Dick, R. (2014). Implicit theories in organizational settings: A systematic review and research agenda of implicit leadership and followership theories. *The Leadership Quarterly, 25*(6), 1079–1186. doi:10.1016/j.leaqua.2014.09.002

Kouzes, J. M., & Posner, B. Z. (2012). *The leadership challenge: How to make extraordinary things happen in organizations* (5th ed.). San Francisco, CA: Jossey-Bass.

Lord, R. G. (2008). Follower's cognitive and affective structures and leadership process. In R. E. Riggio, I. Chaleff, & J. Lipman-Blumen (Eds.), *The art of followership: How great followers create great leaders and organizations* (pp. 255–266). San Francisco, CA: Jossey-Bass.

Northouse, P. G. (2013). *Leadership: Theory and practice* (6th ed.). Thousand Oaks, CA: Sage.

Nye, J. L. (2002). The eye of the follower: Information processing effects on attributions regarding leaders of small groups. *Small Group Research*, *33*, 337–360. doi:10.1177/10496402033003003

Offermann, L. R., Kennedy, J., Jr., & Wirtz, P. W. (1994). Implicit leadership theories: Content, structure, and generalizability. *The Leadership Quarterly*, *5*(1), 43–58. doi:10.1016/1048-9843(94)90005-1

Porth, S. J., McCall, J., & Bausch, T. A. (1999). Spiritual themes of the learning organization. *Journal of Organizational Change Management*, *12*(3), 211–220. doi:10.1108/09534819910273883

Ricketson, R. S. (2014). *Followerfirst: Rethinking leading in the church* (2nd ed.). Cumming, GA: Heartworks.

Winston, B. E., & Patterson, D. K. (2005). An integrative definition of leadership. *International Journal of Leadership Studies*, *1*(2), 6–66. Retrieved from http://www.regent.edu

Yukl, G. (2013). *Leadership in organizations* (8th ed.). Boston, MA: Pearson.

CHAPTER

7 In Whom Do We Invest?

Eric Downing and Jennifer Moss Breen

Sandy Sullivan began to feel that same sense of looming dread that seemed to set in annually as the fiscal year-end approached. Although she had been the head of Organizational Development and Training at LargOrg Corporation for 15 years, the process of deciding where to allocate the corporation's limited leadership training resources never seemed to change. LargOrg Corporation had grown dramatically in the years since she joined the company, and now enjoyed the benefits of being publicly traded and looked upon as an industry leader. Although the amount of resources allocated to leadership training had increased over the years, the allocation process remained static. Sandy knew that a series of meetings with the senior management team would be conducted, shortly before deciding on the final budget allocations for training for the upcoming year.

Usually, several individuals on the management committee would ask a few questions about what was accomplished with the training and development budget from the previous year, and then the discussion would move on to other managerial topics, before coming back to focus on next year's leadership training resource allocations. A slight increase in budgetary allocation, which was in line with the inflationary growth of the overall budget, would be allocated to leadership training. The increase would come with a collective desire from the management team to do better with the resources next year.

Sandy knew there must be a better way to make these important resource decisions. She decided that gathering better information and engaging the middle management of the company to help with the allocation decision might be a useful step in helping the company move forward more efficiently.

Sandy set up a meeting with Robert Marx, Senior VP of Operations, and John Helm, Production Manager, to solicit their feedback and perceptions about the company's past leadership training and development practices. Sandy chose Marx to provide input because of his tenure at the company and his status as a senior manager in the organization. He had often expressed interest in leadership development and had pursued a number of outside leadership training opportunities to help develop his personal leadership style. Hess, on the other hand, was included because he was recently promoted into a middle management position after seeking additional leadership development training inside the organization.

In the meeting, Sandy explained to Robert and John that she was frustrated with the inefficient process that the organization used to allocate resources for annual leadership development training. She made it clear that she wanted honest and open feedback, and that she was taking a "clean slate" approach towards crafting a new leadership resource training allocation policy going forward. She quickly covered familiar ground with Robert and John and lamented, "Much of the leadership development training that we have had in place for many years is centered on providing additional courses in the same old leadership styles to new and existing managers."

John immediately pointed out that the current training tends to be event driven, rather than a systematic and ongoing process that could become part of the longer-term learning culture of the organization. John also pointed out during the five years in which he had engaged in the leadership training provided by the organization, three of those years had focused on a single leadership style. Although John was happy to have the training, he also noted that the transformational leadership style training being offered year after year might not have been the best match for his personality and personal skill set.

Robert agreed with John and added a number of observations that he had been contemplating for some time. Robert shared, "For the last couple of years, I have wondered if we should be trying to train and develop managers internally, or if we would be better off simply attempting to recruit employees who are already trained in leadership skills." He continued, "It is frustrating to know that in almost every other aspect of our corporate strategy, we spend a great deal of time with long-term planning, but we do not seem to have place the same emphasis on determining who among the corporate employees should actually be participating in leadership development."

Towards the end of the meeting, Robert shared an observation that was an epiphany for Sandy. Robert exclaimed, "I could be a much better leader if I had better followers! We spend our entire leadership development budget on just a few formal leaders in the organization and there must be some way to help those that we are leading understand how to work with us better." Robert wraps up his rant by suggesting, "If we want to really get better at overall leadership within this company, we must identify our current leaders and decide how we can also equip our followers to eventually step into these roles. And ultimately, if we are going to invest in training our followers, we are going to have to figure out if it is worth what it costs us." John added, "I can't imagine we're going to get all that done without hiring an outside consultant to help us prioritize our next steps."

The next day, Sandy reached out to Bob Johnson, a well-known leadership consultant, to explain the situation that LargOrg Corp faced. Bob assured Sandy that this situation was not unique and offered to fax her a list of questions to consider before proceeding. Bob sent a number of interesting questions to Sandy to include the following ones:

- Does your company recognize the value of focusing on different leadership styles?
- Is there a focus on developing both leaders and followers in the organization?
- Who takes responsibility for ensuring that the organization understands the needs of the leaders as well as the needs of the followers?
- Are leadership and followership development a strategic or tactical focus of the organization?
- With limited resources, how do we decide which employees will benefit from leadership and followership development the most?
- Does leadership and/or followership development training play a long-term role in employee retention?

Scholarly Commentary

Organizations of all types emphasize the need for excellent leaders. Leadership development programs are plentiful in most major corporations, and billions of dollars are spent annually on leadership development programs. Yet, despite this vast human capital investment, many organizations experience frustration when attempting to meet organizational goals. As this case presents, the question arises of whether we are investing limited human capital development funds in the right people. Regardless of how much we invest in leaders, their followers are essential to achieving stated goals. This interdependence makes followership a key component of our human capital and leadership development investment.

When considering the typical organizational structure, one envisions some sort of hierarchy. Even in the flattest of organizations, some stand out as "leaders," while others contribute as individual team members or associates. Every leader must answer to someone in addition to their designated superiors, whether it is their Board of Directors, their stockholders, team members, or peers. These types of informal reporting structures require every leader to function as a follower as well, generating the need to further develop both leadership and followership skills.

Effective followers and leaders share many characteristics, but they also exhibit unique qualities. Some researchers have researched the unique qualities of followers and the important role they play in organizations. Gardner (1987) discussed the dyadic nature of followership where both leaders and followers have influence. True followers, in Gardner's view, do not just subordinate themselves to the leadership process, rather they are active participants. As a result, we might consider training followers to more effectively influence others as this could be an excellent human capital investment opportunity.

Similarly, Rost (1993) described followers as either active or passive. The passive view of followers is one where we envision the sweaty masses of workers, far-removed from the leadership, unable to act without direct supervision, and passively willing to let others control their lives. In this view, followers may do leadership, but not hold formal leadership roles. Rost's work is helpful because it assists leaders in understanding followers as workers who are satisfied not being the leader. They are comfortable working alongside or behind a good leader. They understand that in some situations, they will need to step up and lead, while in others, they will step back and follow.

To examine this idea further, Relational Leadership Theory (RLT) serves as a viable framework (Uhl-Bien, 2006). RLT posits that leaders and followers exist in a shared social context where social influence affects workplace values, norms, and behaviors. Drawing from the LMX literature (Graen & Uhl-Bien, 1995), the RLT framework supports an "entity" view, meaning that the quality and character of the leader/follower relationship is based upon the individual qualities, previous experiences, and the current context of the interaction. Fairhurst and Uhl-Bien (2012) conclude that leadership and followership are created in tandem, emphasizing the importance of their relationship in the influence process.

Given that recent followership theory emphasizes the notion of a dyadic leader/follower process, then how might we encourage followers to more actively engage in this process? If leaders and followers mirror each other and work together in a collective manner, then ideally, we would invest in follower development in kind. Educating followers on their importance not only socially, but cognitively and behaviorally as well, can create a stronger pool of workers whom work to solve today's difficult organizational problems.

To that end, Gardner's (1987) work offers difficult questions regarding the shared leader-follower influence process. If we are going to develop followers, exactly what skills would we cultivate? Gardner suggests that followers significantly impact the success of leaders, but that leaders are encouraged to be attentive to followers' personal and professional goals. Through this lens, we conjecture that if leaders understand the needs, aspirations, values, hopes, and fears of their team, and then attend to these needs, then leaders will earn a following because followers often ask, "How can this leader help me to get what I want and need?" Leaders who meet those needs encourage everyone's "best self" to emerge. If leaders understand the personalities, traits, goals, and aspirations of followers and attend to them, then a clear path for human capital development could emerge (Dvir, Eden, Avolio, & Shamir, 2002).

Because followership and leadership are relational processes, human capital strategists might consider strategically developing followers alongside leaders by including followership components within an organizational learning and development plan. Drawing from authentic leadership theory and the self-based model of leadership, Gardner, Avolio, Luthans, May, and Walumbwa (2005) suggest that developing leaders and followers simultaneously can create an inclusive, collaborative, and effective work environment. Through a shared leader and follower development process, leaders can model authentic leadership and encourage the same in followers.

Leadership development is a human capital investment (Hitt & Ireland, 2002). Organizations seeking to create a sustained competitive advantage through human capital investment can draw upon both the leadership and human capital literature to derive viable approaches. For instance, Birasnav, Rangnekar, and Dalpati (2011) suggest that organizations who purposefully develop transformational leaders also encourage the development of effective followers because transformational leaders have the ability to encourage employees to engage in human capital development opportunities within the organization. This shared development process is thought to create a learning culture and healthier communication strategies.

A good first step is to analyze exactly whom is currently being developed within the organization (human capital investment) and why this investment is being made. If we can quantify human capital investments and development audiences, we can then try to capture the outcomes of these investments. This is a complicated process, as capturing the return on investment in learning is often nebulous because outcomes of development are usually intangible. So, how do we know when effective leadership (or followership) development has occurred?

By strategically planning learning (human capital investment) for both leaders and followers, we come closer to the goal of fully equipping the organization for achieving optimal functioning. Further reading about the process of creating a business plan for learning can be found in Vance (2011). Once it is understood who is identified for development, why they are a development candidate, and the potential outcomes of their development, we can begin to couple leadership and followership development in a more meaningful way. For instance, developing a strong succession plan can be a useful strategy in creating a stronger leadership pipeline. Understanding our leaders and the roles they play, in turn, provides the groundwork for followership development. We can then create a followership succession plan that aligns with key leadership roles as well as strategic and tactical goals, thereby encouraging and equipping followers to step up to new opportunities.

Using the knowledge gleaned from business leaders and key stakeholders, we can begin to draft a plan that attends to business needs. Leadership and followership development plans should directly align with input from managers and line leaders, creating curriculum that attends to those needs. This process allows business leaders to define what constitutes success and allows for the identification of tangible and intangible outcomes of the learning (Black & Earnest, 2009; Hiller, Dechurch, Murase, & Doty, 2011).

The goal of followership development is to link leaders and followers together in the learning process. How can development programs be created in such a way in which followers and leaders learn collaboratively?

DISCUSSION QUESTIONS

1. How does LargOrg Corp currently view the value of focusing on the development of different leadership styles? Why do you think that LargOrg Corp takes this approach?
2. How might Sandy encourage LargOrg Corp to place greater focus on developing both leaders and followers in the organization?

3. What push-back might Sandy experience when attempting to ensure that the organization understands the needs of the leaders as well as the needs of the followers? How might she develop a plan that addresses these concerns?
4. Does LargOrg Corp consider leadership and followership development to be strategic or tactical in nature? What are the key factors that influence their choice?
5. With limited resources, how could LargOrg Corp decide which employees will benefit from leadership and followership development the most? In other words, how can they earn the greatest return of investment in these initiatives and which initiatives should take priority?
6. If you were consulting LargOrg Corp on leadership and/or followership development training, could you ensure that the human capital investment in leadership development contributes to a long-term role in employee retention? Why or why not?
7. How could you work closely with business leaders to determine their human capital development needs? In other words, what business goals have they set for the year and how can leadership (and followership) development help them to meet these goals?
8. Are you aware of your company's succession plan? If not, how could you gain information about this plan? If a succession plan does not exist, what threat does this create for your organization? How can you assist in alleviating this threat?
9. How could you work closely with business leaders to determine their human capital development needs? In other words, what business goals have they set for the year and how can leadership (and followership) development help them to meet these goals?
10. Does your company focus on developing both leaders and followers in the organization? Why or why not?
11. Within your organization, does anyone take responsibility for ensuring that the organization understands the development needs of the leaders as well as the development needs of the followers?

(*continued*)

12. Does your organization have a process that allows them to decide which employees will benefit from leadership development? If so, what is this process? If not, what suggestions would you make to assist in the development of this process?
13. In your estimation, what is the impact of leadership and/or followership development in your company's long-term employee retention? How might the inclusion of strategic development affect retention?
14. What follower skills, if more fully developed, would be the most beneficial for your organization?

References

Birasnav, M., Rangnekar, S., & Dalpati, A. (2011). Transformational leadership and human capital benefits: The role of knowledge management. *Leadership and Organizational Development Journal*, *32*, 106–126. doi:10.1108/0143773111 112962

Black, A. M., & Earnest, G. W. (2009). Measuring the outcomes of leadership development programs. *Journal of Leadership and Organizational Studies*, *16*, 184–196. doi:10.1177/1548051809339193

Dvir, T., Eden, D., Avolio, B. J., & Shamir, B. (2002). Impact of transformational leadership on follower development and performance: A field experiment. *Academy of Management Journal*, *45*(4), 735–744. Retrieved from http://jtor.org/stable/ 3069307

Fairhurst, G. T., & Uhl-Bien, M. (2012). Organizational discourse analysis (ODA): Examining leadership as a relational process. *The Leadership Quarterly*, *23*(6), 1043–1062. doi:10.1016/j.leaqua.2012.10.005

Gardner, J. W. (1987). Leaders and followers. In J. T. Wren (Ed.), *The leaders companion: Insights on leadership through the ages* (pp. 185–188). New York, NY: Free Press.

Gardner, W. L., Avolio, B. J., Luthans, F., May, D. R., & Walumbwa, F. (2005). "Can you see the real me?" A self-based model of authentic leader and follower development. *The Leadership Quarterly*, *16*(3), 343–372. Retrieved from http:// www.elsevier.com

Graen, G. B., & Uhl-Bien, M. (1995). Relationship-based approach to leadership: Development of Leader-Member Exchange (LMX) theory of leadership over 25 years: Applying a multi-level multi-domain perspective. *The Leadership Quarterly*, *6*(2), 219–247. Retrieved from http://www.elsevier.com

Hiller, N. J., Dechurch, L. A., Murase, T., & Doty, D. (2011). Searching for outcomes of leadership: A 25-year review. *Journal of Management*, *37*(4), 1137–1177. doi:10.1177/0149206310393520

Hitt, M. A., & Ireland, R. D. (2002). The essence of strategic leadership: Managing human and social capital. *Journal of Leadership and Organizational Studies*, *9*(1), 3–14. Retrieved from http://onlinelibrary.wiley.com

Rost, J. C. (1993). *Leadership for the 21st century*. Westport, CT: Praeger.

Uhl-Bien, M. (2006). Relational leadership theory: Exploring the social processes of leadership and organizing. *The Leadership Quarterly*, *17*(6), 654–676. doi:0.1016/j.leaqua.2006.10.007

Vance, D. (2011). *The business of learning: How to manage corporate training to improve the bottom line*. Greeley, CO: Poudre River Group.

CHAPTER

8 Followership and the Paradox of Promotion

Rob Koonce, Kimberley A. Koonce
and Sharon Armstead

Shauna and Grace first met in graduate school. While talking on the phone recently, Grace asked Shauna, "So how is your job going in respiratory therapy?" Shauna replied, "Do you really want to hear me rant about that one?" Grace retorted, "Actually, I would. Can I stop by later this week and talk with you about it over lunch? I am in the process of writing a feature article on workplace promotion dilemmas for a prominent training and development publication." Shauna happily agreed to the interview.

On the day of the interview, Grace began by asking, "Shauna, tell me about the time leading up to your promotion last year. What were you feeling at the time and how did the promotion come about?" Shauna responded, "You know, I distinctly remember feeling that I was at a crossroads where I knew that I either had to leave the industry that I had grown to love or somehow figure out how to help that industry to change by giving the need for change a voice. As you know, I was a respiratory therapist and I had been working for the same organization for over 20 years. All that I could think at the time was surely there is something else for me to do. Fortunate for me, I had a chance conversation with a former manager named Jackie who learned of my dilemma. Jackie personally understood my readiness to leave because she was frustrated too, so she asked if I had time for a quick coffee. During that conversation, Jackie asked if I might ever be interested in a leadership role within the department as a supervisor or educator. I wasn't quite sure where she was headed, but I told her, 'Yes'. Then Jackie asked me, 'If you could choose a leadership role which one would you prefer?' I quickly replied, 'I would take the one where I can apply what I have learned over the past 20 plus years and use it to bring about change'. Jackie smiled, I thanked her for the dialogue, and we returned to work."

"About a month later," Shauna continued, "I found myself thinking again about that conversation with Jackie. I decided that it was time for me to get more serious about my perceived need for change. I went home that night and one of the first things that I did was sign up to receive e-mails from our HR Department, but I did not stop there. I remember thinking as long as I am looking, I am going to sign up to receive similar e-mails from three other area hospitals too where I feel like my experience as a clinician can be used to make a difference." Grace retorted, "Why was making a difference important to you?" Shauna responded, "Making a difference is really all that I ever wanted to do. Within a week of putting my name on that e-mail alert list, a managerial position opened at the hospital where I worked. I was so excited that I called my former manager Jackie and told her that I was going to apply for it. It was so discouraging when I did not get the job; however, only a few days later, another position opened for a dayshift supervisor who would be in charge of the entire department. That department happened to be the one for which I had been working for the past over 20 years. On the day that the position first opened, I could not wait to get home to apply for it. As fate would have it, that position was the one into which I was promoted." Shauna laughed, "I suspect that if I were a dog, you would have seen my tail wagging on the day that promotion occurred. I called my husband to share the news with him. He was so proud; he is my biggest supporter."

Grace probed, "So tell me about your first few weeks in that new job. What were they like?" Shauna replied, "Grace, I was so honored to be chosen to lead that department, but the joy of that experience soon faded when I quickly realized just how little that my past experience as a clinician had prepared me to take on this new position. The real proof of just how unprepared that I was came six months into the job when I received the results of our department's first employee satisfaction survey. [Shauna suddenly teared up.] Employees said the most hurtful things about me and my immediate supervisor in that survey. The comments were so bad that it led to an investigation of our department by the Human Resources Department. I remember immediately thinking that I had not only failed myself, but I had also failed my manager and everyone else in the department. It was a horrible experience. Even worse for me personally was the realization that what was said had come from the very people who were entrusted to my care as a leader. I was totally devastated by what that report revealed about my lack of supervisory skills. That was one of the most humiliating experiences with which I have ever had to deal in the workplace. It emotionally stripped me of my confidence." [Grace held further questions while Shauna recomposed herself.] Shauna continued, "As I sit here thinking about the pain and embarrassment I faced as a result of that negative experience, I also consider that it was probably one of the best things that ever happened to me because it has positively impacted how I lead others to this very day. I swore that I would never make anyone suffer through what I did with that experience."

"In looking back at the day I accepted my new position, the people that I had agreed to supervise also needed for me to immediately know how to manage staff, assist my superior with budgetary concerns, and take disciplinary action as warranted." Shauna added, "I faced all three of those conditions within the first two weeks in my new job. I had no experience with any of them." Grace inquired, "Did your supervisor ever indicate why they had hired you for the position?" "Oh yes," Shauna replied, "she said that it was my passion and drive for the profession, my clinical skills, and the length of time that I had spent in the profession. As I now think about that response, I also find myself asking how any of my prior experiences as a clinician now leave the people who are following me any better off – not as a clinician, but as their leader. To be blunt about it, I was promoted into a position that I was unprepared to lead. The same can be said for the person above me too. In the first meeting that I ever had with my supervisor, she indicated that she came to our department with only six months of supervisory experience. This happened in one of the leading cities in the United States. I also think of the fact that there were no policies in place to follow. No procedures. And even if there had been, I was never exposed to them. How was I supposed to learn about my job? Trial by fire? That is how the person who hired me learned what she was required to do."

Shauna continued, "The only work experience that was required in the job description was five plus years of clinical practice. While I can now see how that experience would help me to relate to the environment in which I would be working, I also realize that it did not prepare me in any way as a leader, nor did any of the classes which I was required to take to obtain my bachelor's degree prepare me for anything more than what I needed to know to be a clinician. Two months after starting my new job, I remember taking my first leadership training workshop. The focus for the first day of that workshop was on servant leadership. I vividly remember a question that was asked of everyone on that first day: '*When you first applied for the position for which you are being trained today, did you respond to a job posting or a calling*?' That question not only helped me to rediscover my calling as a leader, but also it sorely reminded me of the reason that I had become a clinician over 20 years ago."

Grace then asked, "Shauna with what you have learned from this experience, what questions would you pose to the leadership of your profession regarding how people in your profession are currently promoted into leadership roles?" Shauna said, "In healthcare, we look to our clinical staff with an expectation that they will always give of their best. That is a laudable goal which should be commended, but as I sit and ponder the scenario of clinical staff who give of their best, I also ask if healthcare organizations should not expect its leaders and managers to give of their best too? If our answer to that question is yes, then is it not reasonable to assume that we should also attempt to train, educate, or ensure that clinicians have the proper work experience to lead and manage other clinicians prior to promoting them? Without the proper training, education, or prior work experience, how can we expect clinicians to lead or manage with their best? The simple truth of the matter is that we cannot have this expectation – and yet we do."

Scholarly Commentary

U.S. organizations currently spend in excess of $164 billion per year on training and development (Miller, 2013). According to a study by Aguinis and Kraiger (2009), training and development also benefits employee performance, organizations, and society as a whole. Yet, as this case illustrates, how training and development programs are often implemented in organizations offers reason for pause.

According to Edmondson (2011), when executives are asked how many failures in organizations are truly blameworthy, they typically suggest 2–5%; however, when the question changes to one of asking how many are treated by the executives as blameworthy, the response is typically 70–90%. When one considers the potential impact of such a culture on followers who are promoted into positions for which they are untrained to perform, the potential problems associated with such a culture surface and no one is exempt – not the one who is blamed; nor the staff who point fingers at the untrained manager in an employee satisfaction survey; nor human resources who are called to investigate; nor more senior managers who, in a too little, too late performance review may be called to make decisions to fire the untrained manager because the affected departments are underperforming. The impact of the disconnect between follower expectations and traditional work cultures offers additional reason for concern when one considers millennials who are resigning at a more rapid rate than prior generations (Graen & Grace, 2015). Very simply put, the blame game is a no-win situation for all involved. Organizational systems in which information flows uni-directionally from the top down and "subordinate" managers and non-managers are expected to carry out orders and never to question are a challenge for traditional hierarchies (Collinson, 2008; Koonce, 2013, 2016). When one considers the 80% contribution on average that followers make to an organization's success (Hassan, 2011; Kelley, 1992), the implications are clear.

As defined by Salas, Tannenbaum, Kraiger, and Smith-Jentsch (2012), the goal of training is to "create sustainable changes in behavior and cognition so that individuals possess the competencies they need to perform a job" (p. 77). The authors go on to note that while training is related to learning, only learning during training that transfers to an actual job-related application or job performance is relevant to training's impact on an individual and the organization which they represent. This conclusion is supported by a recent study by Aragon, Jimenez, and Valle (2014) in which the authors examined the relationship between training, organizational learning, and performance. Although the authors did not find support for a direct effect between training and performance, they did find support for a positive relationship between training and learning, as well as a positive relationship between learning and performance. This information leads to some interesting questions. For example, what happens when a follower is promoted into a position which requires specific management or leadership knowledge, skills, and abilities (KSAs) for which they do not have prior work experience or training and development? Who is impacted by this decision and where does it leave an employee and her staff, the clients who are served, as well as her supervisor, her department, and her organization?

If the current case is any indication of what should be expected when followers are promoted without prior work experience or training and development, the answer to the latter question is all of the above are impacted. While past work experience as a manager or leader and prior training and development for a particular position can be helpful in performing a job into which one is promoted, Salas et al. (2012) suggest that training should be approached as a system in which the effectiveness of on-going training is influenced, and ultimately measured, by what occurs before, during, and after each training. One should also consider characteristics related to the individual and the work environment. Research suggests that individuals are likely to be more motivated to attend and learn from trainings when they (a) are given the freedom to choose which trainings to attend, (b) asked what they would like to see included in the training, (c) perceive their work climate to be supportive of their attendance, and (d) are provided the opportunity to practice what they learn (p. 78).

For promotion purposes, it is always possible that a particular pool of applicants will not have prior management or leadership work experience as requested for a job opening. It is also possible that existing members of an organization like Shauna represent a hidden talent who has not yet been recognized as one of the organization's future leaders. Despite these potential limitations, it seems reasonable to assume given the responsibilities and accountabilities of leadership and management positions that one needs to have some rudimentary understanding of one's position if one is to be required to perform the tasks that a position entails. Research also suggests that at least a low level of training and experience can be valuable for predicting future performance (Heneman, Judge, & Kammeyer-Mueller, 2015, p. 383). An appropriate level of training or experience appears to be particularly relevant to positions of management and leadership in which one's actions, reactions, or inactions may not only impact the ability to perform the tasks of one's own position, but also set the tone for the group whom one is managing or leading (Barsade, 2002). This knowledge leads us back to the employee satisfaction survey and subsequent performance review in the current case, as well as the culture of blame which so often pervades today's organizational hierarchies.

Conclusion

According to Bender (2005), the clinical ladder design in hospitals is frequently based on a stepwise progression of clinical expertize, years of employment, or education with little to no prior assessment for one's readiness to assume a higher administrative role. An experienced clinician's skill set likely includes strong interpersonal skills, flexibility, and creative problem solving abilities; however, these abilities say very little about a clinician's ability to handle administrative, financial, or regulatory policy issues. According to Bender, it is not uncommon for a clinician who lacks the skills needed to perform their new role to receive guidance from a co-worker who also learned her administrative role on the job.

As described to her friend Grace, the method used to train Shauna following her promotion was "trial by fire," the same method which had been used to train her supervisor prior to her own promotion. Unfortunately, "trial by fire" is reactive and rarely leads to satisfactory workplace outcomes. As a result, Shauna was ultimately faced with a professional situation that left her feeling personally and professionally empty. The demotivation and resultant talk of leaving was preventable. When one considers the 20 plus years of clinical experience that she brought to the table in her new leadership role, the question of how that experience could have been more effectively applied also warrants further reflection.

DISCUSSION QUESTIONS

1. During the interview between Grace and Shauna, Shauna mentions a question that she was asked two months into her new position during her first leadership workshop: "*When you first applied for the position for which you are being trained today, did you respond to a job posting or a calling*?" Do you believe that this question is more relevant to organizational leaders, followers, or both? Make a list of the people whom you believe will be impacted by your response.
2. Assume that you are the HR representative in this case. You just received the results back on Shauna's first employee satisfaction survey? What information should be considered in assessing the survey results?
3. Assume that you are Shauna in this case. You were just contacted by HR to discuss the results of your first employee satisfaction survey. What information should be considered in assessing the survey results?
4. What proactive steps could have been taken by the organization to prevent the investigation?
5. Do you believe that Shauna could have taken any additional steps to prevent the remarks made by the staff that she was called to lead?
6. Write an essay in which you consider your own promotion. Imagine that you are ill-equipped to take on your new role. What measures would you take to become familiar with the requirements for that role as quickly as possible? How would you assess your shortcomings and eventual effectiveness in the new role? How do you believe that your senior manager or leader should assess the same shortcomings and eventual effectiveness?

References

Aguinis, H., & Kraiger, K. (2009). Benefits of training and development for individuals and teams, organizations, and society. *Annual Review of Psychology*, *60*, 451–474. doi:10.1146/annurev.psych.60.110707.163505

Aragon, M. I. B., Jimenez, D. J., & Valle, R. S. (2014). Training and performance: The mediating role of organizational learning. *Business Research Quarterly*, *17*, 161–173. doi:10.1016/j.cede.2013.05.003

Barsade, S. (2002). The ripple effect: Emotional contagion and its influence on group behavior. *Administrative Science Quarterly*, *47*(4), 644–675. doi:10.2307/3094912

Bender, D. G. (2005). Escaping the box: Preparing allied health practitioners for management positions. *The Health Care Manager*, *24*(4), 364–368. Retrieved from http://journals.lww.com

Collinson, D. (2008). Conformist, resistant, and disguised selves: A post-structuralist approach to identity and workplace followership. In R. E. Riggio, I. Chaleff, & J. Lipman-Blumen (Eds.), *The art of followership: How great followers create great leaders and organizations* (pp. 309–323). San Francisco, CA: Jossey-Bass.

Edmondson, A. C. (2011). Strategies for learning from failure. *Harvard Business Review*, *89*(4), 48–55.

Graen, G., & Grace, M. (2015). *New talent strategy: Attract, process, educate, empower, engage and retain the best.* Retrieved from http://www.shrm.org/Research/Documents/SHRM-SIOP%20New%20Talent%20Strategy.pdf

Hassan, F. (2011). The frontline advantage. *Harvard Business Review*, *89*(5), 106–114.

Heneman, H. G., Judge, T. A., & Kammeyer-Mueller, J. D. (2015). *Staffing organizations* (8th ed.). Middleton, WI: Mendota House.

Kelley, R. E. (1992). *The power of followership: How to create leaders people want to follow and followers who lead themselves.* New York, NY: Doubleday.

Koonce, R. (2013). Partial least squares analysis as a modeling tool for assessing motivational leadership practices. *International annual conference proceedings of the American society for engineering management, 2013 international annual conference*, Minneapolis, MN, October.

Koonce, R. (2016). All in "the family": Leading and following through individual, relational, and collective mindsets. In R. Koonce, M. Bligh, M. K. Carsten, & M. Hurwitz (Eds.), *Followership in action: Cases and commentaries*. Bingley, UK: Emerald Group Publishing Limited.

Miller, L. (2013). *ASTD state of the industry report 2013*. Alexandria, VA: American Society of Training & Development.

Salas, E., Tannenbaum, S. I., Kraiger, K., & Smith-Jentsch, K. A. (2012). The science of training and development in organizations: What matters in practice. *Psychological Sciences in the Public Interest*, *13*(2), 74–101. doi:10.1177/1529100612436661

CHAPTER

9 Just in Time Followership

Rhonda K. Rodgers and Michelle C. Bligh

Christine Guerrier is an 18 year old, part-time supervisor who works for J.I.T., a small parcel shipping company. She was recruited through the local community college she attends. Her first job at the company was to unload packages from tractor-trailers at 4 o'clock in the morning. Christine was eager to prove herself as the only female on her crew, and so she made sure to empty more trailers each shift than any of her coworkers. Her productivity and "go-getter" attitude were noticed by her supervisor, which led to several promotions, first to continuously greater responsibilities as an hourly employee, and ultimately to a supervisory role.

Christine's current supervisor, Sean, announced the news of her promotion on Friday afternoon and told her to report for duty on Monday morning. Christine asked what she assumed were thoughtful questions, such as "Where will I be working?" and "What should I wear?" Sean told her that she would be managing the "small sort" – an area in which she had never worked. He also explained the dress code: slacks, a button-down shirt, and a tie. Christine wasn't sure how to make the tie work as a female supervisor. It occurred to her that there were no other female supervisors on her shift. It also occurred to her that there were no female managers at her branch. However, she remained unfazed by these observations; she thanked Sean for offering her this opportunity and walked out of the branch, her last day as an hourly employee.

Monday morning arrived and Christine reported to the manager's office to collect her tan briefcase and employee timecards. Sean grabbed his briefcase and whispered "good luck" as he dashed from the office. Christine stood awkwardly, flowered scarf brightly adorning her neck, anxiously looking for her trainer. The shift manager, Jimmy, caustically scolded, "You'd better get going – you don't want to be late for your first day of work."

Christine reported to the small sort area just as her new employees began to shuffle in. Once the 15 or so employees were assembled around her, she announced that she would be their new supervisor and that she was excited to be in their department and eager to get to know each of them. She also explained that she was unfamiliar with the operation and would be asking for their help until she was up to speed. The employees smiled cordially, welcomed her, and then went to work as parcels began filling the large metal slide that dominated the center of the work area.

Christine shadowed a young male employee and began asking him questions about the small parcel sorting process, his responsibilities in the area, and general "get-to-know-you" types of questions. She was keenly aware of the productivity standards expected of each employee, and she sensed the stress she was causing as he slowed to answer her questions. She thanked him and moved on to another employee. Christine had shadowed three or four employees when a group of managers strolled toward her area. They seemed to be touring the building and one manager pointed to Christine and the others glanced her way. The group continued to move forward, but two managers lagged behind: one was Jimmy, the shift manager, and the other a visitor, perhaps from another branch. Jimmy went to the slide and pulled an urgent letter from the pile of parcels. He walked toward Christine, letter in hand, and asked why the letter had missed the trailer headed to the airport. Christine knew intuitively that this was not the time for criticism or complaints. She stood silently as Jimmy introduced her to his guest, the regional manager of the company. Jimmy explained that this was Christine's first day on the job. The regional manager asked, "Does she want it to be her last?" Christine stood, feeling utterly dejected, as they walked away.

Christine knew that she was in trouble and would need help to survive day two. It was also evident that her manager was not part of the solution. Christine went home that night and created a new strategy. First, she needed someone capable of teaching her the specifics of running the department. She had noticed a senior female employee named Victoria who seemed to be the key person in the department. Whenever someone had a question regarding the operation, she was the one they asked. However, Christine didn't want to burden Victoria with questions during the operation. Her strategy was to go in first thing in the morning and ask Jimmy if she could take Victoria out of the operation so that she could learn more about the department. On the following day, Jimmy's response was "You'd better do something."

Christine approached Victoria openly and honestly. She told her that she needed her help to avoid being fired and Victoria graciously accepted the invitation. Victoria meticulously explained all the pertinent cut-off times for the various package trucks, problem areas in the department, unspoken procedures, and then finally offered that the last department supervisor had been fired on Friday, the same day Christine had been offered the job. Christine then asked Victoria what she could do to reciprocate the favor. Victoria explained that she had been with the company for over a decade, that she was a single mom, and that she hadn't had a raise in two years. After the shift, Christine reviewed Victoria's records for the past year and found her to be a model employee with above average productivity and accuracy. Christine approached Human Resources about the missed performance reviews and potential raises. It was suggested that Christine only give an increase for the past year's review and then reevaluate in six months. Christine ignored this suggestion and submitted the change in pay paperwork for the two missed review periods.

Christine returned the next morning and gave Victoria the news that her next paycheck would reflect her overdue increase. Victoria was grateful, but noticeably reserved. Christine had been with the company for six months and believed that anything was possible. She mentioned to Victoria that she had big plans for the department and that she would like for Victoria to be part of her vision, either as a team leader or as a supervisor. Again, Victoria's lack of enthusiasm was palpable. She simply smiled and thanked Christine and told her that she would help "however she could."

Scholarly Commentary

This case raises a number of issues common in many organizations, including a hostile work environment, gender discrimination, lack of sufficient mentoring and training, standardized HR policies, and a culture of intimidation, and a "throw leaders into the fire" mentality. The case invites us to examine these prevalent themes from the perspective of a follower who is – literally overnight – required to adapt roles from follower to leader, and then must learn to juggle the two roles in different situations. For example, Christine made the decision to proactively make decisions at times in the case yet, at other times, she deliberately chose a more passive role (e.g., when her boss berated her in front of his boss). Over the past several decades, scholars have focused increased attention on followers' needs, personalities, motivations, and attributions as critical aspects of the leadership relationship. These findings suggest that, just as not all leaders are the same, followers vary, sometimes dramatically, in their needs for certain types of leaders and leadership (e.g., toxic, authoritarian, charismatic, authentic, paternalistic, servant), as well as their susceptibility and responsiveness to certain types of leadership (authentic, transformational, dictatorial, directive vs. participative). However, as we clearly see in Christine's experience, these roles are far from static or distinct, and are in reality perhaps best conceived as simultaneous. In the words of Weick (2007), "To treat leading and following as simultaneous is to redistribute knowing and doubting more widely, to expect ignorance and fallibility to be similarly distributed, and to expect that knowledge is what happens between heads rather than inside a single leader's head" (p. 281).

Despite the recent growing interest in followership, the vast majority of research continues to focus on leaders and leadership. Within this broader tradition, those studies that do focus on followers often do so from within a very limited perspective, treating followers such as Christine and Victoria as "an undifferentiated mass or collective" (Collinson, 2006, p. 179). Bligh (2014) divides approaches to followers into three broad categories: (1) follower *attributes* relevant to the leadership process, including follower perceptions, affect, identity, motivation, and values; (2) leader-follower *relations*, such as the active role followers play in dynamic leadership processes; and (3) follower *outcomes* of leadership behaviors such as performance, creativity, or other effects that leaders have on followers. From this framework, we can examine which aspects of Christine's personality and previous experiences shaped her initial approach to the leadership role. We can also highlight how Christine's relationship with Jimmy impacted her leadership style, as well as her proactive development of a relationship with another follower and informal leader, Victoria. Finally, we can ask how both Jimmy and Christine's leadership styles impacted the performance of their followers, both as a hindrance or distraction as well as a facilitator or motivator.

In this case, we also see evidence of the implications of Christine's followership style for her leadership approach. Scholars have examined followers' characteristics and potential biases that influence their approaches to leadership, including individual differences such as gender, age, and personality. Personality traits are conceptualized as stable dispositions that direct beliefs, attitudes, and behaviors and may importantly influence interactions with leaders. Specifically, a closer look at followers' personalities may help to explain preferences for specific leaders. For example, Felfe and Schyns (2006) found that more extraverted followers were more likely to rate a leader as transformational. In addition, Keller (1999) found that the preference for charismatic and transformational leadership is influenced by followers' personality traits on the basis of perceptions of similarity between follower and leader. In this case, it is clear that Christine's personality and perceived lack of similarity to Jimmy impacted her approach to the role and strategies for being successful.

While followers have always been recognized as an important part of the leadership process, the study of followership has emerged as a critical, even "controversial" (Kelley, 2008) research stream that has provided an alternative to the "mainstream" leadership tradition. In the process of its development, it has helped to crystallize what the study of leadership has left out. As Weick (2007) puts it, follower-centered approaches deepen almost any leader-centric analysis: when we shift questions of perception and attention from leaders to followers, then inevitably new issues arise and new questions are raised.

Pearce and Conger (2003) point to the roots of the leader-follower dichotomy in the Industrial Revolution, its emphasis on control and oversight, and scientific management. Within this context, early management scholars emphasized distinctions between leaders and followers, and "spent considerable time trying to figure out ways to prevent followers from shirking responsibilities" (2003, p. 6). This perspective is in marked contrast to the case, which highlight the critical roles of Victoria and the unnamed young male employee that Christine shadows in an attempt to understand her new role. Both of these "followers" demonstrate task- and relationship-oriented leadership in the case, yet in terms of "performance" both are likely to have suffered short-term setbacks. Thus, the case also highlights how shifting from a more passive to active approach to the followership role reflects the array of – relatively unnoticed – influence followers can have on organizational processes. In addition, it is important to realize that the limited and one-sided impression that the regional manager likely took away from his visit may be the only information he has to make future personnel and performance evaluations.

These aspects of the case highlight the importance of attributions for organizational success and failure and the romance of leadership. The work of James Meindl and colleagues addresses these issues directly, marking the beginning of a truly follower-centric approach to leadership. Meindl (1995) articulated a follower-centered approach as "an alternative to theories and perspectives that place great weight on 'leaders' and on the substantive significance to their actions and activities" (p. 330). Meindl did not reject or minimize the importance of leadership, but simply emphasized that "it is easier to believe in leadership than to prove it" (Meindl, 1990, p. 161). His work reminds us to question critically our cultural and societal fascination with leadership, and the prevailing emphasis on heroism, charisma, and the glorification of leadership in the face of any real proof of its efficacy.

Meindl, Ehrlich, and Dukerich (1985) also provided convincing evidence that leaders and leadership issues often become the favored explanations for both positive and negative outcomes in and around organizations. In addition, subsequent research has demonstrated that people value performance results more highly when those results are attributed to leadership. In other words, organizations prefer to emphasize that the regional manager made the right decisions and motivated Christine and Victoria, rather than recognizing Victoria's critical role in the center's performance outcomes and giving her a well-deserved raise. In addition, this research highlights that a halo effect exists for leaders: if an individual is perceived to be an effective leader, his or her personal shortcomings, ethical violations, or poor organizational performance may be overlooked (Meindl & Ehrlich, 1987). Meindl and Ehrlich (1987) pointed out that this one-sided emphasis on the positive forms of leadership can be dangerous, for it suggests that leaders are inherently positive forces for individuals, organizations, and humanity as a whole.

Meindl et al. (1985, p. 100) also asserted that this "continuing infatuation with leadership, for whatever truths it yields about the qualities and behavior of our leaders, can also be used to learn something about the motivations of followers." Work in this tradition has pointed out that a collective desire to believe in an "omnipotent leader" can be very dangerous, and to see leaders simplistically as either heroes or villains to be elevated or blamed for organizational successes and failures (Collinson, 2005) obscures real problems and opportunities. It also points out that the heavy emphasis on leadership effectively mitigates the responsibility and accountability of followers (Uhl-Bien & Pillai, 2007). Other research suggests that leaders may utilize self-deception and impression management techniques to effectively "woo" followers into believing in the inflated potency and efficacy of the leader (Gray & Densten, 2007), encouraging followers to also be passive recipients of outcomes (as in the case of Victoria's raise).

Uhl-Bien and Pillai (2007) offered a corollary to this romance of leadership, which they termed the subordination of followership. Historically, they point out that "follower" often has a pejorative connotation, evoking images of passivity, conformance, compliance, inferiority, and a lack of drive and ambition. They assert that prototypical followership behaviors involve some sort of deference to the leader, and that in more hierarchical contexts, followers are more likely to construct their roles based on status differentials, resulting in reduced responsibility-taking and initiative and increased reliance on the leader for motivation. In contrast, Uhl-Bien and Pillai suggest followers such as those in this case can also more actively construct their roles as partners, participants, and co-leaders and co-followers, as Christine ultimately does in this case. Collinson (2006) echoes this sentiment, pointing out that followers are not "hapless beings" that exist at the mercy of their leaders. Instead, followers are often active, powerful players in the leadership process.

Carsten, Uhl-Bien, West, Patera, and McGregor (2010) distinguish followership approaches from follower-centric approaches to leadership such as Meindl (1995) by proposing that the issue of interest is not follower perspectives of leadership, but follower perspectives of *followership*. Rather than considering how followers view their leaders and their leaders' behaviors, a focus on followership considers how followers view their own behaviors and roles when engaging with leaders (see also Uhl-Bien & Pillai, 2007). Carsten et al.'s (2010) research demonstrates that followership holds "a multiplicity of meaning," in that individuals develop followership schema along a continuum from more passive and obedient on one end to more proactive on the other. Further, they found that followership constructions were related to leadership styles (more authoritarian vs. supportive/empowering) and organizational climate (more bureaucratic/hierarchical vs. empowering). In this case, the more bureaucratic, hierarchical climate of the organization, coupled with the more authoritarian leadership style evidenced by her superiors made a proactive followership style challenging for Christine to enact successfully.

DISCUSSION QUESTIONS

1. In this case, the supervisor was chosen for a management role not for her leadership ability, but because she was an ideal employee. Based on your experience, is this a common issue in organizations? What are some of the factors that lead to ideal employees being promoted into management? What are the implications of this approach to promotions?
2. The supervisor applied the same skills that made her a good follower (hard-working, good attitude) into her leadership role. Which of these skills were more readily adaptable to the leadership role? Which of these skills may have hindered her leadership effectiveness?
3. The new position challenged Christine to grow as a leader and enabled her to positively impact the organization and let her authentic self shine. She ignored HR's advice to only give one year pay increase because she perceived that it was dishonest. Do you agree with her decision? Why are why not? What are the implications of this type of proactive disobedience? If you were Christine's boss and learned of her decision, how would you react?

References

Bligh, M. C. (2014). Followership and follower-centered approaches. In B. Shamir (Ed.), *SAGE benchmarks in leadership series* (Vol. 4, pp. 425–437). Emerging Approaches to Leadership. London, UK: Sage.

Carsten, M. K., Uhl-Bien, M., West, B. J., Patera, J. L., & McGregor, R. (2010). Exploring social constructions of followership: A qualitative study. *The Leadership Quarterly*, *21*, 543–562. doi:10.1016/j.leaqua.2010.03.015

Collinson, D. L. (2005). Dialectics of leadership. *Human Relations*, *58*(11), 1419–1442.

Collinson, D. L. (2006). Rethinking followership: A post-structuralist analysis of follower identities. *The Leadership Quarterly*, *17*, 179–189. doi:10.1016/j.leaqua.2005.12.005

Felfe, J., & Schyns, B. (2006). Personality and the perception of transformational leadership: The impact of extraversion, neuroticism, personal need for structure, and occupational self-efficacy. *Journal of Applied Social Psychology*, *36*(3), 708–739. doi:10.1111/j.0021-9029.2006.00026.x

Gray, J. H., & Densten, I. L. (2007). How leaders woo followers in the romance of leadership. *Applied Psychology: An International Review*, *56*(4), 558–581. doi:10.1111/j.1464-0597.2007.00304.x

Keller, T. (1999). Images of the familiar: Individual differences and implicit leadership theories. *Leadership Quarterly*, *10*, 589–607. doi:10.1016/S1048-9843(99)00033-8

Kelley, R. E. (2008). Rethinking followership. In R. E. Riggio, I. Chaleff, & J. Lipman-Blumen (Eds.), *The art of followership: How great followers create great leaders and organizations* (pp. 5–16). San Francisco, CA: Jossey-Bass.

Meindl, J. (1995). The romance of leadership as a follower-centric theory: A social constructionist approach. *The Leadership Quarterly*, *6*(3), 329–341. doi:10.1016/1048-9843(95)90012-8

Meindl, J. R. (1990). On leadership: An alternative to the conventional wisdom. In B. M. Staw & L. L. Cummings (Eds.), *Research in organizational behavior* (Vol. 12, pp. 159–203). Greenwich, CT: JAI Press.

Meindl, J. R., & Ehrlich, S. B. (1987). The romance of leadership and the evaluation of organizational performance. *Academy of Management Journal*, *30*, 91–109. doi:10.2307/255897

Meindl, J. R., Ehrlich, S. B., & Dukerich, J. M. (1985). The romance of leadership. *Administrative Science Quarterly*, *30*, 78–102. doi:10.2307/2392813

Pearce, C. L., & Conger, J. A. (2003). All those years ago: The historical underpinnings of shared leadership. In C. Pearce & J. Conger (Eds.), *Shared leadership: Reframing the hows and whys of leadership* (pp. 1–18). Thousand Oaks, CA: Sage.

Uhl-Bien, M., & Pillai, R. (2007). The romance of leadership and the social construction of followership. In B. Shamir, R. Pillai, M. C. Bligh, & M. Uhl-Bien (Eds.), *Follower-centered perspectives on leadership: A tribute to the memory of James R. Meindl* (pp. 187–210). Greenwich, CT: Information Age.

Weick, K. E. (2007). Romancing, following, and sensemaking: Jim Meindl's legacy. In B. Shamir, R. Pillai, M. C. Bligh, & M. Uhl-Bien (Eds.), *Follower-centered perspectives on leadership: A tribute to the memory of James R. Meindl* (pp. 279–291). Greenwich, CT: Information Age.

CHAPTER

10 Diversity, Inclusion, and Followership

James H. Schindler and Sonya Rogers

The Jamson Manufacturing Company is a privately held family-owned business in the Midwestern United States. For the past 30 years, it has been manufacturing wiring harnesses for the aviation industry. Jamson is a medium-sized firm with deep roots in the community. The population of the town that it serves is a diverse mix of Caucasians, Native Americans, African Americans, Hispanics, and Asians. Its main plant is located near a large Indian Reserve with a population that is slightly larger than the town itself. While relationships amongst these groups are generally good, each community tends to socialize separately.

The senior leadership team of Jamson Manufacturing is exclusively white and male. The Vice President (VP) of Operations is the brother-in-law of the CEO, the VP of Finance is the son-in-law of the CEO, and the VP of Marketing is the daughter of the CEO. Additionally, the Director of Human Resources (HR), who has accountability for all of Jamson's HR functions and reports directly to the CEO, is married to the VP of Operations. These vested leaders have differing levels of education, all are experienced in their respective areas of responsibility, and the company has been profitable for most of its existence. Other than relatives of Jamson's owners, upper and middle management of Jamson (i.e., VPs and Directors) are also mostly white and male.

One notable exception is Paul Jones, Director of Accounts Receivable, an African-American who earned his MBA at the local state college. Recently, at a company-sponsored senior leadership retreat, Paul noticed that he was the only person of color in attendance. Paul had been vocal about the lack of diversity within the company and suggested to his boss, the VP of Finance, that the company should hire additional African Americans at various levels of the organization including supervisory positions. Paul and his boss get along well; they play golf together regularly and Paul has always been encouraging and supportive of his boss's decisions. While Paul believes the company is ready to embrace greater diversity in its workforce, he has been disappointed by the pace of change and the lack of an HR policy supporting it.

Most employees have worked several years at Jamson and depend upon the security of their employment to support their families. When initially hired, the majority of these employees did not complete an extensive training process; they were expected to learn on the job. Nevertheless, the workforce is mostly competent and experienced thanks to a work culture where helping each other is the norm. Teams form the backbone of Jamson and people recognize that the team's accomplishments are a result of individual commitment combined with the skills and competencies of a few especially skilled staff. Teams act largely as self-contained units, with the team lead not only managing the work of the team but also bridging communications between the teams and supervisory staff. However, relationships between teams are not always strong and some competition at this level is encouraged.

The New Hire

Carl Peterson was recently hired as a supervisor for the first shift on the production floor. With a bachelor's degree in production management and 10 plus years' experience in manufacturing, Carl was well qualified for the position. He was excited about being hired and moved his wife and two children from Duluth, Minnesota, to the town near Jamson's plant. His excitement, however, soon turned to dismay as he noticed a drop in production by the three teams on the shift that he supervised shortly after his arrival. He began to overhear rumors of employees expressing their disappointment that Sally Onida, an internal applicant, was not selected for the supervisory position that Carl had accepted. Carl was also concerned about increasing incidents of detrimental conduct and poor attitude that he personally witnessed on the production floor.

Sally Onida, a Native American, began working for Jamson 15 years ago. She worked as a machine operator for 12 years and was promoted three years ago to one of the company's three team lead positions on the first shift. She has never had any performance issues and her evaluations have all been exemplary. When her supervisor, Mark Rollins, recently announced his retirement from the company, Sally expressed an interest to her male co-workers in applying for his position. As Sally left the break room where everyone was seated, she overheard Mark smirk, "Don't worry guys,

I will do anything that I can to keep an overweight woman from getting my job. I don't care how good she is." Upset by his comment, Sally decided to speak to HR. HR thanked her for the information and told her, "We will take care of it." Mark was not fired over the incident, but he did retire quickly. Sally anticipated that Mark's supervisory position would be offered to her and Sally's team members agreed. Instead, Carl Peterson, who had only recently been hired, was promoted and given Mark's job.

Following Carl Peterson's promotion, Sally began to have problems with the other two team leaders, which escalated into shouting matches and disciplinary action for all involved. Recently, Sally has been late for work and tardy for production meetings. She began criticizing Carl's decisions along with his ability to motivate the team to achieve the shift goals necessary for production. Carl recognized these changes in Sally's behavior and work habits and arranged two counseling sessions with her in an effort to respond to the escalation of conflict between the two of them. One of the sessions was informal and not documented; the second session was brought on by Sally's refusal to abide by Carl's suggestions from the first counseling session. At the end of the second session, Sally broke down and accused Carl of "not wanting fat women on the production floor." Unlike his predecessor, Carl is very aware of the necessity to include Sally in the decision-making process of goal setting and empowerment to help her better lead her team. He is also mindful of the need to address the attitude displayed by Sally before it escalates into an even bigger problem for Jamson Manufacturing.

Scholarly Commentary

To build an inclusive environment within an organization, there must be a commitment from the top, respect for diverse opinions, and equitable policies (Hays-Thomas & Bendick, 2013). These inclusive work environments offer a place where employees are treated in a positive manner, as assets rather than liabilities (Sabharwal, 2014). Employees serve as a key ingredient to the overall process and everyone's input matters for strategic planning purposes and the establishment of short- and long-term goals.

Inclusion in the decision-making process of an organization is an essential component of empowerment, and workplace empowerment is a product of "genuine inclusion of difference" (Prasad, 2001, p. 65). Inclusion has also been described as "the degree to which an employee perceives that he or she is an esteemed member of the work group through experiencing treatment that satisfies his or her needs for belongingness and uniqueness" (Shore, Randel, Chung, Ehrhart, & Singh, 2011, p. 1265).

The feeling of being included facilitates people unifying in order to work as a cohesive group. As Sabharwal (2014, p. 197) notes, "Diversity management is insufficient for improving workplace performance." For this to occur, a greater inclusion of employees is required in a manner that promotes self-esteem and considers everyone's input. The improvement of workplace performance is the result of the fact that diversity focuses on demography, whereas inclusion focuses on the removal of obstacles to the full participation and contribution of employees (Roberson, 2006).

When individuals belong to a group, they become *members* by developing an association, a partnership with others and a social identity. Tajfel (2010) posits that individuals choose to join a group to build self-esteem. This process, however, creates separate and distinct out-groups and in-groups, which divides the population into "them" and "us." As a result of the divide in the population, the in-group, in an attempt to heighten their own self-image, discriminates in some manner against the out-group. When individuals do not feel they are being valued within the organization, their work performances and morale become affected. These individuals can often begin to identify with the out-group and they may not be able to adequately connect with teammates. If this identification behavior continues, out-group workers may display a downward trend of morale and performance. On the other hand, in-group members will continue to act to heighten their own self-image until leadership has brought the issue to their attention, and remedies are put in place.

Social comparison theory (Sabharwal, 2014) suggests that individuals compare their skills and abilities to those attributes in others. However, this constant comparison creates perceptions of inclusion or exclusion based upon social interactions. Feeling safe within a group is sometimes more valuable than being innovative or rewarded.

Creating an atmosphere where all workers feel they are accountable yet valued and appreciated is best for the purpose of organizational growth and excellence. By the early 1980s, American industry began to experience a destabilization of the *status quo*, and to develop toward a more diverse and inclusive workforce. The globalization of business, advancing technological changes for employees, and the ongoing dynamic between business, labor and government put pressure on corporate systems. Dixon and Westbrook (2003) further note that globalization pressure altered organizational culture and also has required a more fluid employee-employer social relationship. Unfortunately, this process of change has been hindered by a preoccupation with leadership and has downplayed the importance of followers to an organization. According to Dixon and Westbrook (2003), "Being a follower is a condition; not a position" (p. 20). Being an exemplary follower is a state in which a person accepts the role of serving others and behaves in a manner that is respectful to others, while at the same time exemplifying the traits and characteristics of effective leadership.

Within any organization, there will be leaders and followers. The two must be cognizant of how to work together in a manner that promotes a connection to the business, a connection to the group, and a connection to each other as leaders and follower. Members who feel connected to a business are proud of the role they are given and willingly support leadership in setting clear and obtainable goals for the success of the organization. If workers feel alienated from the group, they tend to believe their voice is never heard and their competencies are not an essential component for organizational progress. Being that there are more followers than leaders within the framework of a company or business, it is vital that each member feels valued and respected as they contribute to the organizational mission.

Blanchard, Wellbourne, Gilmore, and Bullock (2009) note that leaders are particularly essential to organizational success. However, little attention is paid to the other side of the leadership equation, namely followership. More training time should be focused on how followership is regarded and included within the organization. The two terms, leader and follower, are closely intertwined to the point that effective followers can shape productive leader behavior just as effective leaders can develop people into good followers (Daft, 2008, p. 195). However, without focused training in regards to empowerment and inclusion, neither the leader's nor the follower's behavior can be influenced to help achieve organizational success.

Workplace empowerment is important to the followership side of the leadership equation. Unless leaders or managers have genuinely assessed their own personal feelings and perceptions regarding those they supervise, they might unconsciously experience leadership bias. This bias comes from an attitude of *I know best*, which can cause followers to experience feelings of shame and worthlessness. Self-righteous leadership sabotages inclusion. In order to empower workers, leaders must have a clear understanding of human capital and its significance in the overall prosperity of a business. Effective leaders will consider the diverse sets of skills, personalities, and demographics of each member. Prasad (2001) identifies workplace empowerment as an integral aspect of inclusion, meaning the inclusion of races, ethnicities, genders, classes, and the like. Hollander and Offerman (1990) postulate that workplace empowerment is understood as increased responsibility and more participative decision-making. Workers feel more connected to their teammates and the organization when they are given ample opportunity to have a voice in organizational matters. Conger and Kanungo (1988) conceptualize workplace empowerment as the removal of conditions that lead to the feelings of powerlessness in the workplace. When members feel powerless and weak, they often experience an attitude of helplessness and insignificance in contribution and productivity, regardless of their true potential or worth.

Prasad (2001) argues that empowerment is only a single moment of inclusion. It is necessary to provide a more enduring sense of inclusion than empowerment provides. In the political realm, empowerment is in concert with some values and ideals of democracy and is also linked to the concept that power resides in the citizens. The concepts of empowerment and inclusion do not move easily between the realms of democratic politics to the world of corporate governance. Corporate governance in the United States is vested in the stockholders (i.e., in capital) and not the majority rule of the employees. Democracies work toward the inclusion of all of its citizens in order to achieve success and the legitimacy of the political system. Research in the arena of workplace democracy has emphasized worker inclusion and as a result spurred an increase of empowerment opportunities for employees (Prasad, 2001).

Basically, an inclusive workplace would be one in which leadership embraces diversity and the richness of backgrounds and perspectives of all employees. Equal representation of worker talents and competencies is valued. Today, there is an increased focus on employee rights and representation, as well as women in leadership. Even though this is a work in progress, women are actually thriving in business environments all around the world. Issues such as employee rights and equal representation of women in leadership positions remain a valid concern for the labor-management workforce (Prasad, 2001). Empowering workers to demonstrate their potential with ease can only be accomplished if a business is open to the idea of differing views, gender, and ages. Inclusive leadership leverages diverse talents, where the participation of all members is welcomed. The process of open communication and acceptance of all should result in a winning solution for a multitude of business initiatives.

DISCUSSION QUESTIONS

1. How would you evaluate Sally as a follower? What could Sally have done differently to enhance her position and become a more favorable candidate for job openings in the future? Explain your response in terms of your experiences and the commentary.
2. As the Human Resources (HR) Director, your boss has asked you to develop a plan for employee development

that will improve diversity and inclusiveness. Describe the program you might propose for employee development that will include all employees.

3. Do you believe Carl is aware he is a follower as well as the First Shift Supervisor? If you were the Vice President (VP) of Operations, how would you ensure Carl understands what needs to be done to improve morale on the first shift?
4. Carl is aware of the necessity to include Sally in the decision-making process of goal setting and empowerment to help her better lead her team. If you were Carl, what might you do to continue to defuse the problem of Sally arriving late to work and displaying a negative attitude toward supervisors?
5. If you were the VP of Finance, and you were aware the company should hire a more diverse workforce at various levels of the organization to include supervisory positions, what could you do in the short term to remedy the situation? What could you do in the long term? Develop a plan for each.
6. If you were the CEO of Jamson Manufacturing how would you begin to create an atmosphere where all workers feel they are accountable; yet, valued and appreciated in a way that supports organizational growth and excellence?

References

Blanchard, A. J., Wellbourne, J., Gilmore, D., & Bullock, A. (2009). Followership styles and employee attachment to the organization. *The Psychologist-Manager Journal*, *12*(2), 111–131. doi:10.1080/10887150902888718

Conger, J., & Kanungo, R. (1988). The empowerment process: Integrating theory and practice. *Academy of Management Review*, *13*(3), 471–482. Retrieved from http://www.jstor.org/stable/258093

Daft, R. L. (2008). *The leadership experience* (5th ed.), Mason, OH: South-Western.

Dixon, G., & Westbrook, J. (2003). Followers revealed. *Engineering Management Journal*, *15*, 19–25. Retrieved from https://netforum.avectra.com/eweb/DynamicPage.aspx?Site=asem&WebCode=EMJ

Hays-Thomas, R., & Bendick, M. Jr. (2013). Professionalizing diversity and voluntary inclusion practice: Should voluntary standards be the chicken or the egg? *Industrial and Organizational Psychology*, *6*(3), 193–205. doi:10.1111/iops.12033

Hollander, E. P., & Offerman, L. R. (1990). Power and leadership in organizations: Relationships in transition. *American Psychologist*, *45*(2), 179–189. doi:10.1037// 0003-066X.45.2.179

Prasad, A. (2001). Understanding workplace empowerment as inclusion: A historical investigation of the discourse of difference in the United States. *The Journal of Applied Behavioral Science*, *37*(1), 31–69. doi:10.1177/0021886301371004

Roberson, Q. M. (2006). Disentangling the meanings of diversity and inclusion in organizations. *Group and Organizational Management*, *31*(2), 212–236. doi:10.1177/1059601104273064

Sabharwal, M. (2014). Is diversity management sufficient? Organizational inclusion to further performance. *Public Personnel Management*, *42*(2), 197–217. doi:10.1177/0091026014522202

Shore, L. M., Randel, A. E., Chung, B. G., Ehrhart, K. H., & Singh, G. (2011). Inclusion and diversity in work groups: A review and model for future research. *Journal of Management*, *37*(4), 1262–1289. doi:10.1177/0149206310385943

Tajfel, H. (2010). Cognitive aspects of prejudice. *Journal of Social Issues*, *25*(4), 79–97. doi:10.1111/j.1540-4560.1969.tb00620

CHAPTER

11 The Importance of Followership and Reputation in an HR Consulting Firm

Debra Finlayson and William S. Harvey

Ten years ago, Sarah Randall was captivated and inspired by a conversation with a job candidate, Dan Hartman. During the interview, Dan shared his ideas about being an "Employer of Choice." Sarah was so impressed by the interview that she asked Dan if he would be interested in forming a company that assists other companies to become employers of choice; Dan asked if he could have a day to think about it. When he called back the next day, Dan said yes, and that began a collaboration which continues today. Sarah is now the CEO and Founder of the company they created, Higher Steps HR Consulting.

The core business of Higher Steps is to examine organizations through the use of HR audits, analysis, and recommendations. It consists of senior independent human resources consultants who bring together their unique and extensive individual expertise, which spans the entire body of HR knowledge, to provide a single source solution for clients. Higher Steps aims to close any gaps between client expectations before a project and their experiences during a project. Typically, there is a lot of rhetoric from consultancy firms during the tendering process and Higher Steps ensures it is as transparent as possible and that it only promises what it can deliver on.

Sarah purposely does not micromanage her consultants, but she does occasionally remind them of the dynamic in which they work, and the importance of positioning themselves as a neutral party with clients. A common thread running through the group is their high level of mutual respect for each other. Their notable pride in being part of a reputable firm has resulted in a collective brainpower and expanded suite of resources upon which all who contribute have come to rely. In other words, their collective reputation is greater than the sum of their individual parts.

Collaboration is fundamental to the culture. Sarah brings the consultants together for quarterly team meetings and all eagerly anticipate hearing about the projects on which each person is working. These meetings provide an opportunity for receiving expert input where needed, as well as an opportunity to learn from the expertise and experience of other team members, which would not be available to them if they were solely independent consultants.

Transparency is a key operational strategy at Higher Steps. Sarah maintains that, whenever a decision is to be made, she runs it by the team prior to its implementation. Thus, each consultant is aware of what is going on and they are consulted as a group if a pending decision will affect them.

Sarah brings numerous additional qualities to Higher Steps, but admits that it would not exist today without the tenacity that all have demonstrated in developing and promoting the business. She values the organization's diverse relationships with the business community. Sarah's respect for her team members is mutual; the consultants describe Sarah as a mastermind and visionary, consistently collaborative, transparent, and always respectful. Dan Hartman notes,

> While Sarah remains open to feedback she has always exhibited confidence when it comes to making key decisions. She clearly demonstrates just how much she values her clients and consultants. These abilities help to draw people together to make a difference on behalf of the greater organization. Yet, Sarah is not a pushover and, when needed, has difficult conversations about loyalty to the firm, and maintaining a high standard of quality. (D. Hartman, personal interview)

Reputation is paramount to Higher Steps, especially as it is a service-based business with a lot of competition. The senior consultants have earned reputations as experts in the HR industry; some as generalists and others as specialists in organizational development, recruitment and retention, leadership training, total compensation, and more. All the consultants have built their careers through single or multi organizational paths and have developed successful independent consulting companies alongside working for Higher Steps, which Sarah has encouraged. The Higher Steps team is a cooperative group of HR experts well positioned to support and realize their clients' desire to become employers of choice.

Scholarly Commentary

The literature on leadership has typically focused on leaders and performance while overlooking the importance of followers (Meindl & Ehrlich, 1987). Riggio (2014) argues that we need to better understand how leaders and followers "co-produce" leadership, while other scholars have emphasized a follower-centric approach to overcome the historical bias of only analyzing leaders (Bligh & Kohles, 2012; Haslam, Reicher, Millard, & McDonald, 2015; Uhl-Bien, Riggio, Lowe, & Carsten, 2014). Understanding followership is imperative today given the importance of working in teams, particularly among professional service firms (Gardner, 2015), which are typically less vertical and more horizontal in structure (Carsten, Uhl-Bien, West, Patera, & McGregor, 2010). Therefore, it is essential to understand both leaders and followers in the context of co-leadership because both have a significant impact upon their collective corporate and individual reputations.

Corporate reputation is understood as the aggregated perceptions of an organization held by stakeholders in relation to the organization's competitors. Reputation, that is, "what do stakeholders actually think about us," is also similar to a number of related concepts such as *identity* (who we are as an organization), *intended image* (how we want others to think about us), and *construed image* (what do we believe others think about us) (Brown, Dacin, Pratt, & Whetten, 2006, p. 102). Understanding these different concepts will benefit organizations because there are often subtle differences in how internal and external stakeholders perceive organizations, and yet it is important that these perceptions are consistent otherwise stakeholders will questions such differences.

A positive reputation is vital in attracting and retaining key talent, which enables the firm to charge higher prices and, over time, leads potential and existing clients to assume that the organization provides a high quality service (Fombrun, 1996; Harvey & Morris, 2012). This is important since a positive reputation helps attract and retain the best followers. The reason for this is because individuals want to work for and remain working for organizations and leaders with positive reputations, especially since this casts a halo over their own individual reputations.

Furthermore, the growing emphasis on sound ethics has led to Trevino, Brown, and Hartman (2003) to claim that an executive's reputation for ethical leadership is as important as ever in influencing followers' impressions of these leaders and their organizations, which in turn will affect followers' motivation and performance. Huang, Wang, and Xie (2014) linked leader-member exchange (LMX) with organizational citizenship behaviors (OCBs) discovering that, when a follower has a favorable perception of the leader's external image, one that matches the follower's self-identity, it leads to higher quality relationships and more motivation to perform OCBs. Furthermore, positive leader reputation is built when leaders share their expertise with less knowledgeable followers (Thomas & Hirschfeld, 2015).

Ehrhart (2012) posits followers' self-concepts (self-construal) can be linked to leader and organizational goals, whereby the followers' ILT (implicit leader theories) uniquely vary with their personalities, values, and other characteristics. Proactive followership behaviors can directly enhance a manager's overall effectiveness by directly contributing to the positive reputations of leaders, organizations, and performance outcomes. In short, leader reputation is positively correlated with engaged followership.

One example of engaged followership is a transcendent follower, who is "someone who expresses competence in terms of their management of relations with self, others and organization" (e Cunha, Rego, Clegg, & Neves, 2013, p. 87). In particular, a transcendent follower embraces three critical capabilities: (a) a responsible self-manager, (b) the ability to build and sustain rich constructive relationships with peers and leaders to acquire social capital, and (c) the ability to help build vigilant organizations through extra role behaviors (e Cunha et al., 2013). Moreover, new to the followership literature is the concept of the *zone of stewardship*, which is when followers "go the extra mile" for their organizations and are fully committed and engaged to achieve the best in the interests of their organizations (Hayes, Caldwell, Licona, & Meyer, 2015, p. 275). The authors assert that if leaders treat employees as valued partners, a trust culture ensues which enhances OCBs, and thus to increased profitability through engaged followership. Higher Steps consultants exhibit transcendent follower attributes in having strong self-leadership as independent consultants, bringing social capital from careers full of rich business relationships, and also demonstrating extra role behavior in their willingness to collaborate with stewardship on projects in spite of not being the assigned project lead. These extra role behaviors further enrich their social capital within the Higher Steps team and help to build the firm's reputation among clients.

Arguably, Sarah has become a successful business leader in part influenced by the consultants, who exhibit transcendent followership, contributing within and across each of the levels of self, others, and organization (e Cunha et al., 2013). *Identity strength* (credibility) and *immediacy* (perceived psychological social distance) are key moderators of influence that followers have with leaders (Oc & Bashshur, 2013, p. 924). Followers' influence can be strengthened when leaders have "information dependence," relying on followers for information, or "effect dependence," relying on followers for social affiliation or positive self-regard (Oc & Bashshur, 2013).

It is clear from our interviews and participant observation that it is through Sarah's predisposition for social charismatic leadership (SCL), envisioning a better state for organizations, being collectively orientated, egalitarian and non-exploitive, that she attracts the consultants to engage in realizing her vision. Thus, their intrinsic motivation (susceptibility for meaning, competence, self-determination, and impact) is sparked through their ILT's. Additionally, leaders with a strong reputation for SCL attract proactive followership styles, which further enhance a leader's confidence that their followers will provide the necessary input, so the vision is truly shared (Lapierre, Bremner, & McMullan, 2012). Engagement now becomes reciprocal, perpetual, and generative.

Higher Steps has moved to being an employer of choice by embracing an inclusive talent management approach (Martin, 2009), which sees talent distributed throughout the organization and opportunities for self-development as fundamental through assigned projects and expert peer support in which all members engage. This poses a curious dilemma of determining who leads and who follows. Tanoff and Barlow (2002) noted that the difference between leadership and followership constructs is not as simple as strong followers emulate their leader, and the authors concluded that Kelley's (1992) behaviors of exemplary "proactive" followers were very similar to the behaviors that effective leaders showed.

Conclusion

Sarah's careful choice of who would come onto the team of consultants further illustrates the importance of followership for leadership effectiveness. At the same time, without Sarah's leadership qualities, consultants would not remain working at Higher Steps. This illustrates the impact a leader's reputation has on an organization's followership and vice-versa.

It is difficult to predict exactly where Higher Steps will be in two or even five years given the changing landscapes of organizations today. However, as noted by Martin (2009), "Good governance and leadership, supported by good 'followership', helps to bind an organization together as it changes" (p. 223).

DISCUSSION QUESTIONS

1. What role, if any, does Sarah's reputation with her team play in the overall collaboration of the group? In what ways does her reputation impact the team, and does it extend beyond the organization to its interactions with clients?
2. Based on the evidence from the case, do you believe that Higher Steps is an Employer of Choice?
3. In what ways is Higher Steps' approach to empowering its workers transferrable to other organizations?
4. If you were a human resources consultant, would you want to work for Higher Steps? Why, or why not? What are all the benefits of the Higher Steps approach, and what are the downsides?
5. In what ways can followership influence the reputation of an organization and/or its leaders?

References

Bligh, M. C., & Kohles, J. C. (2012). Approaching leadership with a follower focus. *Zeitschrift Für Psychologie*, *220*(4), 201–204. doi:10.1027/2151-2604/a000114

Brown, T. J., Dacin, P. A., Pratt, M. G., & Whetten, D. A. (2006). Identity, intended image, construed image, and reputation: An interdisciplinary framework and suggested terminology. *Journal of Academy of Marketing Science*, *34*(2), 99–106. doi:10.117/0092070305284969

Carsten, M. K., Uhl-Bien, M., West, B. J., Patera, J. L., & McGregor, R. (2010). Exploring social constructions of followership: A qualitative study. *The Leadership Quarterly*, *21*(3), 543–562. doi:10.1016/j.leaqua.2010.03.015

e Cunha, M. P., Rego, A., Clegg, S., & Neves, P. (2013). The case for transcendent followership. *Leadership*, *9*(1), 87–106. doi:10.1177/1742715012447006

Ehrhart, M. G. (2012). Self-concept, implicit leadership theories, and follower preferences for leadership. *Zeitschrift für Psychologie*, *220*(4), 231–240. doi:10.1027/2151-2604/a000117

Fombrun, C. J. (1996). *Reputation: Realizing value from the corporate image*. Boston, MA: Harvard Business School Press.

Gardner, H. K. (2015). When senior managers won't collaborate. *Harvard Business Review*, *73*(2), 75–85. Retrieved from https://hbr.org/2015/03/when-senior-managers-wont-collaborate

Harvey, W. S., & Morris, T. (2012). A labor of love? Understanding reputation formation within the labour market. In M. L. Barnett & T. G. Pollock (Eds.), *The Oxford handbook of corporate reputation* (pp. 341–360). Oxford: Oxford University Press.

Haslam, S. A., Reicher, S. D., Millard, K., & McDonald, R. (2015). Happy to have been of service: The Yale archive as a window into the engaged followership of participants in Milgram's 'obedience' experiments. *British Journal of Social Psychology*, *54*(1), 55–83. doi:10.1111/bjso.12074

Hayes, L. A., Caldwell, C., Licona, B., & Meyer, T. E. (2015). Followership behaviors and barriers to wealth creation. *Journal of Management Development*, *34*(3), 270–285. doi:10.1108/JMD-09-2013-0111

Huang, J., Wang, L., & Xie, J. (2014). Leader-member exchange and organizational citizenship behavior: The roles of identification with leader and leader's reputation. *Social Behavior and Personality: An International Journal*, *42*(10), 1699–1711. doi:10.2224/sbp.2014.42.10.1699

Kelley, R. E. (1992). *The power of followership*. New York, NY: Doubleday.

Lapierre, L. M., Bremner, N. L., & McMullan, A. D. (2012). Strength in numbers: How employees' acts of followership can influence their manager's charismatic leadership behavior. *Zeitschrift für Psychologie*, *220*(4), 251–261. doi:10.1027/2151-2604/a000119

Martin, G. (2009). Driving corporate reputations from the inside: A strategic role and strategic dilemmas for HR? *Asia Pacific Journal of Human Resources*, *47*(2), 219–235. doi:10.1177/1038411109105443

Meindl, J. R., & Ehrlich, S. B. (1987). The romance of leadership and the evaluation of organizational performance. *Academy of Management Journal*, *30*(1), 91–109.

Oc, B., & Bashshur, M. R. (2013). Followership, leadership and social influence. *The Leadership Quarterly*, *24*(6), 919–934. doi:10.1016/j.leaqua.2013.10.006

Riggio, R. E. (2014). Followership research: Looking back and looking forward. *Journal of Leadership Education*, *13*(4), 15–20. doi:10.12806/V13/I4/C4

Tanoff, G. F., & Barlow, C. (2002). Leadership and followership: Same animal, different spots. *Consulting Psychology Journal: Practice and Research*, *54*(3), 157–167. doi:10.1037//1061-4087.54.3.157

Thomas, C. H., & Hirschfeld, R. R. (2015). Knowing is half the battle: Interdependent effects of knowledge and action on leader emergence. *Leadership & Organization Development Journal*, *36*(5), 512–526. doi:10.1108/LODJ-09-2013-0125

Trevino, L. K., Brown, M., & Hartman, L. P. (2003). A qualitative investigation of perceived executive ethical leadership: Perceptions from inside and outside the executive suite. *Human Relations*, *56*(1), 5–37. doi:10.1177/0018726703056001448

Uhl-Bien, M., Riggio, R. E., Lowe, K. B., & Carsten, M. K. (2014). Followership theory: A review and research agenda. *The Leadership Quarterly*, *25*(1), 83–104. doi:10.1016/j.leaqua.2013.11.007

Section II
Education and the Arts

CHAPTER

12 Dancing Leader

Rens van Loon and Karlijn Kouwenhoven

In 2009, we met John Hall, Head of the Urban Development Department (UDD) of a municipality in a major Dutch city. We had previously worked together on a Management Development Program which he had set up. He asked us to help him and his management team at UDD to improve their shared leadership. The municipality was going through a major new development phase at the time which included the construction of a new city hall – set to house the entire municipal organization. One of the most challenging issues the managers faced was to look beyond the walls of their own department and start to collaborate as one team.

We arranged several one-on-one reflective dialogues with his management team members and two one-day sessions with the full team. After these interventions, we got together and reflected on the transformation through which he, his team, and the entire municipality had moved. John proved to be a man with an intuitive and genuine fondness for the public good.

John made the statement: "If you are a pair, there will always be one taking the lead and another one following this lead. But leading is solely possible if the other party wants to be led." John was a former professional dancer who had also worked as a dance teacher. He said, "I now often use the role of taking the lead in dancing as a metaphor. In my opinion, leading and following is an agreement of wills between two persons. If I dance, I will feel it instantly if the other person does not want to be led. It is noticeable particularly because when I stop dancing, I get kicked in the shins."

Within an organization, this mechanism works identically – although in dancing the person leading and the person following are equally important. Following is an often overlooked factor in organizations, as leaders tend to think they are superior to their subordinates. John continued, "In Latin American dance, the men lead the women. Women lend dances their beauty – they are the ones making the dance beautiful." Analogous to this visual imagery, he said, "The wonderful aspect of the work done in our department is that it is realized by the staff – not by me, the leader. If the staff refuses to be led, the leader is left empty-handed! This instills humility. You have to do it together. The other one needs to be enticed into collaborating."

"Dancing is hard work. People sometimes fail to see it is a top-class sport. The same applies to work. Hard work is first and foremost rewarding because it gives me the feeling I am in a flow, I do not lose energy. And on top of this flow, harvesting applause makes me rise even higher. I do not explicitly use the dancing metaphor in my conversations with people. Dancing is part of my life, but I do not explicitly apply it in my day-to-day affairs." Still, I do apply what I have learned as a dancing teacher. An example is the benefit of having been in front of a group for years.

Experience of a Salsa Dancer.

In salsa dancing, the woman always follows. I, Karlijn, see a few things in my dancing that relates to leadership:

- Leading is about providing direction and taking the initiative.

- Following is being sensitive to the leader at all times.

- I lead myself very consciously.

- I am also conscious of the pushback/strength I have in my body to help the leader in making more complex turns.

- I can follow without leading the other the entire dance, resulting in a beautiful dance together.

- However, if I feel the man (leader) is more sensitive to me (follower), I can play with this leader-follower interaction and take the lead while we are dancing (for example, by refusing a turn or surprising him). This increases awareness and sensitivity to each other and enhances synchronicity, resulting in a more aware and beautiful dance.

- Hence, a good leader in salsa is sensitive to the follower and allows the follower to also lead.

Our rapidly changing and technological society confronts us with complex issues such as the major changes in education systems, the aging population, and the rising cost of health care. Complex issues cannot be solved by simply implementing an unequivocal regulation. This needs dialogue and the power of collaboration. The mutual agreement during a dance between leader and follower about their roles and interaction facilitates collaboration and participation. A world with increasingly complex global issues demands more cooperative solutions. This is a demand for collaborative leadership with the ability to lead and follow at the same time. New public leadership mobilizes collaboration and participation.

This case illustrates how experiences in an individual's life can have a deeply seated influence on one's interpretation of leadership. The creator of the Dialogical Self Theory, Hubert Hermans (Hermans & Gieser, 2012; Hermans & Hermans-Konopka, 2010; Hermans, Kempen, & van Loon, 1992) describes this phenomenon as I-positions. With John Hall, they are the *dancer* and the *director*. Bringing both I-positions into contact with each other has a positive influence on his performance. He becomes aware of the significant role the *dancer* and the dancing teacher play in his life. This has a positive and integrating influence on the role of the *director*. By using the dancer as a metaphor for his role as director, he now applies at a mental level the vital influencing skills he has learned and instructed in physical dancing – unconsciously at first, deliberately later on. Many of the skills he applies derive from dancing. He is not unique in doing so. We know horse riders who enrich their leadership with the metaphor of riding or breaking a horse and captains doing the same with sailing on a ship. By introducing the metaphor into the internal dialogue and making it explicit in the external dialog, the I-positions can be integrated. John Hall became explicitly aware that leading and following are equally important.

Scholarly Commentary

FIRST REFLECTION

By using the dancing metaphor, we can incorporate followership into the leadership equation. Intuitively, you sense and observe that you cannot dance without relationally switching between leading and following. Gergen (2009) and Hersted and Gergen (2013) define leading and following as reciprocally co-constructing reality. Dialogical leadership describes it as "A dynamic *multiplicity* of *I-positions* in the *landscape* of the mind" (Hermans et al., 1992). Alternatively, it can be defined as "flexible movements between a diversity of I-positions that are relevant to the functioning of the organization as a whole" (Hermans & Hermans-Konopka, 2010, p. 326). In Dialogical Self Theory, leading and following are simultaneously viewed as internal movements of the mind. This internal dynamism directly impacts how leaders and followers behave, think, and feel in the external world. Leading and following are equal I-positions in this view. In this case, John Hall adapts a dialogue of equal leading and following I-positions to his professional experience as a public leader and a dancing teacher. Both I-positions are present in the landscape of his mind.

SECOND REFLECTION

Van Vugt (2009) speaks about the "riddle of following." He argues that leadership and followership emerged in human history when groups grew larger and socially more complex, and the potential for conflict increased exponentially. People used to be members of small hunter-gatherer tribes, where they had different roles and where they felt one of the members. These groups were held together by kinship, norms of reciprocity, and fairness. People could experience how they were dependent on each other. This is completely different in large-scale organizations. Understanding evolutionary frameworks is critical to comprehending the relationship between leadership and followership, starting from physical evolutionary findings. Van Vugt, Hogan, and Kaiser (2008) describe why somebody could decide to "follow the leader." Individuals must perceive a need for coordination; they must decide on a collective course of action. There must be situations that require proactive thinking to prevent future dangers which are not yet obvious. According to Van Vugt et al. (2008), "It is possible that well-led groups are so much better at group hunting, food sharing, and warfare that the relatively lower within-group payoffs for followers are compensated for by between-group fitness benefits" (p. 186).

THIRD REFLECTION

In our view, a solid leadership-followership theory and practice should start from the principle that leadership and followership are – by definition – mutually implicated not only in theory but also in practice. You can lead and follow at the same time. The dance metaphor has been chosen to illustrate this point. You cannot move in a certain direction without being connected with your dancing partner. Anybody who has ever danced will affirm this truth. Leading *is* following. Following *is* leading. Following and leading means being connected. In reality, you cannot separate the two activities. This is in line with the leadership process approach described by Uhl-Bien, Riggio, Lowe, and Carsten (2014). Causality is seen as an interconnected network. In interacting, leading and following emerge unpredictably like in a flock of birds. Leading and following are not equated with one's hierarchical position in the organization. As managers, people also follow just as subordinates people also lead. Being aware is challenging for many leaders because they tend to think they no longer follow – they are only leading. The mind-set of following seems to have disappeared from their minds. In our experience, one of the most challenging learnings for leaders is to become aware when, how, and with whom they follow. While hierarchically people lead subordinates in one team, people hierarchically follow in the other, higher ranking team. And with their peers, people constantly switch between leading and following, as they are hierarchically equal. Many leaders consider it to be a challenge because, more often than not, they are inclined to identify with one role: the leadership role. This yields a higher status and more power. We even make the statement that world leaders like Obama and Putin are members of multiple teams and have to adapt to different situations, sometimes leading, sometimes following.

FOURTH REFLECTION

I, Rens, am working as a professor at Tilburg University in the Netherlands and as a Director of Learning, Leadership and Culture at Deloitte Consulting. In those two roles, I have to lead and follow simultaneously. If I push a certain topic too hard, I will meet with resistance. If I lead from a vision and try to convince others to follow me, the result might be collaborative success. Every day, I find that if I use a formal hierarchical approach, I am far less effective than I could be. In Hagel, Brown, and Davison (2012), the *power of pull* is described as the ability to draw out people and resources for different endeavors. In a globalized, cross-cultural, cross-company, and cross-national world, the skill to flexibly follow *and* lead is an expression of this mechanism.

FIFTH REFLECTION

Goffee and Jones (2006) come near to what we propose above. They start with the question, "Why should anyone be led by you?" This question gently forces the leader to take the perspective of the follower. If only all leaders in public and private organizations were to ask themselves this question twice a day. I propose adding another question for leaders to ask themselves every day, "Who did I voluntarily follow today?" This question not only puts leaders in the shoes of the followers but also offers them a glimpse into the followers' motives. Several followership needs have been identified. First, Goffee and Jones suggest that followers want to see authenticity in their leaders. Followers seem to have a sharp eye for inauthenticity (p. 192). Second, followers need to feel significant. Third, they want to be recognized for their contributions. Personalized and here-and-now recognition influences the atmosphere in an organization in a positive way. Followers need to feel they are a meaningful part of the community.

DISCUSSION QUESTIONS

1. How do multiple I-positions as a follower influence one's leadership capabilities in a corporate environment?
2. In this case, John Hall became aware of the leader-follower dynamic by dialoguing with himself about his leadership style. In reality, many people are not aware of how leading and following really works. This brings up the question of whether an agreement is made explicitly or implicitly? How does this agreement affect the quality of the interaction?
3. Which of John Hall's characteristics facilitated his understanding of flexibly switching between leading and following? If you were to write your own leadership story, how would your professional experiences as a leader inform your journey as a leader and follower?
4. In your experience, how does leader-follower agreement influence the quality of a dance or a job? Is leader-follower agreement expressed verbally, nonverbally, or both? Name three reasons why you believe that a better understanding of this agreement is important.

References

Gergen, K. J. (2009). *Relational being: Beyond self and community*. New York, NY: Oxford University Press.

Goffee, R., & Jones, G. (2006). *Why should anyone be led by you?* Boston, MA: Harvard Business School Press.

Hagel, III, J., Brown, J. S., & Davison, L. (2012). *The power of pull: How small moves, smartly made, can set big things in motion*. New York, NY: Basic Books.

Hermans, H. J. M., & Gieser, T. (Eds.). (2012). *Handbook of dialogical self theory*. Cambridge: University Press.

Hermans, H. J. M., & Hermans-Konopka, A. (2010). *Dialogical self-theory. Positioning and counter-positioning in a globalizing society*. Cambridge: University Press.

Hermans, H. J. M., Kempen, H. J. G., & van Loon, R. J. P. (1992). The dialogical self: Beyond individualism and rationalism. *American Psychologist*, *47*, 23–33. doi:10.1037/0003-066X.47.1.23

Hersted, L., & Gergen, K. J. (2013). *Relational leading. Practices for dialogically based collaboration*. Chagrin Falls, OH: Taos Institute.

Uhl-Bien, M., Riggio, R. E., Lowe, K. B., & Carsten, M. K. (2014). Followership theory: A review and research agenda. *The Leadership Quarterly*, *25*(1), 83–104. doi:10.1016/j.leaqua.2013.11.007

Van Vugt, M. (2009). Despotism, democracy, and the evolutionary dynamics of leadership and followership. *American Psychologist*, *64*(1), 54–56. doi:10.1037/a0014178

Van Vugt, M., Hogan, R., & Kaiser, R. B. (2008). Leadership, followership, and evolution: Some lessons from the past. *American Psychologist*, *63*(3), 182–196. doi:10.1037/0003-066X.63.3.182

CHAPTER

13 Shattered Dream of a University Professor

Tanuja Agarwala

"As I think about it, maybe I was mistaken about the world of academia. When I first joined as an assistant professor at one of the best departments of the university where I had been a student, it felt like a homecoming. I was eager to contribute to research and academics which had been my passion. Now, I stand disillusioned and de-motivated." As Ruma penned another line in her diary about her professional experiences, she was startled by a knock at the door. Her colleague Suvashish opened the door. "Care for coffee at the café?" he asked. Ruma readily agreed.

As they settled with their coffee in a quiet corner of the café, Suvashish asked, "Ruma is something bothering you?" Ruma hesitated for a moment. About seven years ago, both of them had joined as assistant professors of the department, but they had progressed very differently through the years. Ruma was not sure whether she should share her thoughts. Yet, she nodded slightly and said, "Yes, I am disturbed. But I do not know if you will understand." Suvashish reassured her. Ruma asked, "What are your views about Professor Ghosh?" Professor Ghosh was the head of the department. Suvashish replied cautiously, "Well, he is academically bright and has a vision for the department. He involves everyone in moving the department forward. But how is that related to your being disturbed?"

"I am not necessarily disturbed," said Ruma, "but I am beginning to feel my potential is not being put to good use. I was always among the top-ranked students throughout my educational pursuits. My doctoral thesis received the 'outstanding thesis' award. I had several job offers and could have joined any university. But I chose my alma mater because I wanted to give back what I had gained. Is it so much to ask of them to provide me an opportunity in return? You may find it hard to understand my feeling of pride and obligation since you did not study here. However, I was full of enthusiasm. Today, I feel completely dejected and disillusioned."

In an attempt to comfort Ruma, Suvashish responded, "Ruma, nothing is perfect. And personally I find that we have great opportunities in this department to further our career. Why do you feel dejected?"

"I find the academic world so hierarchical," Ruma said. "Remember when we joined this department? I was the youngest of the four newly inducted assistant professors. I was not allowed to teach the paper of my specialization. The senior colleagues decided what I would teach and how I will contribute. I tried to speak with Professor Ghosh, but he waived it off by saying that I should first settle down. On the other hand, you and others who had joined with me enjoyed more freedom and autonomy. I knew that I had so much to offer. I did not know with whom to speak. With time, I thought things would change, but they did not." Suvashish intervened, "Ruma, it was not so simple for us either. We made efforts to be involved and took the initiative to interact with senior professors."

"I tried to do the same, but it was not so simple. You know there are groups in this department and I am not identified with any group," Ruma continued. "You were fortunate that Professor Tripathi included you in his group. You received support, exposure, and guidance from him. I find myself isolated and left to fend for myself in this system."

"It was not entirely one-sided Ruma," Suvashish retorted. "I can say for myself. I made efforts to interact with Professor Tripathi and shared my interests. I took the initiative to make it known that I was keen on being a part of various activities. The fact that Professor Tripathi was close to Professor Ghosh certainly helped in getting me the visibility in the eyes of Professor Ghosh; however, I think that is universal to all organizations."

Ruma said, "That is exactly the point. For me, Professor Ghosh was rather inaccessible. When I met him, it was evident that he already had preconceived notions about me based on what others close to him had communicated to him. He believed what he had 'heard' not what I had to 'say'. In fact, I felt that he did not think that I had the capability. I am completely demotivated. I have been left out of all important departmental committees and not assigned any important role by the head of the department. What am I to make of such a thing? You have been involved in all department activities and are acknowledged in meetings. I do not resent that recognition, but I have never been given a chance. It appears that my good credentials do not matter. I am beginning to question my own competence and feel perhaps I am not good enough!"

"I do see what you are trying to say, but you need to reach out. Nothing is handed over naturally in any organization," said Suvashish. As they finished their coffee, the cafeteria grew more crowded. Ruma and Suvashish returned to the department. "Do let me know if I can do something," said Suvashish as they walked toward their respective offices.

Ruma returned to her diary. She began writing a note to Ms. Burgundy, her school teacher and mentor for years. She wrote, "Why did you not prepare me for this difficulty? Why did you not tell me that affiliations matter more than merit or work? Earlier, I looked up to the department head, but how do I respect someone who is unfair and partial? Please tell me."

Taking a deep breath, Ruma continued to write, "My potential is being wasted. I am not being allowed to learn, grow, and develop. I am unable to play their game. I can't join a 'group' since to me this is politicking. I would like to achieve things through hard work and merit and not merely because I am close to someone important. When I joined I thought it was the most ideal place not only because I studied here, but also because I believe that an academic institution has a responsibility to maintain social and moral standards. Is it time to quit? The current situation is very discouraging and I do not wish to continue down this path."

Suvashish was not entirely unaffected by what Ruma had shared. Clearly she was going through emotional turmoil. He knew that Ruma's observation had some merit. He also knew that Ruma was very reserved and did not take initiative to interact with colleagues. Yet he wondered, why can't leaders recognize merit of all subordinates? Why should a bright employee with huge potential not be given a chance to contribute? Does it not affect the outcomes of the organization? He wished he could change things.

Scholarly Commentary

This case highlights the mutuality of the follower-leader relationship. Leadership is not unidirectional (Koonce, 2013), nor is followership meant to be passive. Suvashish's statement, "Ruma, it was not so simple for us either. We made efforts ..." reflects the importance of follower behavior in the leader-follower dyad. At the same time, it is also evident that the same leader may be rated differently by different followers. The case may be examined from three perspectives: quality of the leader-follower exchange relationship, follower characteristics, and the organizational context.

Leaders and followers typically engage in a social exchange of psychological benefits. Social exchange theory suggests that the leaders and followers involve a system of inducements and contributions over time based on dyadic interactions which is reflective of the quality of the relationship (Graen, 1976). The exchange is characterized by mutual trust, respect, liking, and obligation between the two parties (Graen & Uhl-Bien, 1995). When the exchange is viewed as fair, a high-quality leader-member exchange (LMX) emerges (Liden, Sparrow, & Wayne, 1997). In the present case, Ruma betrays a lack of respect for the head of the department, Professor Ghosh, since she believes that he has developed preconceived notions about her skills, knowledge, and abilities, and has denied her opportunities to contribute and demonstrate her competence. Overall, the perception of the relationship quality between Ruma (as follower) and Professor Ghosh (as leader) is poor. The case suggests leader-follower congruence with respect to the experienced quality of the LMX relationship with both members of the dyad perceiving the relationship quality as poor.

According to Atwater and Yammarino's (1997) model of self-other agreement based on the LMX balance framework, four types of leader-follower relationships may be inferred based on two dimensions: (a) leader-follower agreement (balance) on the nature of the relationship and (b) quality of the relationship (low/high). The relationship between Ruma and Professor Ghosh is typically the balanced/low LMX type. This type of relationship is evidenced when both the leader and the follower view the relationship as being one of low quality. In balanced/low LMX relationship, the leader and follower engage in contractual exchanges. Such leader-member relationships are largely defined by formal job roles, are characterized by low affect, trust, and loyalty for each other and influence that is primarily downward (Cogliser, Schriesheim, Scandura, & Gardner, 2009). Low-quality LMX of this nature is expected to be particularly likely early in the development of the leader-follower relationship but may continue even in relationships of longer duration. This type of relationship is consistent with the description of "out-group" relationships. In this type of relationship, neither the leader nor the follower makes significant investments in developing the relationship beyond what is prescribed in the formal employment contract (Cogliser et al., 2009).

It is, however, quite possible that different followers rate the same leader differently. This may be due to the different behavior that the leader demonstrates toward different followers. The quality of LMX relationship between Suvashish and Professor Ghosh is high and may be classified as balanced/high LMX in which both dyad members rate the relationship as being of high quality. The relationship itself is characterized by mutual trust, respect, liking, and reciprocal influence. Such type of relationships is consistent with in-group relationships in which the follower is a trusted ally of the leader who in turn, makes a significant investment in the career of the follower (Cogliser et al., 2009).

Followers' work attitudes and job performance may be related to leader-follower perceptions of LMX (Cogliser et al., 2009). Ruma describes herself as demotivated, dejected, disillusioned, and also states, "I am beginning to question my own competence and feel perhaps I am not good enough." The poor quality of LMX between Ruma and Professor Ghosh adversely affected Ruma's attitude and intentions to stay with the university. In terms of Kelley's (1992) follower types, Ruma is most appropriately seen as an alienated follower.

Fairness is a fundamental characteristic of an effective leader-follower exchange relationship (Bettencourt & Brown, 1997). Perceived fairness reassures the followers that they will receive their deserved reward for their effort and contribution to the organization. Fairness or justice perceptions extend the relationship between the employee and the organization beyond the economic obligations. According to fairness theory, injustice is perceived when an individual is able to hold another accountable for a situation in which her well-being has been threatened (Nicklin, Greenbaum, McNall, Folger, & Williams, 2011). Fairness theory requires three conditions for a situation to be perceived as socially unjust: (1) An unfavorable condition or adversity must be present in the eyes of the victim; (2) the victim must determine who is accountable or responsible for the injustice and whether this person could have acted differently; and (3) whether the harmful actions are unethical in the context of interpersonal interaction. A follower is likely to perceive greater unfairness when the originator of action was knowledgeable and could have acted differently to prevent the situation (Nicklin et al., 2011). Justice perceptions are related to equity and have significant consequences for fairness perceptions in the organization. When the leader is perceived to follow fair procedures in decision-making, followers will consider them as trustworthy. People also judge the fairness of the interpersonal treatment they receive, also called the interactional justice (Bies & Moag, 1986). From this perspective, Ruma is experiencing injustice and unfair treatment at work and considers Professor Ghosh to be responsible for the same.

Another factor that may have influenced Ruma's perception of the relationship quality may be the image of leaders, in general, or of an ideal leader (implicit leadership theory) that Ruma has formed (Schyns, Kroon, & Moors, 2008).

Follower characteristics contribute to LMX quality. Follower extraversion is particularly important for cultivating LMX in the early stages of the relationship (Nahrgang, Morgeson, & Ilies, 2009).

Ruma is an introvert. Suvashish says, "It was not entirely one-sided Ruma. I can say for myself. I made efforts to interact with Professor Tripathi and shared my interests. I took the initiative to make it known that I was keen on being a part of various activities." On the other hand, according to Ruma, "I tried to do the same but it was not so simple. You know there are groups in this department and I am not identified with any group … I find myself isolated and left to fend for myself in this system."

Another follower characteristic that impacts social exchange is self-identity. At the individual level, self-identity is associated with self-definition based on personal sense of uniqueness. The follower derives self-worth from being different, and perceiving self as often better than others (Brewer & Gardner, 1996). Ruma has a strong sense of self-identity (individual) as evident from her diary notations of "Why did you not tell me that affiliations matter more than merit or work?" and "My potential is being wasted." Additional evidence is provided from her conversation with Suvashish: "I was always among the top ranked students throughout my educational pursuits. My doctoral thesis received the 'outstanding thesis' award. I had several job offers and could have joined any university" and "I knew I had so much to offer." Individuals with strong self-definition are motivated by goals that maximize their personal uniqueness and pay attention to the fairness of personal outcomes at work (Holmvall & Bobocel, 2008; Johnson, Selenta, & Lord, 2006). Individual level self-identity motivates the follower to focus on maximizing personal outcomes rather than those of the social group, and hence is not expected to relate to LMX quality (Jackson & Johnson, 2012).

Suvashish, on the other hand, demonstrates a strong relational identity where self-definition is based on dyadic connections with specific others, such as co-workers or leaders. Evidence from the case suggests that Suvashish made efforts to reach out to superiors and to be involved in department activities. Such individuals derive self-worth from having high-quality relationships and derive satisfaction and commitment from the quality of interpersonal exchange they receive from others (Johnson et al., 2006). Thus, quality LMX is expected to be cultivated when leaders and followers have strong relational identities.

Within the organizational context, the followership, as it has evolved in this case, may be examined with respect to breach of psychological contract. Psychological contract is based on an employee's beliefs about the reciprocal obligations (perceived promises, both implicit and explicit) between them and their organization in an employee-organization exchange relationship (Morrison & Robinson, 1997; Rosen, Chang, Johnson, & Levy, 2009); it extends beyond the formal employment contract. Each party in the psychological contract relationship develops a set of beliefs about the reciprocal exchange, that is, what either party in the dyad should expect to receive, and obligated to give in exchange for the contributions of the other (Levinson, Price, Munden, Mandl, & Soller, 1962). An employee may experience breach of the contract when she believes that her organization has failed to meet one or more obligations of the psychological contract commensurate with her contributions (Morrison & Robinson, 1997). Ruma's dejection and disillusionment are suggestive of the expectations that she had about the unfulfilled obligations on the part of the department, university, and Professor Ghosh toward her. On the other hand, she believes that she has fulfilled her side of the contractual obligations of the relationship through rejecting other job offers in favor of her alma mater, bringing her academic credentials and awards and being enthusiastic to contribute.

Breach of psychological contract may be due to reneging or incongruence (Morrison & Robinson, 1997). Reneging occurs when the organization recognizes that an obligation exists but knowingly fails to meet an exchange obligation either due to inability or unwillingness. Incongruence occurs when the employee believes that the organization has a certain obligation but has not fulfilled the obligation. On the other hand, the organization sincerely believes that it has fulfilled all obligations that it had toward the employee. This suggests that the employee and the organization have different understandings of whether an obligation exists or the nature of the obligation. Reneging and incongruence create a discrepancy between the employee's perception of what was promised and what was experienced (Rosen et al., 2009). Clearly, then Ruma defines the breach in terms of reneging ("I have been left out of all important committees of the department and not assigned any important role by the head of the department"; "I have never been given a chance"); as well as incongruence ("I tried to speak with Prof. Ghosh, but he waived it off by saying that I should first settle down"). Once the breach has occurred, the follower's response to the breach depends on how they interpret the nature of the breach. Responses may range from feelings of hurt, anger, betrayal, and resentment (Morrison & Robinson, 1997; Rousseau, 1989). Ruma experiences all of these emotions.

Professor Ghosh is not aware of Ruma's state of mind. Ruma is a high potential and it is important that the university retains talent. A high-quality relationship results in positive outcomes for all – the follower, leader, and the organization. Suvashish can play an important role in transforming the quality of the relationship between Ruma and Professor Ghosh.

DISCUSSION QUESTIONS

1. Do you support the decision which Ruma is contemplating? Do you agree or disagree with the course of action she is considering? If you were in her place, what would you have done?
2. Compare the perceptions that Ruma and Suvashish have of Professor Ghosh. Also consider the organizational context.
3. Evaluate the quality of the leader-follower relationship between Professor Ghosh and Ruma and between Professor Ghosh and Suvashish. Was Professor Ghosh an effective leader? Did he do anything wrong? If you were Professor Ghosh, what could you have done differently? Why is this important?
4. Do you believe that the department and the university stand to lose anything if Ruma leaves the university?
5. What lessons do you draw from this case about the role of followership in leader effectiveness and performance?

References

Atwater, L. E., & Yammarino, F. J. (1997). Self-other rating agreement: A review and model. In G. R. Ferris (Ed.), *Research in personnel and human resources management* (Vol. 15, pp. 121–174). Greenwich, CT: JAI Press.

Bettencourt, L. A., & Brown, S. W. (1997). Contact employees: Relationships among workplace fairness, job satisfaction and prosocial service behaviors. *Journal of Retailing*, *73*(1), 39–61. doi:10.1016/S0022-4359(97)90014-2

Bies, R. J., & Moag, J. S. (1986). Interactional justice: Communication criteria of fairness. In R. J. Lewicki, B. H. Sheppard, & M. H. Bazerman (Eds.), *Research on negotiation in organizations* (Vol. 1, pp. 43–55). Greenwich, CT: JAI Press.

Brewer, M. B., & Gardner, W. (1996). Who is this 'We'? Levels of collective identity and self representations. *Journal of Personality and Social Psychology*, *71*(1), 83–93. doi:10.1037//0022-3514.71.1.83

Cogliser, C. C., Schriesheim, C. A., Scandura, T. A., & Gardner, W. L. (2009). Balance in leader and follower perceptions of leader-member exchange: Relationships with performance and work attitudes. *The Leadership Quarterly*, *20*(3), 452–465. doi:10.1016/j.leaqua.2009.03.010

Graen, G. B. (1976). Role-making processes within complex organizations. In M. D. Dunnette (Ed.), *Handbook of industrial and organizational psychology* (pp. 1201–1245). Chicago, IL: Rand-NcNally.

Graen, G. B., & Uhl-Bien, M. (1995). Relationship-based approach to leadership: Development of leader–member exchange (LMX) theory of leadership over 25 years: Applying a multi-level multi-domain perspective. *The Leadership Quarterly*, *6*(2), 219–247. doi:10.1016/1048-9843(95)90036-5

Holmvall, C. M., & Bobocel, D. R. (2008). What fair procedures say about me: Self-construals and reactions to procedural fairness. *Organizational Behavior and Human Decision Processes*, *105*, 147–168. doi:10.1016/j.obhdp.2007.09.001

Jackson, E. M., & Johnson, R. E. (2012). When opposites do (and do not) attract: Interplay of leader and follower self-identities and consequences for leader-member exchange. *The Leadership Quarterly*, *23*(3), 488–501. doi:10.1016/j.leaqua.2011.12.003

Johnson, R. E., Selenta, C., & Lord, R. G. (2006). When organizational justice and the self-concept meet: Consequences for the organization and its members. *Organizational Behavior and Human Decision Processes*, *99*(2), 175–201. doi:10.1016/j.obhdp.2005.07.005

Kelley, R. (1992). *The power of followership*. New York, NY: Doubleday.

Koonce, R. (2013, October). *Partial least squares analysis as a modeling tool for assessing motivational leadership practices*. International annual conference proceedings of the American Society for Engineering Management, 2013 International Annual Conference, Minneapolis, Minnesota.

Levinson, H., Price, C., Munden, K., Mandl, H., & Solley, C. (1962). *Men, management, and mental health*. Cambridge, MA: Harvard University Press.

Liden, R. C., Sparrow, R. T., & Wayne, S. J. (1997). Leader–member exchange theory: The past and potential for the future. In G. R. Ferris (Ed.), *Research in personnel and human resources management* (Vol. 15, pp. 47–119). Greenwich, CT: JAI Press.

Morrison, E. W., & Robinson, S. L. (1997). When employees feel betrayed: A model of how psychological contract violation develops. *Academy of Management Review*, *22*(1), 226–256. Retrieved from http://www.jstor.org/stable/259230

Nahrgang, J. D., Morgeson, F. P., & Ilies, R. (2009). The development of leader–member exchanges: Exploring how personality and performance influence leader and member relationships over time. *Organizational Behavior and Human Decision Processes*, *108*, 256–266. doi:10.1016/j.obhdp.2008.09.002

Nicklin, J. M., Greenbaum, R., McNall, L. A., Folger, R., & Williams, K. J. (2011). The importance of contextual variables when judging fairness: An examination of counterfactual thoughts and fairness theory. *Organizational Behavior and Human Decision Processes*, *114*, 127–141. doi:10.1016/j.obhdp.2010.10.007

Rosen, C. C., Chang, C.-H., Johnson, R. E., & Levy, P. E. (2009). Perceptions of the organizational context and psychological contract breach: Assessing competing perspectives. *Organizational Behavior and Human Decision Processes*, *108*, 202–217. doi:10.1016/j.obhdp.2008.07.003

Rousseau, D. M. (1989). Psychological and implied contracts in organization. *Employee Responsibilities and Rights Journal*, *2*(2), 121–139. doi:10.1007/BF01384942

Schyns, B., Kroon, B., & Moors, G. (2008). Follower characteristics and the perception of leader-member exchange. *Journal of Managerial Psychology*, *23*(7), 772–788. doi:10.1108/02683940810896330

CHAPTER

14 Artist as Apprentice: Reexamining Distance in the Leader-Follower Relationship

Kimberley A. Koonce

Artists are often asked whose art their work most resembles or to whom they are drawn. Almost every artist relates to this question. When asked, most are quick to respond with the name of a teacher who first inspired them at an early age, or, better yet, the name of a single artist who sparked their love to create and influenced their process and style. When approached with this question, my answer is simple: "As an artist, I follow Rembrandt."

In the context of what I and other artists create, I find myself asking how this unspoken desire to recreate and redefine a similar creative flow of those that we admire transforms us into followers if, indeed, it is correct to refer to artists as followers. Do we possess the same qualifiers that are commonly recognized by scholars of followership?

I cannot recall the exact moment or circumstance that lured me to Rembrandt's work. However, in the absence of the master artist himself, I do know that there is something that deeply moves me about his drawings and etchings – how the fluidity and looseness of the lines, their width, and their placement – create a shadow, reflect light, or define space. I am not alone. In her book entitled *The Language of Drawing from an Artist's Viewpoint*, world-renowned artist Sherrie McGraw recounts the evening when she was guarding a special drawing by Rembrandt at the Metropolitan Museum of Art in New York City. As a make-shift apprentice in a post-Rembrandt era, McGraw began to copy the piece because "it kept demanding [her] attention ... The drawing's simplicity kept me coming back in a way that more elaborate drawings by very impressive draughtsmen could not. How could he say so much with so little?," she wondered (McGraw, 2004).

I can relate to McGraw's puzzlement. A similar experience happened to me in a Santa Fe gallery when I first laid eyes on the Millennium Impressions, a modern collection of etched prints produced from eight of Rembrandt's original copper plates. I found myself in reverent awe as I pondered how he was able to produce images with such precision and visual dimension by simply scratching tiny lines on a metal plate.

When I am not painting, I tend to check out a book at least once every year or two entitled *Rembrandt and His Time: Masterworks from the Albertina, Vienna* (Bisanz-Prakken, 2005) from the public library. It is filled with Rembrandt's sketches and etchings of landscapes and everyday life in 17th century Holland, in addition to scenes from his imagination. Each time that I interface with that book, I find myself carefully examining each page as if I were viewing it for the first time. Admittedly, photographs of those drawings on aged and discolored paper embellished with black and red chalk, pen, and brush ink renderings, automatically initiate romanticizing about what it must have been like to have studied under the instruction of Rembrandt himself with the intent of creating similar masterpieces.

My adoration for Rembrandt extends beyond his splendid drawings and etchings to his paintings. Why am I so drawn to his work? Is it the curiosity surrounding the scenes of unfamiliar life in large rooms? Is it my fascination with how he illuminated focal points amidst spaces of darkness? Or, is it the mystery of how he so eloquently captured the human spirit on a flat surface? Maybe, it is the pleasantry of his unexpected, yet respectful depiction of ordinary, curvy, or chubby women which unveils a connection. Although not visible, the source of my fascination is far from imaginary.

A short time ago, I was asked to paint the subject for a poster that was used in conjunction with a large annual event for a state association. Just prior to this time, I had begun studying Rembrandt in an effort to achieve a greater familiarity with his work and improve my technical skills. It was the perfect occasion to manifest what I was learning through what might be described as a *post-humous followership*. While referring to an article that had been published in a well-known magazine for artists, I experimented with ways to replicate surfaces and paint palettes which had supposedly been used by Rembrandt in his own studio. In an attempt to recreate elements used in his own designs, I also began relying on countless pages of Rembrandt's imagery for reference.

My fixation with this master artist even permeates my art studio. In one room hangs a print that bears Rembrandt's name and an embossed signet from a German print house entitled *Der Mann mit dem Goldhelm.* With the stern expression of a weathered man, it is not the type of piece to which I normally gravitate; however, there is a beauty in the earthy dark hues, impasto texture of the golden helmet, and the strong chiaroscuro (bold contrasts between light and dark) effect for which Rembrandt is so well known. Interestingly, one of Rembrandt's students, whose aspiration was to become as skilled and accomplished as Rembrandt himself, is speculated to be the painter of *The Man in the Golden Helmet* (Friedrich, 1985).

Scholarly Commentary

Much has been written about dyadic relationships between leaders and followers in organizations, but how does one explain the type of followership that occurs between a master artist – either living or dead – and a living artist who strives to follow his or her prior work?

Does followership explain the influence of a master artist on another artist's work?

Meindl's (1995) social constructionist theory suggests that in a follower's construction of a leader's personality, the follower's perception of the leader's personality is more influential than the leader's actual personality. Can the personality of an artist be perceived through an artist's collection of works, or is a more suitable explanation found in mission-driven followership? Keim (2014) asserts that mission-driven followers choose to follow out of their support for a mission, leader, or organization. The same rationale could conceivably be applied to artists' who construct their calling of following the mission of a great craftsman like Rembrandt. Alternatively, based on the perception of Rembrandt as a leading figure in the art world, an artist as follower could be drawn not only to the artist as a leading figure, but also to the mission of recreating or reimagining his work through her own creations based on inspiration received from her attachment to his work.

For centuries, artists have turned to other artists for guidance and apprenticeship, seeking to emulate admired skills. Aspiring artists must exert tremendous dedication to their craft if they are to reach what Bayles and Orland (1993) refer to as *self-acceptance* as an artist. This acceptance frees artists to begin producing distinctive authentic work. In an attempt to arrive at uninhibited self-expression, artists may learn from other artists. As noted by Leeds (1984), copying other artists can play an essential part of that learning as long as the student also aims to "deepen and broaden his [or her] own powers of invention" (p. 43). It is my belief that artists follow other artists as mentees until they are able to recognize their own accomplishments as artists. This phase operates much like Higgins' (1997) regulatory focus theory in which followers align themselves with prevention or promotion goals. Promotion goals are representative of obtaining the ideals of one's "hopes, wishes, and aspirations" (Higgins, 1997, p. 1281). According to Kark and Van Dijk (2007), followers can be persuaded to center on their ideal self through inspirational and visionary messages (p. 511). Centering on the ideal self may inspire followers to have a promotion focus by which energy can be channeled into work tasks which help them to achieve goals that they perceive they have set for themselves. If followers can be persuaded by using image-based language to illustrate an organizational goal (Kark & Van Dijk, 2007, p. 511), it seems plausible that following another artist's work may serve to prime an artist's promotion focus and therefore assist in their goal of becoming an accomplished artist.

Upon reaching self-acceptance, an artist's followership shifts to a form of *inspiration seeking* by continual engagement with things that bring forth interpretations of what artists admire and what they see. An example of this transformation is evidenced by the success of another famous Dutch artist, Vincent van Gogh. Van Gogh's inspiration seeking came through his study of Japanese culture and nature designs created on woodblocks by Japanese artists. Through experimentation, "not only [did he] construct an image of an ideal primitive Japan – he also fashioned an ideal primitive self in relation to Japan" (Walker, 2008, p. 87). Although van Gogh invested a lot of his time and energy into following traditional Japanese woodblock artists, he did not impersonate their style; instead, his success came from mimicking what Japanese artists had created and then producing his own artistic representations of individual natural phenomena (Walker, 2008). The intent of artists who follow others artists may be to gain knowledge and self-acceptance. However, the benefit of following to acquire meaning through connectedness and self-discovery cannot be overlooked.

While standing in front of one of Rembrandt's paintings a few years ago in La Musee des Beaux Arts de Montreal, I made a reflective comment regarding what he had captured in the work of art before me. When my husband asked me to repeat what I said, he exclaimed, "Kim, that is followership!" At that moment, I gained a deeper appreciation for followership as the result of my experiences and progression as an artist. While writing the current case, I was recently reminded of that experience while reading a thought provoking piece in *The New York Times*. In *The Art of Slowing Down in a Museum*, Rosenbloom (2014) describes the surprise discovery of a student while taking a positive humanities course. The instructions for the assignment required the student to observe a painting for at least 20 minutes, so she chose a piece of art whose subject had red hair like her own. This deliberate observation stirred her inner skeptic to imagine the subject's hidden story in the painting. Beautifully recounted by Rosenbloom, the observer thought that perhaps the woman in the painting was unhappy, felt trapped, not yet having discovered that the window behind her could offer her an escape. What ultimately resulted from that brief moment in time was the learner's self-discovery as she came to realize that she was projecting her own life's experience into artist Toulouse-Lautrec's work.

Conclusion

According to Adler (2015), art and its processes provide "the power to offer us hope" and "guide us in rediscovering and creating beauty in our fractured world" (p. 481). As I sense the student's connection to Toulouse-Lautrec's art in Rosenbloom (2014), I am also reminded of van Gogh's inspiration seeking through his study of Japanese culture and nature designs, as well as my own self-discovery through my long-standing connection to the work of Rembrandt. From self-acceptance to inspiration seeking, artists and those who follow artists learn to self-regulate and find purpose in their lives. As I consider the possibilities associated with these discoveries, I am left to explore the expansive role that art may eventually play in the lives of followers and leaders in organizations.

DISCUSSION QUESTIONS

1. According to Kark and Van Dijk (2007), followers can be persuaded to center on their ideal self through inspirational and visionary messages. Centering on the ideal self may inspire followers to have a promotion focus by which energy can be channeled into work tasks which help them to achieve their goals. How could art be used in organizations to help followers achieve organizational goals?
2. Following other artists may result in self-discovery which, in turn, can lead to authenticity in one's work. How could

(*continued*)

this self-discovery be used to positively impact how individuals contribute to organizational processes?

3. How could art be used in organizational settings to teach followers and leaders about diversity and inclusion?
4. Exercise: Conduct an online search for an art collection. Find a particular piece of art that appeals to you and observe it for 20 minutes. After 20 minutes, write an essay about your experience. Alternatively, conduct a similar exercise in a larger group, and then spend time discussing the experiences of each person in the group. How could this exercise be used in a classroom or an organizational setting to creatively dialogue about a current challenge?

References

Adler, N. J. (2015). Finding beauty in a fractured world: Art inspires leaders—Leaders change the world. *Academy of Management Review*, *40*(3), 480–494.

Bayles, D., & Orland, T. (1993). *Art and fear: Observations on the perils (and rewards) of artmaking*. Santa Cruz, CA: The Image Continuum.

Bisanz-Prakken, M. (2005). *Rembrandt and his time: Masterworks from the Albertina, Vienna*. Manchester, VT: Hudson Hills.

Friedrich, O. (1985). The man with the golden helmet. *Time*, *126*(24), December. Retrieved from http://content.time.com

Higgins, E. T. (1997). Beyond pleasure and pain. *American Psychologist*, *52*(12), 1280–1300. Retrieved from http://www.apa.org

Kark, R., & Van Dijk, D. (2007). Motivation to lead, motivation to follow: The role of the self-regulatory focus in leadership processes. *Academy of Management Review*, *32*(2), 500–528. doi:10.5465/AMR.2007.24351846

Keim, S. (2014). Mission-driven followership and civic engagement: A different sustainable energy. *Journal of Leadership Education*, *13*(14), 76–87. doi:10.12806/V13/I4/C9

Leeds, J. A. (1984). Copying and invention as sources of form in art. *Art Education*, *37*(2), 41–46. Retrieved from http://www.arteducators.org

McGraw, S. (2004). *The language of drawing from an artist's viewpoint*. El Prado, NM: Bright Light.

Meindl, J. R. (1995). The romance of leadership as a follower-centric theory: A social constructionist approach. *Leadership Quarterly*, *6*(3), 329–341. doi:10.1016/1048-9843(95)90012-8

Rosenbloom, S. (2014). The art of slowing down in a museum. *The New York Times*, October 9. Retrieved from http://www.nytimes.com

Walker, J. A. (2008). Van Gogh, collector of "Japan". *The Comparatist*, 32, 82–114. doi:10.1353/com.0.0025

CHAPTER

15 Online Cybersecurity Courses: Dissent and Followership

Steven Lee Smith

Sandra is a member of the undergraduate academic committee that reviews degree program proposals submitted by university deans. The development and approval process is often cumbersome and drawn-out due to compliance with academic standards, curriculum development, and review of faculty qualifications. Like other members of the committee, Sandra appreciated the manner in which Donald, the Chairperson, kept everyone informed about programs under development that would eventually come to the committee for review. When the committee reviewed a degree program and specialization, members often took the time to examine and question various aspects of the proposal. One morning, Sandra along with the other committee members, received an e-mail from Donald that degree proposals in three fields of specialization were ready for a committee vote. Instead of conducting a face-to-face meeting, Donald informed members that the review, discussion, and vote would be via e-mail. Included in Donald's e-mail were three attachments, one for each degree program proposal. Sandra made a note on her calendar regarding Donald's request for each member to review the proposals, submit discussion points for all members to read, and submit a vote within 72 hours recommending either approval or disapproval.

A few hours after the e-mail was sent, Sandra began receiving e-mail messages in her inbox from a majority of the committee members who were already casting their votes – all recommending *approval*. Sandra, a retired military officer, was intrigued that members cast their votes quickly and without discussion on the cybersecurity degree. It was her understanding that there would be vetting among members regarding the cybersecurity proposal before a formal vote. Since Sandra had three days before her vote was required, she decided to spend at least a couple of days researching which, if any, American universities were already offering an online cybersecurity degree programs. Her research both surprised her and troubled her due to the number of institutions offering the degree, but also the level of cyber information. She mulled over potential national security concerns; attempting to understand the reasoning behind online cyber programs. What concerned her the most was the realistic probability that online cyber programs were educating adversaries, criminals, and terrorist with the tools to commit cybercrime or terrorist activities. She wondered if her institution, as well as other institutions, had given this serious consideration. In her search, she uncovered the following passage containing information from a government website, the National Initiative for Cybersecurity Careers and Studies (NICCS) (http://niccs.us-cert.gov/):

> In the first two decades of the 21st Century, the cybersecurity industry has experienced unprecedented growth in the professional job market. The growth is due, in no part (sic), to cybercrime, cyber-attacks, rogue employees, and the need for constant innovation within cyber security/defense. Because of the need for cybersecurity professionals, academic institutions are developing degreed programs with various specializations. In conjunction with the National Security Agency (NSA) and the Department of Homeland Security (DHS), National Centers of Academic Excellence (CAE) are in place at a select number of universities "to reduce vulnerability in [the] national information infrastructure by promoting higher education and research, and producing a growing pipeline of professionals with information assurance expertise in various disciplines."

When Sandra submitted her vote, she gave approval for recommendations two and three, but for the first recommendation for the cybersecurity degree, she added a message for discussion: "Recommendation #1: approve with trepidation and grave concern – for those who want to read my concerns – please continue, otherwise ignore." In less than 500 words, Sandra presented a reasoned and cautionary argument against offering an online cybersecurity degree. Based on her analysis of the course content and program outcomes, she argued for a strictly face-to-face classroom experience. Furthermore, since the university's online program reached a global population, she wanted to know how they could effectively scrutinize the intent and background of degree seeking students. Her final comment was an appeal for a vibrant and deliberative assessment by the university. Sandra was concerned that the university might be rushing to compete with other institutions for cybersecurity students without first pausing to consider the potential severity of its implications. Sandra could not justify recommending that the institution follow suit.

A few members of the committee hailed her response; a couple of members went so far as to include her e-mail when they cast their vote. However, the majority of the committee members dismissed her concerns, with a couple of them e-mails privately e-mailing her to say that her arguments were hypothetical and unfounded. Even though Sandra had a position of authority within the university, she knew the committee operated in a congenial and collaborative decision-making process. Furthermore, she was aware of the pressure on the university to create marketable degree programs that also became a means for much needed revenue. Overall, Sandra was baffled that no committee member submitted comments for discussion on any of the three proposals other than casting approval votes.

Scholarly Commentary

FRAMING THE ISSUE TO COMMAND ATTENTION: DISSENTERS SPEAK FROM KNOWLEDGE

Chaleff (2009) notes how leaders intentionally or unintentionally fail in being attentive to the input of followers. An intentional decision indicates a personal unwillingness to act, while an unintentional decision is a personal failure in attentiveness to information. Sandra's experience demonstrated the intentional failure of Donald and the majority of the committee members to hear and discuss her concerns about online cybersecurity degrees. As Kelley (2008) noted, followers – like Sandra – can and do "establish themselves as independent, critical thinkers whose knowledge and judgment can be trusted" (p. 11). In Sandra's case, there was an immediate collective failure to trust her professional judgment coupled with the minimization of her argument. Furthermore, since the committee procedures operated in an *ad hoc* manner, the result was followers acting in a passive manner that permitted a flawed decision-making process.

Sandra's experience brings up two highly interrelated and interconnected elements associated with the activity of being an exemplary follower which entails having the ability to frame an issue in such a way that it commands the attention of the leader and other followers engaged in the issue at hand, as well as the ability to address the issue from a foundation of knowledge (Chaleff, 2009; Craig, 2014; Havel, 1985; Kelley, 2008; Reed, 2015). Operating in such a manner not only protects institutional integrity but challenges *groupthink* along with the diffusion of responsibility often prevalent in groups (Kelley, 2008).

According to Kelley (2008), there are followers who possess a "courageous conscience," which Sandra's actions demonstrate via a thoughtful and knowledgeable socialization of her concerns. As noted by Reed (2015), a follower must be mindful of the manner they present their dissent, which is inclusive of demonstrating a level of prudence and restraint (p. 15). Chaleff (2009) argues there is a "seismic shift … in organizational structures" where people of knowledge permeate the organization (p. 190). In effect, this shift results in organizations recognizing the breadth of knowledge throughout the organization and capitalizing on it via instructional briefings or presentations to those who are decision-makers. Because of this shift, followers must demonstrate to leaders their knowledge and intelligence through diligent preparation and confident presentation in the subject matter (Chaleff, 2009; Reed, 2015). Furthermore, when meeting with leaders, it is imperative for followers to have conducted thorough research before making comments or recommendations.

Sandra took the time to conduct internet research on cybersecurity courses offered via online classrooms. By raising a series of questions, Sandra laid a foundation for Donald and the committee to understand the issue and potential ramifications (Chaleff, 2009, p. 191). Overall, Sandra was attempting to educate Donald and other committee members about the potential for abuse of an online cybersecurity degree. But it was an uphill battle for Sandra because of the time constraints given for the vote by the committee.

HELPING LEADERS TO LEAD WELL: ADVISING

The case study raises one final matter, which can be classified as helping leaders to lead well. This concept, whether explicit or implied, is alluded to in many places including Bennis (2009), Bennis and Nanus (1985), Chaleff (2009), Craig (2014), Johnson (2015), Kelley (1988, 2008), and Reed (2015). In reality, helping leaders to lead well is a multifaceted and dynamic process undertaken by followers. Bennis (2008) encapsulates one overarching rule for followers who want to help by "speaking truth to power" (p. xxv). Speaking truth to power, in part, is an art of mastering clarity, style, and even "impoliteness" (Chaleff, 2015, p. 166) via the various communication channels available.

Another powerful facet of helping the leader to lead well includes the requirement of followers to be experts in *advising* leaders. Advising is a complex matter because it may include a variety of elements with significant ramifications that are moral, economic, organizational, or human in nature. Furthermore, advising implies a thorough review of pertinent information, an extensive and detailed examination of the situation, and proper presentation which, when done properly, helps the leader to sharpen their own thinking and assists them in making informed judgments on critical issues (Reed, 2015; "U.S. Department", 2003).

In this context, advising is the process of *moving a leader* to consider additional insights on an impending decision or a matter under review while simultaneously constructing a frame of reference whereby the leader is able to view decisions or matters from a spacious perspective. This process fills in the gaps of missing information as well as halts the misinterpretation of the interconnected and interrelated facets of an issue. Within the advisement role, however, there is the ever-present reality that others who also sit at the table or have the ear of the leader selectively edit, disregard, or fail to support advisory recommendations. In part, these other followers may very well recognize, in metaphorical language, that *the emperor has no clothes* but they still fail to speak truthfully (Argyris, 1991). This self-imposed and collective silence, regardless of reason, is a moral failure. Ethically, silence by others is culpability in wrongdoing (Havel, 1985). Because leaders are fallible and limited in their perspective regarding all the nuances of a matter, they can and do make flawed decisions. Faulty decisions, more often than not, set in motion a series of events that others rightly perceive as absurd, dangerous, or irresponsible – yet, those individuals remain silent.

Sandra experienced the dilemma of speaking truthfully in a gracious and diplomatic manner without sounding like an alarmist or engaging in the degrading of other members' perspective. Even though she presented a reasoned argument for opposing the cybersecurity program, she not only failed to persuade others on the committee, but also did not effectively communicate the depth of meaning regarding their role and responsibility as committee members (Argyris, 1991). Conversely, with the negation of her voice, Donald and her colleagues voided their opportunity to examine a moral quandary, thereby turning away from an honest appraisal of the recommendation.

DISCUSSION QUESTIONS

1. How does this case study present a different and possibly emerging role of advising and its relation to followership?
2. In a lecture at the London School of Economics and Political Science in 1933, Mary Parker Follett stated, "[The follower's] part is not merely to follow, they have a very active role to play and that is to keep the leader in control of a situation." Discuss the role that Sandra played in an attempt to keep the leader and other members of the committee in control of the issue.
3. Given the time constraints imposed on Sandra to make her case known to the committee, were there other actions she might have taken to delay the vote? Would it have been prudent for an all-out dissent? Should she have cast a "no" vote because of her objections?
4. Does a university have a moral obligation to forgo the offering of an online degree programs that might endanger national security?
5. Should Sandra speak directly to the NSA about such programs and try to get something done at a level that results in a system-wide impact?

References

Argyris, C. (1991). Teaching smart people how to learn. *Harvard Business Review*, *69*(May–June), 99–110.

Bennis, W. (2008). Introduction. In R. Riggio, I. Chaleff, & J. Lipman-Blumen (Eds.), *The art of followership: How great followers create great leaders and organizations* (pp. xxiii–xxvii). San Francisco, CA: Jossey-Bass.

Bennis, W. G. (2009). *On becoming a leader*. New York, NY: Perseus Pub.

Bennis, W., & Nanus, B. (1985). *Leaders: The strategies for taking charge*. New York, NY: Harper and Row.

Chaleff, I. (2009). *The courageous follower: Standing up to and for our leaders*. San Francisco, CA: Berrett-Koehler.

Chaleff, I. (2015). *Intelligent disobedience*. San Francisco, CA: Berrett-Koehler.

Craig, T. (2014). Leveraging the power of loyal dissent in the U.S. Army. *Military Review*, *94*(6), 97–103.

Havel, V. (1985). The power of the powerless. In J. Keane (Ed.), *The power of the powerless: Citizens against the state in central-eastern Europe* (pp. 23–96). Armonk, NY: M.E. Sharpe.

Johnson, C. E. (2015). *Meeting the ethical challenges of leadership: Casting light or shadow* (5th ed.). Thousand Oaks, CA: Sage.

Kelley, R. (1988). In praise of followers. *Harvard Business Review*, 66(6), 142–148. Retrieved from https://hbr.org/1988/11/in-praise-of-followers

Kelley, R. (2008). Rethinking followership. In R. E. Riggio, I. Chaleff, & J. Lipman-Blumen (Eds.), *The art of followership: How great followers create great leaders and organizations*. San Francisco, CA: Jossey-Bass.

Reed, G. (2015). Expressing loyal dissent. *Public Integrity*, *17*, 5–18. doi:10.2753/PIN1099-9922170101

U.S. Department of the Navy, Office of the Chief of Naval Operation, Navy Warfare Publication. (2003). Religious ministry in the United States Navy. (NWP 1–05). Navy Warfare Publication. Retrieved from http://www.marforres.marines.mil/Portals%20/116/Docs/Chaplain/instruction/NWP%20RELMIN%20IN%20THE%20USN.pdf

CHAPTER

16 Who's in Charge of a Residential College?: Student-led Seminars as an Example of Followership in Action

Eric K. Kaufman

In 2011, Virginia Tech opened its first residential college, a place "where undergraduates, graduate students, and faculty could live together in a facility dedicated to learning" (Johnson, 2011). As articulated by Frank Shushok, Associate Vice President for student affairs, "The residential college reflects all aspects of student learning ... It touches intellectual life, social life, and contemplative life. It gives students a space they can govern themselves, in collaboration with faculty and student affairs personnel" (DeLauder, 2010). The newly created Honors Residential College (HRC) includes 320 Junior Fellows who are undergraduate students in the University Honors program, as well as over 30 Senior Fellows, composed of faculty, staff, and community members. The HRC accommodates nearly three times as many students as the previous Honors-designated residence halls. So, while the HRC could benefit from some existing structure and standards, the new community required a different approach.

University Honors requires all residents in Honors housing to participate in a one-credit seminar, each semester that they live in the community. For the first two years of the HRC, the faculty administration tried to continue the "Colloquium Magnum" format of the seminars that existed in other Honors living-learning communities. Although the Colloquium Magnums were generally student-led, they relied upon regular interaction with academic faculty to ensure rigor, and the larger community made faculty oversight more difficult. So, in year three of the HRC, the director of University Honors, Terry Papillon, mandated a change to a more structured seminar with mandated reading and writing assignments. The approach related in part to Papillon's desire that the HRC "be very intentional and very intense with how it encourages students to grow and broaden" (DeLauder, 2010). The syllabus described the seminar as follows:

> The Honors Residential College Seminar (HRCS), which is replacing Colloquium Magnum, lies at the core of the academic mission of honors in the residential college model and serves two important purposes: it brings Junior Fellows together in community, and it provides a forum to hone your reading, writing, and debate skills. These are both key goals of University Honors. These common core readings serve to unify conversation and community. It is our goal that conversations about these readings and topics will spill outside the parameters of HRCS and lead to long discussions over dinner, intense arguments late at night in lounges, and blog posts that provoke online conversations and debates.

While the Honors administrators were hopeful the new structure would achieve the desired results, the Junior Fellows (i.e. students) expressed dismay and frustration with the heavy-handed approach. The backlash from the Junior Fellows was so extreme that the administration took the unprecedented approach of allowing the seminar to be optional during the second semester of that academic year. They acknowledged the need to revamp the seminar structure and worked with students to develop a new plan. Whereas the prior year's effort to improve the seminar was authoritative, the administration resolved to be more inclusive. This began by hosting a series of town hall style meetings that focused on the following questions:

- What is and is not working? Do you have a sense of why?
- Honors students are capable of holding high-level discussions without a faculty member guiding them – what do you need to make this happen?
- Keeping in mind that the courses represent honors and university credit – how can we ensure that work done in these courses is deserving of this credit?

The fellows who participated in these meetings were able to share their perceptions and suggest new changes and structures, but they also identified more questions to ponder. The HRC's director of academic enrichment (a student-elected position) accepted the challenge to improve the seminars for the next academic year and solicited a student committee to join him in the design process. In cooperation with the faculty principal (the HRC's live-in academic faculty leader), the committee engaged in several video conference calls throughout the summer, allowing student committee members to participate from geographic locations around the world. The committee developed consensus around the following course description:

> The Community and Discussion Seminar (CaDS) is designed to encourage communication, collaboration, and connectivity among fellows of the HRC. Throughout this course, you will be tasked with improving your discussion and debate skills through presentation, facilitated discussion, and a group project to be showcased late in the semester.

The syllabus describes the course format as follows:

> The course is designed to be student led. So, although we have identified an instructor of record and teaching assistant in this syllabus, do not be surprised when we are not present for the meetings of your individual section. What we will do is help provide the appropriate structure and answer questions that surface. Each section will select a "moderator" that can manage some of the logistics and serve as a point-person for communication between the instructor(s) and the group/section. The moderator is NOT responsible for leading the discussion each week; instead, the discussion leader role will rotate among all Junior Fellows enrolled in the section.

In addition, the syllabus offers the following guidance for the discussion facilitator role:

> Each week, the discussion facilitator should introduce a topic and facilitate discussion surrounding that topic. The format is far from rigid; the desire is to allow individuals enough leeway to craft exciting experiences that will both interest their peers and provoke academic discussion. After choosing a topic, the discussion facilitator should prime the discussion by posting in the online discussion forum at least three days before the next meeting. The class meeting should begin with a 5–10 minute introduction that sparks dialogue between the presenter and participants. The discussion facilitator is then responsible for guiding conversation through the remainder of the hour-long class meeting.

Students have appreciated the empowerment that occurs with the new approach. One student wrote, "This has been the best experience I have had with an honors dorm-related class since the beginning of the HRC, and I think a big part of that is how the class was organized."

Scholarly Commentary

Living-learning communities expand the potential for learning because they include both curricular and co-curricular learning opportunities (Grohs, Keith, Morikawa, Penven, & Stephens, 2013). Although the residential college model promotes close faculty interaction, a fundamental advantage of the residential college system is "the way students in the colleges educate one another" (Ryan, 2001, p. 24). This is a shift from traditional approaches to leadership. In response, we need to consider the potential of emerging discourses of leadership and ways to facilitate appropriate interactions.

The Eco-Leadership Discourse

Reflecting on a century of leadership literature, Western (2007) identified an emerging "eco-leader discourse" that is characterized by collective decision-making, collaboration, shared leadership, and grassroots organization. According to Western (2010), this discourse blurs the lines between leader and follower, emphasizing a more collective approach to leadership. Wielkiewicz and Stelzner (2005) note that positional leaders are now encouraged to assist in the emergence of leadership rather than dictating change through unilateral decision-making. This new eco-leadership approach gives a larger number of stakeholders a stronger voice, creating the potential for both better decisions and greater commitment to those decisions (Allen, Stelzner, & Wielkiewicz, 1999). This is what occurred with the Honors Residential College (HRC) seminar. Immediately prior to the current seminar format, the University Honors director mandated a new format that clearly dictated both content and format. The students rebelled against the executive orders and were motivated to contribute to the leadership process in ways they had never previously contributed. The followership in action has clearly resulted in the eco-leadership identified by Western (2007).

These premises of eco-leadership are changing the way leadership is conceived and taught. Instead of the "Great Man" theories, with leaders that were seen as controllers, therapists, or messiahs, which tended to centralize power as a sign of structural strength, this new approach sees power at the margins as beneficial

(Western, 2010). "Eco-leadership shifts the power from individual leaders to leadership ... in an attempt to harness the energy and creativity of the whole system" (Western, 2010, p. 44). Rather than focusing on leader-created change, eco-leadership focuses on "a reciprocal relationship between leadership and its environment. It decenters individuals and challenges centralized power, claiming that by creating the right culture and conditions, leadership will emerge in plural forms and unexpected places" (Western, 2010, p. 36). What remains to be seen, though, is how to structure the environment in a way that optimizes the potential for eco-leadership. For that endeavor, we can turn to the OBREAU Tripod.

Obreau Tripod

The OBREAU Tripod is a structure for helping groups and individuals work through challenging conversations. "OBREAU" is a composite of the first two letters of three guiding words: Observation, Reasonableness, and Authenticity. According to Dunoon (2014), the tripod is an aid for engaging in conversations with a broad range and depth of intelligence on an issue; it discourages default patterns of reactive thinking, negative judgment, passive engagement. The first leg of the tripod, Working from Observation, is intended as a counterpoint to the common default behavior of reacting to new information or experience. When we work from what we observe or hear directly, we keep ourselves open to different meanings – as well as minimize the threat associated with talking about difficult issues. The second leg of the tripod, Attributing Reasonableness, requires imagining what the issue might look like from another person's perspective. We all bring our mindsets to conversations, and having some awareness of these helps achieve a more rounded, holistic appreciation of an issue. The third leg of the tripod, Speaking Authentically, means that what we say what is true for us also connects with our observations (the first tripod leg) and reflects the assumption that others involved are capable of reasonableness (the second tripod leg). This third tripod leg helps to overcome a common default behavior of "dancing around": speaking in euphemisms, avoiding or sugar-coating the difficult topics, and holding back on what we would like to say (Dunoon, 2014).

The OBREAU Tripod appears to be a useful tool for engaging in eco-leadership and a natural fit for structuring student-led conversations within the Honors Residential College's Community and Discussion Seminars. Benefits include:

- introducing a level of structure to help sort through the messiness of virtually any thorny issue,

- bringing a degree of clarity to what otherwise can seem an intractable problem,
- promoting creativity by enabling new ways to frame an issue,
- reducing the risks and threat of speaking up, and
- strengthening the capacity of users to build shared understandings with others (Dunoon, 2015).

With the OBREAU Tripod as a foundation for face-to-face discussion, a final consideration is the opportunity to build upon this through writing.

Shared Leadership in Reflective Discussion Forum

While face-to-face discussions can cause some students to fall into a passive follower role, we know that shared engagement in the application of course material enhances students' learning (Comer & Lenaghan, 2013). Therefore, it is helpful to consider the theory and practice of shared leadership as a guide. Fletcher and Kaufer (2003) note the importance of relational interactions in shared leadership, and they emphasize the need to distribute tasks and responsibilities in order for collective learning to occur. The key to success, then, is to provide forums with sufficient structure and opportunity for shared leadership in the reflective and generative dialogue.

According to Berger (1999), electronic communication allows students to participate more and be more revealing than typically occurs in a classroom setting. Research also suggests that students' online discussion can be better than face-to-face discussions for fostering ideas, interaction, and in-depth consideration of others' viewpoints (Rainsbury & Malcolm, 2003). Educational researchers speculate that the benefit from asynchronous discussions comes from the added time students have to reflect on what they want to convey (Berry, 2005). However, discussion forums without clear expectations can lead to low-quality, high-quantity posts that are both unproductive and overwhelming (Rollag, 2010). Comer and Lenaghan (2013) encourage a strategy that ensures students: (a) apply course concepts to their own experience in ways that provoke meaningful discussion, (b) analyze classmates' posts to provide useful advice or solutions, and (c) evaluate classmates posts by critiquing them. To accomplish this strategy, Comer and Lenaghan (2013) propose involving a balance of original examples (OEs) and value-added comments (VACs).

The Honors Residential College's Community and Discussion Seminars incorporated this guidance for electronic communication, requiring students to contribute to an online discussion forum between the weekly face-to-face meetings. The assigned/selected presenter was instructed to begin the discussion with an "original post" that was multifaceted and unbiased with sufficient depth. Then, all other participants were asked to contribute "value-added comments" that were characterized as insightful, pertinent, and respectful, with sufficient depth. The comments, then, would build upon one another, expanding far beyond the original post. In this way, the students' engagement in followership was not a passive role but an active adoption of eco-leadership, blurring the lines between leader and follower.

DISCUSSION QUESTIONS

1. A review of the leadership literature reveals "the majority of leadership theories and studies have tended to emphasize the personal background, personality traits, perceptions, and actions of leaders" (Shamir, 2007, p. x). In what way(s) is the case of the Honors Residential College's Community and Discussion Seminar different? In what ways is it the same?
2. Shamir (2007) argues for "a balanced perspective on leadership, one that is neither entirely leader-centered nor entirely follower-centered, but views both leaders and followers as co-producers of the leadership relationship and its consequences" (p. xi–xii). Does the case of the Honors Residential College's Community and Discussion Seminar reflect a balanced approach? What evidence supports your conclusion?
3. Some scholars argue for a "shared leadership approach [that] is neither leader-centered nor follower-centered because it rejects the distinction between leaders and followers" (Shamir, 2007, p. xvii). Does the case of the Honors Residential College's Community and Discussion Seminar reflect a shared leadership approach? What evidence supports your conclusion?
4. In what ways does the eco-leaders discourse identified by Western (2007) enhance our understanding of the successful emergence of the Honors Residential College's Community and Discussion Seminar?

(*continued*)

5. Some scholars have investigated the notion of "leaderless work groups" but conclude "humans still need direction, control, rules, hierarchy, predictability, routine, and so on" (Jackson & Parry, 2011, p. 108). In what way might Dunoon's (2014) OBREAU Tripod provide the necessary structure? What about the online discussion forum?
6. As Jackson and Parry (2011) conclude their review of critical and distributed perspectives on leadership, they argue "groups cannot do without a formal leader, but team leadership reduces the pressure on the formal leader to produce all of the leadership" (p. 110). How does this perspective relate to the Honors Residential College's Community and Discussion Seminar?

References

Allen, K. E., Stelzner, S. P., & Wielkiewicz, R. M. (1999). The ecology of leadership: Adapting to the challenges of a changing world. *Journal of Leadership & Organizational Studies*, *5*(2), 62–82. doi:10.1177/107179199900500207

Berger, N. S. (1999). Pioneering experiences in distance learning: Lessons learned. *Journal of Management Education*, *23*(6), 684–690. doi:10.1177/10525629990 2300606

Berry, G. R. (2005). Online and face-to-face student discussion: A comparison of outcomes. *Journal of the Academy of Business Education*, 6(Fall), 27–35. Retrieved from http://www.abeweb.org/

Comer, D. R., & Lenaghan, J. A. (2013). Enhancing discussions in the asynchronous online classroom: The lack of face-to-face interaction does not lessen the lesson. *Journal of Management Education*, *37*(2), 261–294. doi:10.1177/105256291 2442384

DeLauder, R. (2010). *University launches new residential colleges to foster student-faculty engagement [Press release]*. Retrieved from http://www.vtnews.vt.edu/articles/ 2010/09/090110-dsa-rescollege.html

Dunoon, D. (2014). Mindful OD practice and the OBREAU Tripod: Beyond positive/ problem polarities. *OD Practitioner*, *46*(1), 18–25. Retrieved from http://www.odnet work.org

Dunoon, D. (2015). *The OBREAU Tripod: Enabling challenging conversations*. Retrieved from http://www.dondunoon.com/the-obreau-tripod.html

Fletcher, J. K., & Kaufer, K. (2003). Shared leadership: Paradox and possibility. In C. L. Pearce & J. A. Conger (Eds.), *Shared leadership: Reframing the hows and whys of leadership* (pp. 21–47). Thousand Oaks, CA: Sage.

Grohs, J., Keith, C., Morikawa, A., Penven, J., & Stephens, R. (2013). Living learning communities: Models of authentic community. Paper presented at the Conference for Higher Education Pedagogy, Blacksburg, VA, February 6.

Jackson, B., & Parry, K. (2011). *A very short, fairly interesting and reasonably cheap book about studying leadership* (2nd ed.). Thousand Oaks, CA: Sage.

Johnson, J. (2011). Virginia Tech dorm becomes a learning experience. *Washington Post*, September 21. Retrieved from http://www.washingtonpost.com

Rainsbury, E., & Malcolm, P. (2003). Extending the classroom boundaries – an evaluation of an asynchronous discussion board. *Accounting Education, 12*(1), 49–61. doi:10.1080/0963928032000049366

Rollag, K. (2010). Teaching business cases online through discussion boards: Strategies and best practices. *Journal of Management Education, 34*(4), 499–526. doi:10.1177/1052562910368940

Ryan, M. B. (2001). *A collegiate way of living: Residential colleges and a Yale education.* New Haven, CT: Jonathan Edwards College, Yale University.

Shamir, B. (2007). From passive recipients to active co-producers: Followers' roles in the leadership process. In B. Shamir, R. Pillai, M. C., Bligh, & M. Uhl-Bien (Eds.), *Follower-centered perspectives on leadership: A tribute to the memory of James R. Meindl* (pp. vii–xxxix). Greenwich, CT: Information Age.

Western, S. (2007). *Leadership: A critical text.* Thousand Oaks, CA: Sage.

Western, S. (2010). Eco-leadership: Toward the development of a new paradigm. In B. W. Redekop (Ed.), *Leadership for environmental sustainability* (pp. 36–54). New York, NY: Routledge.

Wielkiewicz, R. M., & Stelzner, S. P. (2005). An ecological perspective on leadership theory, research, and practice. *Review of General Psychology, 9*(4), 326–341. doi:10.1037/1089-2680.9.4.326

CHAPTER

17 Followership in Service Organizations: An English Secondary School Case of Distributed Leadership

Andrew Francis and Thomas Bisschoff

Jubilee Secondary School is an all ability secondary school based in a leafy suburb in the east of England. It is a larger than average comprehensive school with approximately 1,100 learners. In 2014, it received a positive government-driven inspection report. The head teacher (principal) has worked effectively for the last three years with senior leaders, staff, governors, parents, and learners to improve the school. The school has an experienced senior leadership team and has grouped subject leaders into broader faculties to encourage discussion and joint planning.

The case of Jubilee Secondary School is part of a bigger research project. The school is anonymized and the reporting is done in such a manner that confidentiality will be maintained.

John Smith the school leader started his teaching career as a mathematics teacher in a school in Greater London and quickly moved up in the ranks to become the assistant head teacher. During quite a troubled period in the history of the school, he took on the role of deputy head. John indicated that he had a superb head teacher as a mentor at that school. As a result, John learned a lot of skills, underwent substantial professional development, and landed up as the head of Jubilee Secondary School. At the writing of this case, John has been in his post for three years.

In a conversation with John, he said:

> I think they see me as a leader, I hope they do because what I try to model is good leadership as opposed to just managing situations. The nature of a school is that you do need lots of schedules and duties and timetables and management skills. I obviously do have, you know, a fairly good brain for that ....

He describes his staff as committed and dedicated with a clear sense of their role and place in the school and they know how important the role that they play is to the school's success.

He indicates that the staff component includes newly qualified teachers (NQTs) and others with a substantial amount of experience. The latter, according to him, is an inspiration to the others because they lead a number of teams. He emphasized that all the team members have the opportunity to lead (in ideas and implementation of decisions) as well as to follow. It is not only the team leader who leads.

He acknowledges that the staff who did not buy into the vision of the school eventually moved on to other schools. When asked whether he thinks the staff is 100% behind his vision, he said:

> Probably not 100% of the staff because some of the staff leave, you know, so maybe they reach the realisation that perhaps this isn't the organisation that they wanted to be in.

In the appointment of new staff, John indicated that he was looking for people with subject knowledge, passion, creativity, critical thinking, and commitment. He was not considering gender, age, or even personality as such:

> No, I think it just comes down to who it is, you know, who has been lucky enough to be exposed to very high standards themselves because essentially I just want really good quality people.

He acknowledges that in the career paths of some individual staff members moving on to another school might be the right thing to do and he would not stand in their way.

He emphasized that he did not view his staff as subordinates. When asked what he meant by this, he said, "The staff has a voice, are engaged, and know how to lead themselves."

The school improvement plan was developed around the vision of the school or the so called 6Ps, namely professionalism, profile, personal development, personalized experience, performance, and physical and human resources.

Through each priority, we aim to achieve:

- *"Professionalism" and facilitate high quality teaching and learning to maximize learner achievement. As we create our learning culture, we will ensure that students become effective, enthusiastic, independent learners committed to life-long learning, who achieve, enjoy, and excel in life.*
- *High "Profile" and be a leader in education for our local community, in local district and nationally. We expect our learners to play a positive and active part in these communities.*
- *The "Personal Development" of all our learners, through a focus on our three core values of respect, responsibility, and relationships, so that they can achieve their aspirations while making positive contributions to both the school and the wider community. For learners to fulfill their potential, they should be stretched, challenged, and supported in all of their experiences at the school.*
- *Outstanding "Performance" for all learners and ensure that they achieve their aspirational targets in every aspect of school life while enjoying the challenges that learning brings through careful monitoring and tracking of their progress.*
- *A "Personalised Experience" for our learners through a structured, differentiated curriculum with a wide variety of extra-curricular activities, which enables all students to realize their potential. There will be opportunities for social, personal, health, and cultural development within and across the curriculum.*
- *Best value for our "Physical and Human Resources" and provide an inspirational learning environment by introducing modern well equipped interactive classrooms; inspiring staff and learners to share the responsibility of maintaining their environment.*

For each of these visionary statements, strategic targets were formulated to enable the realization of the vision. These were further broken down into tasks to achieve the target, staff responsibilities, time scales, resources needed, performance indicators, and who would monitor the process.

John indicated that he is a strong believer in empowering the staff by giving them "the opportunity and responsibility" to be critical, but he reserves the final decision for himself. In his own words:

> My job is to ultimately say, right, I've listened to what you're saying, this is what we've got to do, so challenge as long as it's helpful and it's constructive, and as long as it's

> not undermining, I've got no problem with that. Then it's a case of I've listened to you, I love what you're saying, we're going to move with it, or I've listened to you, and unfortunately we're not going to do that at this time.

He insists that his staff consists of willing followers and not subordinates. He supports this on the one hand with a view that staff must voice their views and that "managing from the middle" is encouraged.

> You can't micro-manage, what you really want to do is to get people in the zone most of the time, driving their area of the school forward. And, you know, I see very much myself being a conductor orchestrating what is going on.

On the other hand, he states that he wanted to make it clear to staff that he is in charge and indeed doing what he is saying:

> Walking the floor and walking the talk.
>
> I think it's much better to be outside, you know, rather than being tucked away and suddenly problems and issues arising as a result of it. So presence outside supporting the staff on duty! At lesson changeover, I would generally always try to be outside to make sure people are getting where they should be.

Scholarly Commentary

Uhl-Bien Riggio, Lowe, and Carsten (2014) point out that confusion and misconceptions lie within the notion that leadership is a process that is co-created in social and relational interactions between people (Fairhurst & Uhl-Bien, 2012). It follows that if leadership is about actively influencing other people to action, followership involves allowing oneself (as follower) to be influenced by the leader. Shamir (2007) suggests that followership should not be confused with shared or distributed leadership. It is about followers accepting the disproportionate non-coercive influence of leaders on them. This argument is crucial in the debate on the relationship between distributed leadership and followership.

The next crucial argument is that leader-centric research is on its own not sufficient to provide a complete picture of leadership and should be supported by follower-centric research to obtain that ever elusive holistic view of leadership. A lot of the leader-centric research paints a negative picture of followers. We find in early works the likes of Taylor who references followers as subordinates and "mentally sluggish" (Uhl-Bien et al., 2014).

The follower-centric research drew attention to the role of the follower in constructing leaders and leadership. Uhl-Bien et al. (2014) provide a complete taxonomy of the different strands within leader and follower-centric research. Their paper maps the journey from the early leader-centric stance, through to the role-based and constructionist approaches to the study of followership which dominate its study today.

It is clear that followers were never completely invisible in leadership research, but placing the focus on followership is a fairly recent phenomenon (Carsten, Uhl-Bien, West, Patera, & McGregor, 2010; Collinson, 2006; Sy, 2010). In the emerging field of followership research, the role of the follower is one of privilege in the leadership process. Followership is now a topic equally worthy of study to leadership and followership contributes to our fuller understanding of leadership (Uhl-Bien et al., 2014).

This brings us to the followership styles already documented in the literature. For the purposes of this case school commentary, we need to know how they are enacted in an educational setting.

Followership Styles in an Educational Setting

In this study, the authors claim that while studies have been conducted on followership in higher education, particularly at the university level (Smith, 2009), few studies have been undertaken at the school level. In light of this need, Ye (2008) suggests that studies at different educational levels should be carried out. The findings of his study in an educational setting are interesting and worthy of further investigation; however, the focus in this scholarly commentary will be on the theoretical implications to assist with better understanding the case context.

Al-Anshory and Mohd. Ali (2014) examined the followership of primary and high school teachers using the Followership Questionnaire (TFQ) developed by Kelley (1992) and found that the majority of teachers were identified as exemplary followers. They also report that leadership of the schools became aware of the need to manage the followership style of teachers to achieve the organizational goals. The researchers declare:

> In this research, the teachers are delegated with the responsibilities to assess the school performance using

> the followership style theory. Regardless of the approach, teachers should know and understand the essential importance of followership roles in schools. Ultimately, the aim is to build relationships and tasks with other members of the school so that they can achieve greatness. This study sought to extend the body of knowledge around followership, especially, operationalizing courageous followership theory. (Al-Anshory & Mohd. Ali, 2014, p. 78)

Followership Styles and the Link with Distributed Leadership in the Case Study School

Two aspects unique to the case school are the element of distributed leadership and leading from the middle. Both concepts are in vogue in English schools. The conceptual problem, however, is that both are in a way viewed as related to followership and often used to gloss over the leadership–followership conundrum.

Gronn (2000) outlined the concept of distributed leadership (DL) as a potential solution to the tendency of leadership thinking to be all about leaders and not leadership. According to Gronn, the focus must be shifted away from the attributes and behaviors of individual leaders to a more leadership perspective emphasizing that it is about interactions between multiple actors. From this perspective, it is argued:

> Distributed leadership is not something "done" by an individual "to" others, or a set of individual actions through which people contribute to a group or organization … it is a group activity that works through and within relationships, rather than individual action. (Bennett, Wise, Woods, & Harvey, 2003, p. 3)

Even though distributed leadership is highly regarded in the schooling system in England it is not without its shortcomings as Storey indicated in 2004 and Hartley in 2007.

In the case of leading from the middle (Blandford, 2006) a similar problem arises. Is it all about leadership or indeed of a special kind of leader–follower relationship considering the hierarchical nature of a school with a head teacher (principal) and heads of departments?

DISCUSSION QUESTIONS

1. Is every leader not just a follower of somebody higher up in the hierarchy?
2. When is a leader indeed a leader but not just a quasi-leader?
3. Is there in a socially constructed space a continuum between leader and follower, with two hypothetical extremes (not to be found in reality) that implies that at any given time the same person can move from left to right on this continuum?
4. Is distributed leadership just a nice way to say to teachers you are not followers but a type of leader in your own right?

References

Al-Anshory, A. S., & Mohd. Ali, H. (2014). The gap between primary and secondary school teacher followership styles at Adni Islamic school, Malaysia. *Journal of Educational Studies*, *2*(2), 59–83.

Bennett, N., Wise, C., Woods, P. A., & Harvey, J. A. (2003). *Distributed leadership*. Nottingham: National College of School Leadership.

Blandford, S. (2006). *Middle leadership in schools: Harmonizing leadership and learning*. London: Pearson.

Carsten, M., Uhl-Bien, M., West, B. J., Patera, J. L., & McGregor, R. (2010). Exploring social constructs of followership: A qualitative study. *The Leadership Quarterly*, *21*, 543–562. doi:10.1016/j.leaqua.2010.03.015

Collinson, D. (2006). Rethinking followership: A post-structuralist analysis of follower identities. *The Leadership Quarterly*, *17*, 179–189. doi:10.1016/j.leaqua.2005.12.005

Fairhurst, G. T., & Uhl-Bien, M. (2012). Organizational discourse analysis (ODA): Examining leadership as a relational process. *The Leadership Quarterly*, *23*, 1043–1062. doi:10.1016/j.leaqua.2012.10.005

Gronn, P. (2000). Distributed properties: A new architecture for leadership. *Educational Management and Administration*, *28*(3), 317–338. doi:10.1177/0263211X000283006

Hartley, D. (2007). The emergence of distributed leadership in education: Why now? *British Journal of Educational Studies*, *55*, 202–214. doi:10.1111/j.1467-8527.2007.00371.x

Kelley, R. E. (1992). *The power of followership*. New York, NY: Doubleday.

Shamir, B. (2007). Leadership research or post-leadership research: Advancing leadership theory versus throwing out the baby with the bath water. In M. Uhl-Bien & S. Ospina (Eds.), *Advancing relational leadership research: A dialogue among perspectives* (pp. 477–500). Charlotte, NC: Information Age.

Smith, J. S. (2009). *Followership behaviors among Florida community college faculty.* Unpublished doctoral thesis. University of Florida, Gainesville, FL.

Storey, A. (2004). The problem of distributed leadership in schools. *School Leadership and Management, 29*, 353–371. doi:10.1080/1363243042000266918

Sy, T. (2010). What do you think of followers? Examining the content, structure, and consequences of implicit followership theories. *Organizational Behavior and Human Decisions Processes, 113*(2), 73–84. doi:10.1016/j.obhdp.2010.06.001

Uhl-Bien, M., Riggio, R. E., Lowe, K. B., & Carsten, M. K. (2014). Followership theory: A review and research agenda. *The Leadership Quarterly, 25*, 83–104. doi:10.1016/j.leaqua.2013.11.007

Ye, Y. (2008). *Factors relating to teachers' followership in international universities in Thailand.* Unpublished MA dissertation, Graduate School of Education, Assumption University of Thailand.

Section III
Ethics, Government, and Military

CHAPTER

18 The Interplay of Follower and Leader Ethics: A Case Study of the Film "The Wave"

Kae Reynolds

A group of typical high school seniors are entering "project week" at their post-Berlin-Wall high school in Germany. Amidst normal teenage cliques, couples, rivalries, and parties there is an absence of goals, a lack of direction, and widespread indifference among the youth. Their somewhat atypical teacher for project week is Rainer Wenger, the water polo coach, a former house squatter and fan of punk rock who prefers tattered jeans and Ramones t-shirts to business suits or chinos. The class is on a first name basis with Rainer, although such casual forms of address are highly unusual in German classrooms. In contrast to their other teachers who look down on Rainer as a second class intellectual, the students sense a bit of rebelliousness in Rainer and feel they can relate to him on their own level.

Despite the young adults' rapport with Rainer, their project week on autocracy promises to be particularly dull. On top of a general apathy for schoolwork, they have had the historical atrocities of the Hitler dictatorship stuffed down their throats for 13 years and are genuinely sick of the same guilt trip every year. By now, they get the message, the Nazis "sucked," and see no point in regurgitating it all over again. Educated modern young people like themselves are much too enlightened to fall for fascist propaganda. Just because a few skinheads have popped up in the former East

German states does not mean a National-Socialist movement akin to pre-WWII Germany is ever going to happen again. Unimpressed by the start of their school week, the students go on a break.

They return to find their desks no longer arranged in groups but set up in rows. When Rainer announces they will try an innovative approach to their autocracy project week the group is somewhat skeptical, but intrigued by the prospect of diversion. They play along at first, not taking anything too seriously. The class discussion begins with defining autocracy: the absolute power of an individual or group over the masses. They jokingly elect Rainer as their "central figure." Some new ground rules are set. For the entire week, the group must address Rainer as Herr Wenger; no one speaks unless called on. The classmates slowly adjust to Wenger's uncharacteristic strictness as they are instructed to sit up straight in their chairs, focus on breathing, stand up, and speak clearly when responding to questions. Students are reminded calmly and politely about the new rules, as well as the associated intellectual and health benefits to proper breathing and posture. Although there is some resistance among the group, anyone who does not want to participate is free to change project groups. The week starts under the motto "strength through discipline." Students are gaining confidence and energy as they brainstorm social circumstances that favor the emergence of dictatorship: high unemployment, social injustice, inflation, political disillusionment, and extreme nationalism.

On Day 2, the project develops under the principle: "strength through community." Themes such as solidarity, unity, and interdependence come to the forefront. In addition, there is a new objective: to beat the project group "anarchy" led by Wenger's ultra-conservative colleague Herr Wieland. Students earning higher grades are paired with students earning lower grades to improve performance as project autocracy relishes the thought of outperforming the competitive lone wolves of project anarchy. In a participative dialogue, the group agrees on a simple uniform. Although there is a noticeable division in the group and some leave Wenger's project, there is also an emerging feeling of collective identity and self-confidence. A few students from Wieland's anarchy project even request to switch to Wenger's group.

On Day 3, the maxim is "strength through action." The class votes democratically to name the group "The Wave." Together, the class begins strengthening their collective identity with a logo and a slogan. Even outside the classroom "The Wave" is starting to surge. Students begin to stand up for Tim, an outsider who has often been bullied. Dennis, the school play director, had been unable to assert himself but finds new confidence to advance his vision. Even Kevin, the rebel who left the group, is recruiting younger kids to "The Wave" at the skate park. Tim channels his newfound motivation in producing Wave stickers, graffiti stencils, and a web site. That night a pack of Wave members spread the symbols throughout town and Tim far exceeds the group's expectations in a dangerous attempt to spray a Wave tag at the apex of a town landmark.

Day 4 sees Wave create their own salute. The school is buzzing with enthusiasm. However, Wave member Karo's misgivings mount when she catches her 10-year old brother harassing his classmates for not being a Wave member, and she decides to stop Wenger. Wenger dismisses Karo's concerns, but when the principal, Dr. Kohlhage, calls Wenger to her office, Wenger fears a reprimand. To his surprise Kohlhage expresses her approval of the project, reinforcing Wenger's conviction. Wenger is on cloud nine and pumped up for the upcoming water polo match during which his project group will be supporting the team as a united fan section for the first time.

On Day 5, the students are keyed up for the match. However, their mood swiftly tips when Wenger rebukes them angrily for the Wave's vandalism that he learned about in the newspaper. In silence, Wenger's students write their final essays to complete project week. Nevertheless, the atmosphere at the match is electric and Wave fans are going wild with every goal. The game is close and tensions high. When violence suddenly breaks out, first between two players then among fans, Coach Wenger is enraged. Already concerned about the dubious dynamic of his classroom experiment, Wenger's pregnant wife Anke tries to open his eyes to the impact the project has had on his ego. Wenger, however, is blinded by the positive results he has observed in students' attitudes, motivation, and performance. The rush of success and finally being respected has gone to his head. He rationalizes Anke's criticism as jealousy. Repulsed by her husband's lack of reflection, Anke walks out on the heels of a cruel emotional exchange. When Karo becomes embroiled in a heated argument with her boyfriend Marco over her dissent Marco violently strikes her. Shocked and confused by his own loss of control, Marco flees to Rainer and pleads with him to stop "The Wave." Wenger finally realizes he must take action, and the story culminates with Wenger instructing all members to assemble the following day for an important address about the future of the movement. The ensuing events at the assembly leave the students, Wenger, and the entire community in shock.

Scholarly Commentary

The ubiquitous Hitler-debate in leadership ethics is portrayed with fresh eyes in Becker and Gansel's (2008) German language film *The Wave*. Set in a typical post-Berlin Wall German high school, this cinematic depiction of Jones' (1972, 2008) experiment in 1960s California makes palpable the subtle yet strong undercurrent of destructive followership. The story presents a charismatic leadership situation in which the leader's ethical motivation is corrupted by the enthusiasm and conviction of the followers. This modern-day dramatization exposes the tendency to underestimate the powerful influence followers have in leadership processes, and presents a poignant argument for the need to address followership ethics to students and practitioners of leadership across contexts. The following commentary will examine follower influence on leaders in the context of ethics. Instead of assuming that followers have a passive role in ethical leadership, it is argued that followers have equal responsibility in determining the ethical or unethical nature of follower-leader dynamics as well as holding themselves and their leaders accountable. Discussion also demonstrates the need for followers to practice critical reflexivity particularly in charismatic leadership relationships.

Leadership is a responsibility that is shared by group members and a process of influence that is multidirectional (Johnson, 2014). As such, unethical leadership is made possible in part because of followers' misguided motivations, need for belonging, susceptibility to manipulation, and other toxic relational dynamics (Johnson, 2014). Uhl-Bien and Carsten (2007) added that emergent conceptualizations of leadership view the process as multidirectional and independent of positional roles. Furthermore, followers have a choice to respond either actively or passively to unethical influences of those in authority (Uhl-Bien & Carsten, 2007). In *The Wave*, Wenger takes on his role in the experiment with noble intentions. He has a pedagogical objective: to demonstrate the dynamics of social movements in the context of autocracy. Neither the leader nor the followers begin the project with unethical motives. As the story develops, students' roles begin to shift until their motives and actions cross the line between ethical and unethical. As the followers' motivations become more misguided, Wenger is also drawn into a space of ethical limbo. Considering that people will follow unethical leaders out of common human needs and fears, the same should be true for leaders: leaders can be negatively influenced by the behavior of followers. The followers' needs to belong or to simply be acknowledged fueled the leader's needs for achievement, recognition, and admiration.

As long as leader-centric approaches dominate leadership theory questions raised about unethical leaders will continue to revolve around the leader. This approach, however, ignores the impact of followers in deferring responsibility, attributing heroism, and granting others the approval to dominate. Uhl-Bien and Carsten (2007) supported this view in their assertion that followers are active participants rather than passive recipients in the leadership process. They underscored the importance of the role followers have in co-creating ethical organizations. Uhl-Bien and Carsten (2007) argued further that hierarchical schemata of direction, decision-making, and responsibility are culturally inculcated, legitimizing the condemnation, punishment, and ostracism of dissidents. As Johnson (2014) pointed out, followers equally face ethical challenges and must make decisions about their behavior, reputations, and survival. However, powerlessness can breed cynicism which, in turn, breeds indifference and the lack of courage to challenge, question, or deliver bad news to authority (Johnson, 2014). Uhl-Bien, Riggio, Lowe, and Carsten (2014) noted that, in essence, leadership emerges from followers' willingness to defer to the disproportionate influence structures and systems of dominance. By extension, unethical leadership is created through followers' willingness to defer responsibility for unethical behavior to leaders. Infused with assumptions of subordination, followers' sense of obligation and obedience may cause them to sacrifice their own integrity.

Based on voluntary abdication of responsibility and acceptance of subordination, the follower-leader process entails mutual role taking (Kempster & Parry, 2013). Intentional role taking and identity assertion in social leadership exchange will also cause followers to assign charismatic attributes to leaders (Kempster & Parry, 2013), thus reifying leaders' superiority and justifying their dominance. Furthermore, Nietzsche (as cited in Rosenbaum, 2014) stated that charismatic rhetorists like Hitler persuade people through performative conviction; the performance of the leader role through conviction is then magnified and reflected back to the leader in the follower role. In terms of moral reasoning, the degrees of charisma and destructiveness displayed by an unethical leader simply amplify the blameworthiness of followers (Flanigan, 2013). As such, follower actions can be examined for varying degrees of blameworthiness according to the level of follower deliberation:

- has the follower bypassed moral deliberation (unreflective, dissociative behavior),
- made a deliberative error, or,
- despite deliberation, failed morally on volition (Flanigan, 2013).

Krasikova, Green, and LeBreton's (2013) discussion emphasized volition as a defining aspect of destructive leader behavior. In terms of follower behaviors, this was analogous to the students of "The Wave" who first engaged destructive acts of their own will. For example, students identified destructive goals (bullying, using weapons); and used destructive actions to mobilize each other to attain goals set by the leader or inferred by followers (vandalizing public property, recruiting younger pupils). The students, however, were not held accountable. Such lack of accountability can be attributed to the abdication of responsibility, role-taking dynamic, and identity assertion characteristic of leader-centric perspectives.

Other psychological dynamics can also come into play when followers abdicate responsibility and accountability. Krasikova et al. (2013) further observed that goal blockage, real or imagined, is a central element of destructive leadership. Goal blockage can trigger unethical behavior, that is, negative experiences associated with an individual's inability to achieve their goals (Krasikova et al., 2013). The same principle can be applied to followers. Considering the social status and personalities of the most vulnerable students, goal blockage was a contributing factor in their susceptibility to the seduction of "The Wave." Egalitarianism, solidarity, and collective spirit came as a welcome change to the social strata of cliques of charismatic jocks, queen bees, and rebels. Particularly the outsiders and those who felt disadvantaged or invisible slowly gained status and acceptance in the group through "The Wave." The hierarchies, in-groups, and grading systems that blocked their goals were washed away as "The Wave" evolved, and so were the blocks to Wenger's goals.

Numerous dangers can be associated with followers' deferring responsibility to charismatic leaders. As Flanigan (2013) pointed out, psychological research and experiments have provided evidence that charisma is neither correlated with expertise nor moral authority. These findings suggest that the emotional influence of charisma bypasses both cognitive and moral systems and taps directly into instinctual systems. As such, followers not only allow their sense of autonomy and moral identities to be manipulated in the charismatic leadership process, they also abdicate their obligation of ethical deliberation, effectively replacing their own independent critical thinking and personal responsibility with the perception of the leader's omnipotence, and in doing so seek to legitimate their abnegation of conscientiousness (Flanigan, 2013). An additional danger for both followers and leaders is the conviction of being immune or invulnerable to unethical dynamics. Wenger and his students were misled by a similar sense of superiority over the primitive behavior they associated with fascism. Therefore, critical thinking and reflexivity are crucial skills particularly in the context of ethics and follower-leader processes. Indeed, Cunliffe (2009) placed the capacity for critical reflection at the core of effective followership stating, "Ethical and moral action are embedded in a relational understanding, and enacted through self- and critical-reflexivity" (p. 94). In *The Wave*, only a few of the students in Wenger's autocracy project demonstrate courage and reflexivity; lack of critical reflection added to the momentum of the others' unethical actions as well as the devolution of Tim, Marco, and Wenger.

The courage and strength to make unappealing but morally correct decisions requires self-leadership (Steinbauer, Renn, Taylor, & Njoroge, 2014) and a sense of personal responsibility (Carsten & Uhl-Bien, 2013) in addition, or as opposed, to external leadership and displaced responsibility. Acknowledging and developing the role of followers proactively can create opportunities for effective partnership with leaders through which followers accept accountability (Steinbauer et al., 2014). Kelley (1992) advocated empowering people to be active and engaged followers capable of practicing courageous conscience. Followers must also cultivate independence through critical reflection as well as increasing their personal power and value, be it their marketability, competence, visibility, reputation, indispensability, expertise, credibility, self-esteem, or alliances (Carsten & Uhl-Bien, 2012). Whether they were conformists, colluders, or activists (Johnson, 2014), "The Wave" swept away those characters who were missing something in their lives. They may have been seeking acknowledgment, admiration, the feeling of being special or simply worthy, but most of all, they needed direction and wanted to belong. In the end, the confidence, status, and sense of community Wenger offered his students through the movement was reflected back to him in admiration, obedience, motivation, and respect. Wenger's inadequacies and lack of willingness to self-reflect allowed him to lose control and be pulled under the tow of several manifestations of unethical leadership described by Johnson (2014), rigidity, insularity, and intemperance. The students had transformed Wenger into the role he was playing to the extent that it no longer felt like a role.

Followers have power. They have the power to surrender their own power to others but may forget their own accountability in that exchange. As depicted in *The Wave* and as noted by Uhl-Bien and Carsten (2007), the ramifications of ethical scandals are far too great to limit responsibility solely to leaders. The slow, subtle corruption of Wenger's motives in *The Wave* offers testimony for the urgency of followers *and* leaders to be aware of the ethical and unethical influence followers have on leaders. By examining the follower-leader influence process in the context of ethics, a rationale for viewing followers' roles as active and potent in follower-leader dynamics can be developed. This case illustrated how misattribution of responsibility, follower susceptibility to unethical behavior, as well as misguided follower motivations can lead to the ethical failure of leadership. Commentary asserted that followers must develop and practice critical reflexivity to better uphold their ethical responsibility in follower-leader relationship. Being set in a reunified German nation that was borne of a historically unique peaceful revolution, Becker and Gansel's (2008) cinematic re-contextualization of the Hitler dilemma offers viewers a truly compelling statement on the power of followers. How organizations are to determine the blameworthiness and accountability of followers in unethical group behaviors, however, is left to the cineaste's imagination.

DISCUSSION QUESTIONS

1. Consider the motivations of the characters: Tim, Marco, Lisa, Karo, Mona, Kevin, Sinan, and (Rainer) Wenger. What drives each to participate in or reject "The Wave"? At what point does the behavior of the followers (the project students) become unethical? At what point do the actions of the leader (the teacher) become unethical?
2. Describe the means by which the followers use power and influence among each other, outsiders, and the leader. What is the impact of the students who disagree with Wenger's approach of leaving the group? How might the story have developed differently if Karo and Mona had stayed in the group and continued to express their concerns?
3. In which forms of unethical behavior did Wenger choose to engage? How are the principal and other teachers complicit? Blameworthy? Imagine the school was a business and everyone involved were adults. Would this consideration change the attribution of responsibility?
4. Consider an organization or interest group to which you have belonged. How was your group identity symbolized? How did typical shared gestures, greetings, catch phrases, clothing, logos, or other forms of communication represent your group values? How was your group's identity characterized? If there was an ethical/unethical component to the group identity, how would you describe it? What is the difference between your group's identity forms and their impact and those observed in *The Wave*?
5. Think of a situation in which you felt powerless. What was your emotional response to that sense of powerlessness? Consider possible options you might have had to reclaim power. Have you experienced a situation in which you sensed an unethical situation unfolding? How did you respond? Why?

References

Becker, C. (Producer), & Gansel, D. (Director). (2008). *Die Welle (The Wave)*. [Motion picture]. Germany: Rat Pack Filmproduktion.

Carsten, M., & Uhl-Bien, M. (2012). Follower beliefs in the co-production of leadership: Examining upward communication and the moderating role of context. *Journal of Psychology*, *22*(4), 210–220. doi:10.1027/2151-2604/a000115

Carsten, M., & Uhl-Bien, M. (2013). Ethical followership: An examination of followership beliefs and crimes of obedience. *Journal of Leadership & Organizational Studies*, *20*(1), 45–57. doi:10.1177/1548051812465890

Cunliffe, A. L. (2009). The philosopher leader: On relationalism, ethics and reflexivity – A critical perspective to teaching leadership. *Management Learning*, *40*(1), 87–101.

Flanigan, J. (2013). Charisma and moral reasoning. *Religions*, *4*, 216–229. doi:10.3390/rel4020216

Johnson, C. E. (2014). *Meeting the ethical challenges of leadership: Casting light or shadow* (5th ed.). Thousand Oaks, CA: Sage.

Jones, R. (1972, 2008). *The third wave, 1967: An account*. Retrieved from https://libcom.org/history/the-third-wave-1967-account-ron-jones

Kelley, R. (1992). *The power of followership*. New York, NY: Doubleday.

Kempster, S., & Parry, K. (2013). Charismatic leadership through the eyes of followers. *Strategic HR Review*, *13*(1), 20–23. doi:10.1108/SHR-07-2013-0076

Krasikova, D. V., Green, S. G., & LeBreton, J. M. (2013). Destructive leadership: A theoretical review, integration, and future research agenda. *Journal of Management*, *39*(5), 1308–1338. doi:10.1177/0149206312471388

Rosenbaum, R. (2014). *Explaining Hitler: The search for the origins of his evil*. Boston, MA: Da Capo Press.

Steinbauer, R., Renn, R. W., Taylor, R. R., & Njoroge, P. K. (2014). Ethical leadership and followers' moral judgment: The role of followers' perceived accountability and self-leadership. *Journal of Business Ethics*, *120*, 381–392. doi:10.1007/s10551-013-1662-x

Uhl-Bien, M., & Carsten, M. K. (2007). Being ethical when the boss is not. *Organizational Dynamics*, *36*(2), 187–201. doi:10.1016/jorgdyn.2007.03.006

Uhl-Bien, M., Riggio, R. E., Lowe, K. B., & Carsten, M. K. (2014). Followership theory: A review and research agenda. *Leadership Quarterly*, *25*, 83–104. doi:10.1016/j.leaqua.2013.11.007.

Additional Resources

Del Valle, R. (Producer), Neel, P., & Jeffery, D. H. (Directors). (2011). *Lesson plan: The story of the Third Wave* [Motion picture]. United States: State of Crisis Productions.

Grasshoff, A. (Director). (1981, October 4). *The wave* [Television short]. TAT Communications Company. New York, NY: American Broadcast Company (ABC).

Metaxas, E. (2011). *Dietrich Bonhoeffer: Pastor, martyr, prophet, spy*. Nashville, TN: Thomas Nelson.

Schöne, J. (2009). The peaceful revolution: Berlin 1989/90 – The path to German unity *(E. F. S. Zbikowski, Trans.)*. Berlin: Alles Über Berlin Gmbh.

Strasser, T. (2013). *The wave*. New York, NY: Ember.

CHAPTER

19 Leaders, Followers, and Failures at the VHA

Heather Getha-Taylor

In 2014, the Veterans Health Administration (VHA), a division of the U.S. Department of Veterans Affairs, was scrutinized for a variety of alleged performance problems, including excessive patient wait times, inadequate staffing levels, data manipulation, and even wrongful deaths. The federal response to the scandal included passage of the Veterans Access, Choice, and Accountability Act of 2014 and a change in leadership at the Department of Veterans Affairs. Other implications included changes in funding and performance metrics, removal or punishment of staff members, and a push for public updates. Behind the headlines, however, is a more nuanced story that requires attention to the relationship between leaders and followers.

The VHA is the nation's largest integrated health care system, serving more than 8.3 million veterans each year via a system of medical centers and clinics that employ over 50,000 health care practitioners (http://www.va.gov/health/aboutVHA.asp). The mission of the VHA is: "To honor America's veterans by providing exceptional health care that improves their health and well-being." This important mission exists within a complex and dynamic environment that has been characterized by doctor shortages and difficulty with hiring (Somashekhar, 2014) along with low salaries and poor working conditions in some medical centers (Kupersmith, 2014). At the same time, demand for VHA services has increased following wars in Iraq and Afghanistan. Together, these opposing forces created organizational problems that may have festered for years (Reed, 2014).

Problems emerged in early 2012 when emergency room (ER) physician, Dr. Katherine Mitchell, warned the incoming director of the Phoenix VA Health Care System that the ER was dangerously overwhelmed and understaffed. Mitchell's subsequent transfer out of the ER – and her later associated complaint against the VA – revealed the first evidence of organizational dysfunction and cover-ups. Later in 2012, the problems became more pronounced when the Government Accountability Office (GAO) told the VHA that improvements were needed for the reporting of outpatient medical appointment wait times (The Arizona Republic, 2015).

Medical appointment wait times are key performance indicators for the VHA. The organization's timelines guideline is that appointments should be set within 14 days of the patient's requested appointment date (Somashekhar, 2014). Further, first time enrollees into the system are expected to have an initial appointment within a similar timeframe. These and other performance metrics are published annually and used for organizational assessment, improvements, as well as employee incentives (Reed, 2014). Given the value of these expected outcomes, the VHA implemented the successful *Wildly Important Goals* program designed to reduce the wait between scheduling the appointment and the appointment date.

It was later revealed that the program's success was deceptive: veterans may have waited 6–20 weeks to set an appointment. In 2013, whistleblower and internal medicine physician, Dr. Sam Foote, filed a complaint with the VA Office of Inspector General alleging that data manipulation had tragic effects: veterans were dying while waiting for care (The Arizona Republic, 2015). Specifically, VHA appointment schedulers were instructed to falsify data and hide the actual amount of time to be seen by a doctor. Supervisors directed this manipulation in order to meet organizational performance goals, which determined individual bonuses (Devine, Turk, & Bronstein, 2014).

As the story developed, attention increasingly focused on Phoenix, the site of the first rumblings of trouble. In an April 2014 hearing, Rep. Jeff Miller, R-Fla., chairman of the House Committee on Veterans Affairs, indicated that the Phoenix VA Health Care System kept two sets of records to conceal actual wait times with patients in the Phoenix system waiting an average of 115 days for an appointment. The VA's Office of Inspector General confirmed mismanagement and data manipulation in a review report. As the scandal began to unravel, calls for a change in leadership grew and a new director, Steve Young, was named for the Phoenix VA Health Care System in May 2014. Shortly thereafter, VA Director Eric Shinseki resigned and was replaced by Michael McDonald.

As time passed, it was increasingly clear that VHA's problems were systemic and not confined to Phoenix (Somashekhar, 2014).

A 2014 VA report found that medical centers across the United States misrepresented or sidetracked patient scheduling for more than 57,000 veterans. In addition, the Office of Special Counsel found that the VA ignored whistleblowers' complaints and did nothing to address identified problems. Notably, the organization has the highest number of whistleblower complaints within the federal government: it has been described as having a "retaliatory culture" where complaints are ignored, whistleblowers face punishment, and their punishers are not held accountable (Wax-Thibodeaux, 2015).

As a result of these findings, major reform was proposed to enhance accountability and transparency. The resulting 2014 Veterans' Access, Choice, and Accountability Act, which was described as an "overhaul" (Kupersmith, 2014), makes it easier for veterans to get health care from private providers, sets limits on employee bonuses, provides additional funding for hiring, and also provides avenues to fire senior executives more easily. In an August 2014 statement on the scandal, President Obama said, "If you engage in an unethical practice, if you cover up a serious problem, you should be fired. Period. It shouldn't be that difficult" (Katz, 2014).

Following passage of this legislation, the VA settled with over two dozen employees who alleged retaliation as a result of voicing concerns. Further, the VA moved to fire four senior executives, including a purchasing agent, two directors of VA hospitals in Georgia and Pennsylvania, and a regional hospital director in Alabama. However, at least one of the individuals simultaneously announced his retirement, spurring harsh remarks from Rep. Jeff Miller, R-Fla., chair of the House Veterans Affairs Committee: "Bragging about the proposed removal of someone who has already announced his retirement can only be described as disingenuous." He continued: "The only way the department can regain the trust of veterans and taxpayers is if VA employees who preside over malfeasance and mismanagement are held accountable. Quite simply, any VA administrator who purposely manipulated appointment data, covered up problems, retaliated against whistleblowers or who was involved in malfeasance that harmed veterans must be fired, rather than allowed to slip out the back door with a pension" (Associated Press, 2014).

While leadership changes and organizational reform were identified as solutions for what ails the VHA, at the time of this writing, it seems that little has changed in the aftermath of these efforts. A 2015 Associated Press report indicates that in the months following the scandal, nearly 894,000 medical appointments failed to meet the VA's timeliness goals. Given these and other enduring struggles at the VHA, what additional organizational and/or individual considerations should be examined to understand this challenge?

Scholarly Commentary

The reactions to the scandal have focused primarily on reforms at the organizational level. However, these issues should also be examined at the interpersonal level. Although it appears that the VHA's timeliness metrics were not aligned with organizational realities, leaders understood that they would be held accountable for performance or lack thereof. It is perhaps not surprising, then, that some pushed for success (or at least illusions of success) and followers adapted accordingly.

While much attention has focused on leaders' actions in the VHA case, a more nuanced story is one that focuses on followers and why they might engage in practices they know are inappropriate. It has been reported, for instance, that systems in place at the VHA may have put employees in the difficult position of choosing between helping patients or preserving their own jobs (Reed, 2014). This survivalist mentality is one explanation among many. This commentary considers other potential explanations, including those related to understanding the pressures for obedience and conformity, ethical decision-making, and the exercise of power. Each lens is presented below to consider the complex relationship that exists between leaders and followers as well as the impacts of this relationship on behaviors and outcomes.

To begin, it is important to consider the natural human tendency to follow authoritative directives. While it could be expected that VHA employees may have followed directives of leaders they respected (or feared), Milgram's (1963) electro-shock experiments demonstrated how easily individuals could be moved to potentially harmful actions, even in the absence of a close relationship with a leader. In the classic experiment, study subjects who were referred to as teachers were instructed to deliver electric shocks of increasing degree to other participants who were referred to as learners when they made mistakes in repeating a string of words.

While some teachers defied orders to shock the learner, it was reported that 65% of participants followed orders all the way to what they perceived to be severely dangerous levels. The experiment revealed that just being in a position of authority is sufficient to influence others. When applied to the VHA case, Milgram's experiments underscore the importance of shared responsibility rather than blindly following orders. The experiments also highlight the importance of organizational cultures that promote open, candid communication between leaders and followers; this includes a climate that encourages questioning. For leaders, it is also a reminder of the importance of being responsible stewards of power and authority.

While these experiments revealed that the pressure to follow orders and obey authority figures is critical, one cannot ignore the pressure for conformity within groups and organizations which may also surface under these conditions. Asch's (1951) classic work illustrated the power of groups on individual decision-making and revealed that, even when it is wrong, individuals are easily swayed toward the majority opinion. In Asch's experiment, study subjects were asked to respond to a series of questions in a panel setting. The experiment's findings focused on the tendency of study subjects to give incorrect answers when others also gave incorrect answers.

This tendency can be explained by a desire to fit in with the group or even the tendency to question one's own perception. When applied to the VHA case, inappropriate actions among employees could easily become widespread due to any pressure that existed for conformity over individuality. Asch's work also demonstrated the power of alternative means of communication. Namely, in the experiments, the use of written answers diluted the conformity effect on individual answers. This finding reminds us of the importance of providing multiple, safe channels to communicate individual views that may go against the general consensus.

Being able to communicate one's own views starts with an understanding of the underlying values and ethical principles that undergird those views. Public managers are faced with a web of priorities, including democratic and administrative values, rule of law, and a commitment to balancing individual, organizational, and societal needs. At the same time, managers face resource constraints, declining confidence in government, and increased expectations for productivity and performance (Berman, Bowman, West, & Van Wart, 2012). Tough choices must often be made when facing incompatible goals; sometimes those choices have negative effects. As Reed (2014) notes, "In a system already operating beyond the limits of its resources, it appears the easiest way to improve scores is to cheat. The end result is a process that rewards outcomes regardless of the methods used or even the integrity of the data."

Given this assessment, specifically regarding the evidence of VHA data falsification, the lens of ethical development may help to explain leader and follower actions. According to Van Wart (1998), there are three levels of ethical consciousness: unconsciousness (Level 1), elementary (Level 2), and advanced (Level 3). Those operating at Level 1 lack the understanding or basic awareness of agency values, missions, or standard operating procedures which may result in knowingly or unconsciously taking inappropriate or illegal actions. While it is difficult to imagine that VHA leaders were operating without proper knowledge of values, missions, or standard operating procedures, their subordinates may not have fully understood the broader ethical implications of the directives they were following.

Those who are operating at Level 2 are described as having a basic grasp of missions, laws, and rules, and these individuals focus on conforming to avoid legal violations. A potential illustration in the VHA case is the *Wildly Important Goals* program in which metrics were shifted to meet timeliness expectations although it actually served to effectively disguise the true wait time for patients. When considering the perspective of followers in this scenario, meeting these program goals may have masked or displaced other legal or ethical priorities.

Individuals operating at Level 3 have a thorough understanding of their missions, values, and mandates and take actions that reflect that understanding. In the VHA case, we might characterize those individuals who faced a conflict between organizational performance expectations and individual ethics as operating at Level 3 consciousness. These employees may have informed others or acted as whistleblowers at great personal and professional risk.

In addition to these lenses, the power dynamics at play between leaders and followers at the VHA should also be considered. French and Raven's (1959) classic work on this topic identified a variety of power bases, including legitimate, reward, coercive, information, referent, and expert. Within traditional organizational settings, the use of legitimate, reward, and coercive power is very much intertwined with hierarchical position and chain of command. In the VHA case, there was a link between data manipulation and performance rewards for leaders and their subordinates; this may have contributed to a symbiotic, but dysfunctional, power relationship.

In addition to positional sources of power, personal power bases such as referent and expert power can influence actions in ways that operate independently of organizational structures. In the VHA case, leaders clearly had a powerful influence on followers' actions, which ultimately contributed to a variety of negative organizational outcomes, including whistleblower retaliation, a tarnished organizational reputation, and impacts on patient care. Given the significance of these effects, it is reasonable to ask whether employees who went along with data manipulation respected – or feared – their supervisors on a personal level which then influenced their actions.

In summary, the call for legislative change and organizational reform is not unexpected in the context of the VHA scandal. However, viewing change from the macro level alone misses the nuanced interactions between leaders and followers that are equally important and worthy of attention. A variety of relevant scholarly lenses – including authoritative influence and the pressure for conformity, ethical consciousness, and the exercise of power – can together provide valuable insights on organizational failures as a product of the complex relationship between leaders and followers.

DISCUSSION QUESTIONS

1. Analyzing organizational problems requires attention to both the *internal* (organizational, interpersonal) and *external* (political, societal) forces that promote and resist dysfunction.
   a. What were some of the dominant internal and external forces that promoted data manipulation in the VHA case?
   b. What would you recommend as steps for identifying and supporting internal and external forces to resist unethical behavior?
2. It is easy to think that we would resist the pressure to follow directives that might harm others. Conduct a web search for a video on the Milgram experiments (e.g., https://www.youtube.com/watch?v=y9l_puxcrlM). Watch it and discuss the following questions.
   a. Have you ever been in a situation in which you blindly followed the directions of an authoritative figure? What were the implications?
   b. How can leaders effectively exercise authority and also remain good stewards of their positional power?
3. VHA whistleblowers faced considerable personal and professional risk when raising organizational problems. At the same time, countless others did not come forward. Conduct a web search for a video on the Asch conformity experiments (e.g., https://www.youtube.com/watch?v=NyDDyT1lDhA). Watch the video and discuss the following questions.
   a. Have you ever been in a situation where you followed the consensus of the group even though you knew they were wrong? Why or why not? What were the implications of your action or inaction?
   b. How can organizations and individuals balance the need for effective cooperation and independent thinking?

(*continued*)

4. There are a variety of universal, democratic, and administrative values that influence individual decision-making in public organizations.
   a. What were the most relevant universal, democratic, and administrative values in the VHA case?
   b. Which values did leaders and subordinates prioritize – and violate – in this case?

References

Asch, S. E. (1951). Effects of group pressure upon the modification and distortion of judgments. In H. Guetzkow (Ed.), *Groups, leadership, and men* (pp. 222–236). Pittsburgh, PN: Carnegie Press.

Associated Press. (2014, October 6). *VA fires four senior executives in response to major scandal*. Retrieved from http://www.foxnews.com

Associated Press. (2015, April 9). *Report: Nothing has changed at VA a year after scandal*. Retrieved from http://www.newsmax.com

Berman, E. M., Bowman, J. S., West, J. P., & Van Wart, M. R. (2012). *Human resource management in public service: Paradoxes, processes, and problems*. Thousand Oaks, CA: Sage.

Devine, C., Turk, M., & Bronstein, S. (2014, July 30). *More VA employees said they were told to falsify data*. Retrieved from http://www.cnn.com

French, J. R., & Raven, B. H. (1959). The bases of social power. In D. Cartwright (Ed.), *Studies in Social Power* (pp. 150–167). Ann Arbor, MI: Institute for Social Research.

Katz, E. (2014, August 7). *Federal appeals board has major concerns with firing provisions in new VA law*. Retrieved from http://www.govexec.com

Kupersmith, J. (2014, October 2). *The VA post-scandal: New law and new leadership* [Web log post]. Retrieved from http://healthaffairs.org

Milgram, S. (1963). Behavioral study of obedience. *The Journal of Abnormal and Social Psychology*, *67*(4), 371–378.

Reed, H. (2014). Desperate measures: Probing the incentive for scandal at the VHA. *Journal of the American Academy of Physician Assistants*, 27, 12. doi:10.1097/01.JAA.0000455650.96800.23

Somashekhar, S. (2014). Some of the internal problems that led to VA health system scandal. *The Washington Post*, May 30. Retrieved from http://www.washingtonpost.com

The Arizona Republic. (2015). Timeline: The road to VA wait-time scandal. *The Arizona Republic*, March 12. Retrieved from http://www.azcentral.com

Van Wart, M. (1998). *Changing public sector values*. London: Garland.

Veterans Access, Choice, and Accountability Act of 2014, H.R. 3230, P.L.113-146. (2014).

Wax-Thibodeaux, E. (2015, April 14). *Isolated. Harassed. Their personal lives investigated. That's life as a VA whistleblower, employees tell Congress*. Retrieved from http://www.washingtonpost.com

CHAPTER

20 To Follow or not to Follow? A Tale of Corrupt Power and Unethical Leadership

Melissa K. Carsten

As an executive of Garamond Global Research, Sam Stokes had made it to the top. He had worked hard over the years, devoting his life to growing and developing a high impact and highly regarded global research organization. The company was extremely profitable, working mostly with small client organizations looking to conduct market research and analysis. What Sam didn't know, was that he had lost the respect, loyalty, and support of his followers long ago. As a leader, his actions were deemed unacceptable, and even unethical, however few followers had the guts to stand up and voice their frustration.

Over the many years that he worked at Garamond, Sam amassed a great deal of power and influence over major company decisions, use of company resources, as well as hiring and firing decisions. As he continued to gain power, Sam's subordinates began to notice that he became more secretive about how resources were being used, and much more selective about who received the resources. The company also began experiencing greater amounts of turnover from Sam's direct and indirect reports, with the average tenure of his employees being only 2.5 years. As more and more employees left the organization, rumors stemming from ex-employees began to surface. The stories told of Sam's misuse of company funds, favoritism with certain employees, and seemingly unethical actions with client projects. It wasn't long before current employees began noticing his indiscretions too.

For example, on one occasion, Sam was confronted by Terry, one of his subordinates who asked why his request for more project funding was denied. Terry explained that the funds were necessary to complete work that had been requested by his client organization. According to the budget documentation, the increased funds would support a second phase of the project that could potentially bring the company a great deal of revenue. Sam's response to the inquiry was coarse and defensive. He told Terry that fund allocation was none of his business, and that he had to complete the project with the original budget. When Terry asked for more explanation, and requested a meeting with Sam to rework budget money and perhaps come to a solution together, Sam replied, "It's not your money, so you don't have a say in how it is spent."

On another occasion, a subordinate named Morgan confronted Sam on his decision to promote an employee who had poor levels of productivity, shirked his responsibilities, and took credit for work that he did not complete. The promoted employee was selected over others who had stellar performance records and went above and beyond their minimal work responsibilities. Sam was offended that Morgan would question his decision, and became angry at the implication that he used favoritism to fill the position. When Morgan explained that she simply wanted to understand the reasoning behind the decision, and that she feared others would become disillusioned at the perceived inequity, Sam replied "If others have a problem with it, then they can find their way to the door. I am not here to make people happy, I am here to ensure the success of the company."

Perhaps the most abrasive of Sam's actions was one that directly affected a project team who worked long days and put in many hours to meet a short deadline for a high profile client. As the team completed their work, Sam insisted on seeing the final report so he could make modifications. Perceiving that they had little choice in the matter, the team handed over their report to Sam believing that he would improve upon their work. Instead, Sam deleted major sections of the report that were not seen as positive or favorable for the company, and replaced them with falsified data that demonstrated a larger market impact than the client was actually having. When the team requested a final version of the report, Sam simply told them that they no longer had to worry about it, and that he "took care of it." One member of the team confronted Sam on his secrecy, stating that he did not feel comfortable delivering the final report to the client without cross checking all the findings. The subordinate also stated that he worried the report might be painting an overly positive picture of their research. Sam told him: "We do what we have to do to survive. Do you think I worked my way to the top by doing things the 'right' way? Sometimes you just have to give the client what they want rather than what they need."

Although a few employees confronted Sam directly about his decisions and use of resources, most of them remained silent. They were uncomfortable questioning Sam's actions due to his level of power and status in the company. They felt that confronting a manager of Sam's stature would be inappropriate and perhaps lead to negative consequences. Although Sam had never fired anyone for asking questions, most of the subordinates feared that, at the very least, they would fall out of his favor if they ever crossed him.

With so few subordinates willing to challenge Sam's actions, his indiscretions only grew more bold and overt. He would fly his family first-class on extravagant vacations using company funds. He was also witnessed falsifying productivity reports, and providing raises to himself and his selected in-group. Others in the company had not received raises or recognition for their work, while Sam favored a small group of insiders without merit.

Meanwhile, the rest of the employees felt as though they lacked positive and supportive leadership. They began to turn to one another as a sounding board and reached out to each other to discuss their projects, challenges they were facing, and for advice on how to manage clients and staff. Over time, one of them named Clara Rogers began to emerge as the "best" go to person. When an employee had a problem, needed advice, or expertise, the suggestion that was made was "go see Clara."

Clara Rogers had only been an employee for five years, but had quickly earned the respect and admiration of her co-workers. They saw her as the "expert" and the one they could count on for both good advance and compassion. Although she did not know it at the time, Clara had earned a great deal of informal power among her coworkers and was clearly regarded as a leader amongst her peers, even though her position title afforded her no legitimate authority. Over time, the employees began to identify with Clara, support her vision for the company, and invest personal energy in her ideas or agenda.

While Sam continued to demonstrate duplicitous behavior, Clara emerged as an informal leader with numerous followers. One employee stated: "We follow Sam because we have to, but we follow Clara because we want to." The company was able to stay in business for many years despite Sam's indiscretions. Although they did suffer losses in terms of turnover, many employees remained with the organization because they identified so strongly with Clara, and because they saw hope and meaning in the vision and direction she offered for the company.

Scholarly Commentary

> Leadership is not about titles. It is not about seniority. It is not about status, and it is not about management. Leadership is about power, and the ability to know when and how to use it to influence the people around you to do and become more. (Terina R. Allen, President & CEO ARVis Institute)

In the thousands of books and articles written about leadership, it is often forgotten that followers are an essential part of the equation. As depicted in the case above, followership can take many different forms. Some followers may be silent, deferent, and blindly obedient, while others challenge their leaders, question their decisions, and stand up against tyranny. Still others can decide that they don't want to follow at all and reserve their energy and enthusiasm for leaders who are truly inspiring and trustworthy. These different forms of followership are at the discretion of the individual employee, influenced by the leader and context, and can have profound effects on the success of an organization.

In their review of followership theory, Uhl-Bien, Riggio, Lowe, and Carsten (2014) discuss the role-based approach to followership as an investigation of the follower beliefs, actions, and outcomes of followers (subordinates), working in relation to leaders (managers) in the organization. This approach builds on the notion of follower role orientations, or the beliefs followers hold regarding the tasks, responsibilities, and competencies that should be demonstrated while serving in a follower role (cf. Parker, 2000, 2007; Parker, Wall, & Jackson, 1997). According to studies conducted by Carsten and colleagues (Carsten & Uhl-Bien, 2012; Carsten, Uhl-Bien, West, Patera, & McGregor, 2010), followers may assume one of three different types of role orientations: a coproduction orientation, a passive orientation, or an antiauthoritarian orientation.

A coproduction orientation is the belief that the follower role involves actively engaging with leaders by relaying important information, identifying and solving problems, and even constructively challenging the leader when appropriate (Carsten et al., 2010). These individuals believe that leadership is enhanced by the engagement of followers, and that followers have something valuable to contribute to the leadership process. With regard to the case, this type of follower is exemplified by the individuals who confronted Sam's indiscretions and challenged his decisions. While there is undoubtedly an element of risk that accompanies this type of challenge and confrontation, these followers believe that it is their job to challenge leaders when they feel that the leader is headed down the wrong path, or making decisions that could potentially hurt the organization (Carsten & Uhl-Bien, 2012). They embrace the opportunity to get involved and see their engagement with the leader as a chance to help advance the objectives of the organization. These followers can have a positive impact on the organization because they think critically about the mission of the organization and evaluate the means through which the organization works to achieve it.

Conversely, a passive follower role orientation is characterized by the belief that leaders are more knowledgeable, powerful, and proficient than followers (Baker, 2007; Carsten et al., 2010), and that followers should remain silent and deferent as a result of their subordinate status (Carsten et al., 2010). These individuals believe that the leader's power should not be challenged and that the leader has ultimate discretion to make decisions, even hurtful ones, because they have earned it. In the case of Sam Stokes, the followers who remained silent, refrained from standing up to him, and followed all of his directives would be said to have a passive role orientation. According to Uhl-Bien and Carsten (2007), these followers may be complicit in unethical behavior initiated by the leader and contribute to wrongdoing in the workplace because the leader ordered them to engage in disruptive practices.

The third category is that of the antiauthoritarian follower. These individuals are considered "non-followers" because they resist the influence and authority of the leader, and believe that leaders will use their power to manipulate others. These individuals are not insubordinate; they will follow directives and fulfill their role responsibilities, but thwart any influence attempts made by the leader. Under these circumstances, we have to ask ourselves if the leader is really *leading*. Instead, it may be that leaders can only engage in management when working with individuals who believe in non-following.

Although not identified in the follower role orientation literature advanced by Carsten and colleagues, another important role orientation of followers may be the "leading-up" orientation. Upward leadership or "leading-up" occurs when a follower with no formal power or authority engages in leadership behavior with superiors and inspires others to adopt ideas or initiatives important to the organization. These individuals believe that they can make a difference in the organization and help advance the mission. However, with no formal power or authority, followers must be very careful when they engage in leading-up. In the case above, Clara became an influential leader among her peers because the formal leader was corrupt and not worth following. Although Clara had no formal power or authority, she saw an important opportunity to engage others with her vision and support others through their work processes. Her peers grew to trust her and followed voluntarily. There is no doubt that Clara played a role in retention of the company's talented employees. She gave the employees hope and instilled meaning in their work. She led from the bottom up believing that she could make a difference and feeling as though she was called to service.

The case above demonstrates the different role orientations maintained by followers, and how those role orientations may result in followership behavior. Just as leaders come in many different forms and demonstrate many different styles, followers also bring unique perspectives, beliefs, and behaviors to their interactions with leaders. As we continue to devote energy to understanding multiple follower role orientations, our hope is that it will ultimately lead to a better understanding of the leadership process. Leadership is created through the interactions of leaders and followers working together to advance the mission of an organization (Shamir, 2007). As we continue to study and learn about leadership, it is equally important that we pay close attention to the role of followers and better understand how they contribute to the leadership process.

DISCUSSION QUESTIONS

1. How can people lead without formal power and authority? What skills are required to be an effective "bottom-up" leader?
2. Which of the follower role orientations discussed in the commentary were most/least beneficial for the staff of Sam Stokes? Which follower role orientations do you believe would be most/least beneficial in your own organization? Why? Which follower role orientations do you believe are most/least beneficial to organizations in general? Why?
3. What types of leaders would be best working with followers who have a coproduction orientation? How about a passive or antiauthoritarian orientation? Which of these follower orientations do you believe would work best with Sam Stokes?
4. What other follower role orientations might exist? Can you think about another category of beliefs that people may hold regarding the follower role?
5. If you worked with a superior like Sam Stokes, how would you approach him regarding his unethical behavior? What would be the potential benefits and drawbacks involved? Why do you believe more people do not stand up to unethical leaders?

References

Baker, S. D. (2007). Followership. *Journal of Leadership & Organizational Studies, 14*(1), 50–60. doi:10.1177/0002831207304343

Carsten, M. K., & Uhl-Bien, M. (2012). Follower beliefs in the co-production of leadership: Examining upward communication and the moderating role of context. *Zeitschrift Fur Psychologie [Journal of Psychology], 220*(4), 210–220. doi:10.1027/2151-2604/a000115

Carsten, M. K., Uhl-Bien, M., West, B. J., Patera, J. L., & McGregor, R. (2010). Exploring social constructions of followership: A qualitative study. *The Leadership Quarterly, 21*(3), 543–562. doi:10.1016/j.leaqua.2010.03.015

Parker, S. (2000). From passive to proactive motivation: The importance of flexible role orientations and role breadth self-efficacy. *Applied Psychology: An International Review, 49*(3), 447–469. doi:10.1111/1464-0597.00025

Parker, S. K. (2007). That is my job: How employees' role orientation affects their job performance. *Human Relations, 60*(3), 403–434. doi:10.1177/0018726707076684

Parker, S. K., Wall, T. D., & Jackson, P. R. (1997). "That's not my job": Developing flexible employee work orientations. *Academy of Management Journal, 40*(4), 899–929. doi:10.2307/256952

Shamir, B. (2007). From passive recipients to active co-producers: Followers' roles in the leadership process. In B. Shamir, R. Pillai, M. C. Bligh, & M. Uhl-Bien (Eds.), *Follower-centered perspectives on leadership. A tribute to the memory of James R. Meindl* (pp. ix–xxxix). Greenwich, CT: Information Age.

Uhl-Bien, M., & Carsten, M. K. (2007). Being ethical when the boss is not. *Organizational Dynamics, 36*, 187–201. doi:10.1016/j.orgdyn.2007.03.006

Uhl-Bien, M., Riggio, R. E., Lowe, K. B., & Carsten, M. K. (2014). Followership theory: A review and research agenda. *The Leadership Quarterly, 25*, 83–104. doi:10.1016/j.leaqua.2013.11.007

CHAPTER

21 Followership, Hierarchies, and Communication: Achieving or Negotiating Buy-in within the Public Sector?

Rachael Morris and Sandra Corlett

Cranston City Council is a large public sector organization based in the United Kingdom, which provides a range of public services for the local area. It operates within a difficult and ever changing environment, with multiple internal and external stakeholder pressures and regulations with which to deal while delivering high-quality services to local residents. The council employs 10,000 individuals, the majority of whom are based at its central offices. However, many employees work off-site on a regular basis conducting visits to local sites and residents. The council is hierarchically structured with numerous levels of management and reporting lines spanning its many service areas and functional departments. Interaction between organizational levels is somewhat restricted by predetermined channels of communication, overreliance upon emails, and top-down briefings with those who are running the council. Increasingly important is the need for the council to gain employee support and engagement.

Cranston City Council has experienced severe financial pressure stemming from the centralized governmental environment in which it operates. Budget cuts have been made which directly impact the resources that are available to deliver local services. Multiple rounds of budget cuts have led to three major lay-offs over the last two years. Employees are now speculating about the possibility of further redundancies. Rather than find new ways to deliver services to the community, workers spend valuable time speculating about the possibility of further staff reductions while passively resisting change.

Recently, the council has been subjected to an increasing number of external regulatory reviews because of issues regarding its service delivery, issues that are regularly reported by the media. For example, an entire row of council flats had to be evacuated when a water main burst – much of the infrastructure in the town is over 100 years old – and crews were unable to restore water for over a week. This incident even made a brief appearance on national television news. For all these reasons, employee engagement and morale are at an all-time low.

One response to the recent situation has been the formation of a change management team tasked with implementing changes to the ways in which the council's service areas and functional departments are operating. The chief executive and her senior management team selected long-standing employees from different levels within the council who had significant experience and expertise which they could contribute. A few external specialists were also hired from an internationally recognized consulting firm to provide the team with expertise on how to plan, conduct, and evaluate a change management program. The team faces a number of additional challenges other than employee morale and engagement. First, because of the imminent budget shortfall, the team only has a short time to conceive and implement significant change across this highly diverse organization. Second, there is expected to be scrutiny of the changes by all stakeholders including council executive, employees, media, and residents. Finally, the team is broad and diverse – both in skills and experiences – and, as such, they have struggled to agree on a best course of action.

They have plotted out three broad strategies for determining what change management projects to introduce: (1) service reviews in targeted areas of high cost, value, and volume, including exploration of alternative service delivery methods, such as outsourcing delivery to other providers; (2) functional department reviews, including consideration of centralizing or merging the work done by Information Technology, Finance, and Human Resources employees; and (3) work process reviews, including the introduction of technology, to enable more efficient service and function delivery. The chief executive informed employees about the formation of the change team via a brief organization-wide email. She explained the importance of the team's work in responding to the council's current challenges and asked for employee participation.

The change team has held several meetings in the different service areas and functional departments of the organization. The meetings have been variously received with some workers adamantly opposing any change and others recognizing the need. Recent briefings were held to outline the third strand of the change management program and to stress the importance of introducing or extending the use of technology to improve current work processes. All employees were expected to attend one of the briefings and had been asked to sign up for a preferred date and location. However, attendance at the briefings has been poor and comments made by employees who were present reflected feelings of concern and low morale, as well as frustration and anger. One employee was overheard saying, "It feels like the goalposts are always changing. It's different every day and they haven't got a clue what they're doing." Although they attended the briefing, others seemed to be unengaged. For instance, one such employee commented, "Well if they can't be bothered to ask for our ideas on how practically we can make more use of technology, then to be honest I can't be bothered either." In a similar vein, another employee said, "How can they expect us to be engaged with the proposed changes if they don't allow us to have any real say in the change management decisions?" A small minority of the audience did engage in discussions with the team, asking challenging questions and proposing additional aspects to be considered, which were noted by those presenting the brief.

After one of the briefings, Martin, a middle manager in the Finance Department, decided to hold a meeting with his own team to hear their thoughts and to discuss any questions or concerns they may have. During this meeting, individuals made several suggestions that would be useful technology-based replacements for the department's working processes, and so he decided to email these to the change management team. However, shortly after sending his message, Martin received a response thanking him for his suggestions, but informing him that the team had already drawn up change plans with which they would be moving ahead. Upon updating his own team of the response, Lorna who had actively given ideas to Martin commented, "Oh well, you know how it is in this organization. You can have your say here, but try and get it any further up and you've got no chance."

Scholarly Commentary

This case study provides insight into the complexities of achieving and negotiating buy-in to change within large UK public sector organizations. Giving a particular focus on communication and organizational change, we offer two ways of interpreting the case.

The first perspective builds on Carsten, Uhl-Bien, West, Patera, and McGregor (2010) and similar studies that explore followership as a process of (unequal) partnering with leadership (Carsten & Bligh, 2008). The second perspective challenges the often assumed role of leader power and control (Collinson, 2008; Tourish, 2014) to give a more critical reading which acknowledges "the complex, interactional relationships between leaders and followers" (Collinson, 2008, p. 369).

A PSYCHOSOCIAL PERSPECTIVE ON CONSTRUCTIONS OF FOLLOWERSHIP

A psychosocial perspective focuses attention on followers' constructions of leadership (Meindl, 1995) and of followership (Carsten et al., 2010). Studies from this perspective consider the diverse meanings followers give to followership (and leadership) and explore how these meanings are shaped by an individual's cognitive and social schema, and by the contexts in which the individual is embedded (Carsten et al., 2010; Meindl, 1995). Both schema and context influence how followership is socially constructed and how the follower role is enacted (Carsten et al., 2010). Therefore, followers hold different schema of followership, ranging from followership as subordination, reinforced by social constructions of hierarchy in terms of status inequalities and power differentials between levels (Carsten et al., 2010), to more active, and indeed proactive, schemas which may lead followers to construct and enact their role with leaders as partners (Carsten et al., 2010; Chaleff, 1995) or collaborators (Rost, 2008).

When applied to the case study, rather than relegating followers to a passive role of conforming to organizational change, as traditional leadership approaches might suggest (see Van Wart, 2011), the psychosocial perspective proposes the need to examine *both* leader and follower behaviors and processes in order to understand this important partnership (Carsten & Bligh, 2008). Partnering might include discussing the need for change and cocreating, monitoring, and evaluating the change strategy and implementation plan which Carsten and Bligh (2008) recommend for achieving active followers' buy-in to an organization's vision. Hurwitz and Hurwitz (2009) also advocate followers as active partners in a relationship. Their generative partnership model (Hurwitz & Hurwitz, 2015) includes key leadership and followership communication behaviors of, respectively, *cascade communicating,* that is, keeping team members informed and stimulating the right followership initiative, and *dashboard communication,* that is, keeping your partner well informed and stimulating the right leadership action.

Public sector organizations have undergone significant structural changes in recent years (Pedersen & Hartley, 2008), including reducing top-heavy management levels. However, Cranston City Council's hierarchical structures seem to pose difficulties in achieving follower support, with communication-specific issues including poor attendance at briefings, as well as lack of interaction and engagement with the change management team. Collinson (2008) discusses how followers may oppose leader-initiated change programs because they construct leaders as being out of touch with organizational realities. In hierarchical terms, Martin can be construed as a proactive leader, but also as a proactive follower who attempts to actively influence [his] leaders through constructive challenge and upward communication in an attempt to advance positive change in [his] department (Carsten et al., 2010). As Carsten and her colleagues (2010) and Collinson (2008) discuss, such proactive followership behavior is consistent with Chaleff's (1995) notion of courageous followership, which involves enabling followers to voice constructive criticism, particularly if they believe the leader is not acting in the organization's best interests. From a follower perspective, we interpret Martin's behavior of engaging with the change management team by putting forward his team's suggestions as an act of courageous followership. However, the management team's response to his proactivity, and the organization's structural conditions, may cause Martin to reconstruct his understanding and resultant behaviors of followership (and leadership) to become more passive (Carsten et al., 2010).

This partnership perspective on followership and leadership, therefore, emphasizes the ways in which leaders communicate change and involve followers, enabling multidirectional communication throughout (Carsten & Bligh, 2008). By encouraging followers to voice disagreement and to pose alternative suggestions, followers can become innovative implementers of change (Michaelis, Stegmaier, & Sonntag, 2010) rather than resisters of it. The perspective might suggest that resistance is due to a lack of achieving follower buy-in (Carsten & Bligh, 2008) due to ineffective communication. However, rather than seeing communication with others as tools to be used within a change process, April (1999) argues that change is a social construct and that communication, conversation, and dialogue are the contexts in which change occurs. This perspective, which focuses attention on how leadership, followership, and change occur in a context of human social interactions, which constitute and are constituted by communication (April, 1999) offers a more nuanced perspective on the complex, interactional nature of follower and leader relationships, as suggested by researchers such as Collinson (2006, 2008) and Tourish (2014) whose work we now consider.

A COMMUNICATION-BASED PROCESS PERSPECTIVE ON FOLLOWERSHIP

Langley and Tsoukas (2010; as cited in Tourish, 2014) describe process perspectives through which followership and leadership are understood as being constituted by complex, ongoing, interaction processes among organizational actors. Studies from this perspective explore how meaning making is done together through interacting, communicating, and interpreting the actions and responses of individuals in a given context (McNamee & Hosking, 2012). Therefore, whereas existing studies conducted from the first perspective might focus exclusively on followers (e.g., Carsten et al., 2010; Meindl, 1995), process perspectives consider the practices of followers and leaders as inextricably linked, mutually reinforcing, and shifting within specific contexts (Collinson, 2008; Hurwitz & Hurwitz, 2015) and regard meanings as emergent, fluid, and potentially contested (Tourish, 2014). Such perspectives often focus attention on the dynamics of power, control, and communication of followership and leadership (Collinson, 2008; Tourish, 2014).

From his process- and communication-oriented perspectives, Tourish (2014) understands leadership (and followership) as a fluid process centered on the interactions and communications of organizational members. He suggests that research from the perspective discussed above tends to locate power and control with leaders rather than followers (Tourish, 2014). Our reading of the social constructions on followership literature supports Tourish's claim that asymmetrical power is taken for granted. For instance, Carsten et al. (2010) suggest that followers may be reluctant to pass negative information upward because of a perceived lack of power. In a similar vein, Carsten and Bligh (2008) state that promoting follower participation in the vision creation process requires that leaders relinquish some of the control that they have over processes and procedures. Hurwitz and Hurwitz (2015), however, believe that process and procedures are fundamental to leadership. Rather than taking away control, engaged followers add meaning and content. In other words, rather than acting on followers, leaders need to appreciate that they act collaboratively alongside them (Tourish, 2014).

As communicative processes (Cunliffe & Eriksen, 2011; Tourish, 2014), theories of leadership and followership acknowledge the productive potential of dissent (Tourish, 2014). Although advocating and seeking agreement on particular perspectives are important, formal leaders should value followers' critical ideas (Tourish, 2014). Collinson (2008) suggests followers' demands for greater information, accountability, and openness, which he refers to as strategies of resistance through persistence, may be relatively effective in achieving change. Collinson discusses how followers may psychologically withdraw if their attempts to voice suggestions are ignored by those in leader positions. Collinson refers to such a response and related behavioral changes such as restricting effort and communication as "resistance through distance" (p. 318). This highlights the need to look beyond verbal communication to wider practices including nonverbal gestures (Talley & Temple, 2015), silence (Tourish, 2014), and doing nothing (Collinson, 2008) through which followers can undermine change initiatives. Therefore, in cases of resistance through persistence or distance, followers are active, powerful players in the leadership process and not passive, compliant, obedient sheep at the mercy of their leaders (Bligh & Kohles, 2009).

DISCUSSION QUESTIONS

1. What are the similarities and differences in understanding the role of communication in change from the psychosocial and process perspectives on followership?
2. What role does Cranston City Council's public sector context play in the followers' constructions of their role and in their followership behaviors? Discuss the ways in which hierarchical structures and leadership styles may be influencing passive, active, or proactive social constructions of followership within Cranston City Council. Compare and contrast these influences in your own organization.
3. Given Cranston City Council's hierarchical structure, what are the communication challenges in achieving follower buy-in to the changes and how might their impact be minimized?
4. How might mutual partnership between leaders and followers be negotiated in Cranston City Council, and in your own organization?
5. What examples of resistance through persistence and resistance through distance can you see in the case study?
6. From psychosocial and process perspectives on followership, in what ways might Lorna's comment be interpreted differently? How might she adapt her behavior in the future?

References

April, K. A. (1999). Leading through communication, conversation and dialogue. *Leadership & Organization Development Journal, 20*(5), 231–242. doi:10.1108/01437739910287108

Bligh, M. C., & Kohles, C. J. (2009). Romance of leadership. In J. M. Levine & M. A. Hogg (Eds.), *Encyclopedia of group processes & intergroup relations* (pp. 718–720). Thousand Oaks, CA: Sage.

Carsten, M. K., & Bligh, M. C. (2008). Lead, follow, and get out of the way: Involving employees in the visioning process. In R. E. Riggio, I. Chaleff, & J. Lipman-Blumen (Eds.), *The art of followership: How great followers create great leaders and organizations* (pp. 277–290). San Francisco, CA: Jossey-Bass. doi:10.1016/j.leaqua.2010.03.015

Carsten, M. K., Uhl-Bien, M., West, B. J., Patera, J. L., & McGregor, R. (2010). Exploring social constructions of followership: A qualitative study. *The Leadership Quarterly*, *21*(3), 543–562.

Chaleff, I. (1995). *The courageous follower: Standing up to and for our leaders.* San Francisco, CA: Berrett-Koehler.

Collinson, D. (2006). Rethinking followership: A post-structuralist analysis of follower identities. *The Leadership Quarterly*, *17*(2), 179–189. doi:10.1016/j.leaqua.2005.12.005

Collinson, D. (2008). Conformist, resistant, and disguised selves: A post-structuralist approach to identity and workplace followership. In R. E. Riggio, I. Chaleff, & J. Lipman-Blumen (Eds.), *The art of followership: How great followers create great leaders and organizations* (pp. 309–324). San Francisco, CA: Jossey-Bass.

Cunliffe, A. L., & Eriksen, M. (2011). Relational leadership. *Human Relations*, *64*(11), 1425–1449. doi:10.1177/0018726711418388

Hurwitz, M., & Hurwitz, S. (2009). The romance of the follower part 2. *Industrial and Commercial Training*, *41*(4), 199–2016. doi:10.1108/00197850910962788

Hurwitz, M., & Hurwitz, S. (2015). *Leadership is half the story: A fresh look at followership, leadership, and collaboration.* Toronto: University of Toronto Press.

Langley, A., & Tsoukas, H. (2010). Introducing "perspectives on process organization studies". *Process, Sensemaking, and Organizing*, *1*(9), 1–27. doi:10.1093/acprof:oso/9780199594566.001.0001

McNamee, S., & Hosking, D. M. (2012). *Research and social change: A relational constructionist approach.* New York, NY: Routledge.

Meindl, J. (1995). The romance of leadership as a follower-centric theory: A social constructionist approach. *Leadership Quarterly*, *6*(3), 329–341. doi:10.2307/255897

Michaelis, B., Stegmaier, R., & Sonntag, K. (2010). Shedding light on followers' innovation implementation behavior. *Journal of Managerial Psychology*, *25*(4), 408–429.

Pedersen, D., & Hartley, J. (2008). The changing context of public leadership and management: Implications for roles and dynamics. *International Journal of Public Sector Management*, *21*(4), 327–339. doi:10.1108/09535508108802014

Rost, J. (2008). Followership: An outmoded concept. In R. E. Riggio, I. Chaleff, & J. Lipman-Blumen (Eds.), *The art of followership: How great followers create great leaders and organizations* (pp. 53–65). San Francisco, CA: Jossey-Bass.

Talley, L., & Temple, S. (2015). How leaders influence followers through the use of non-verbal communication. *Leadership and Organizational Development Journal*, *36*(1), 69–80. doi:10.1108/LODJ-07-2013-0107

Tourish, D. (2014). Leadership, more or less? A processual, communication perspective on the role of agency in leadership theory. *Leadership*, *10*(1), 79–98.

Van Wart, M. (2011). *Dynamics of leadership in public service: Theory and practice* (2nd ed.). Abingdon: Routledge.

CHAPTER

22 A Mistake in the Numbers

Marc Hurwitz

On the third business day of every month, DDS Systems Consulting held their executive review meeting (ERM). It was a high profile, high pressure meeting where branch office executives presented the month's activities to the Senior Vice President of Sales and Marketing. At the top of the ERM agenda were the sales result and sales outlook by branch office – the part of the meeting that sent even the most audacious and successful sales executives into distress.

Working at DDS Systems Consulting

Branch offices all had similar structures: heading up each of the eight offices was a branch vice president who was in charge of sales and service for a defined region of the country. Reporting directly to the branch vice president were the sales executives and an office manager. Each sales executive had a team of customer service consultants (CSCs) reporting to him or her. While the sales executive dealt with decision makers at client companies, her CSC staff dealt with counterparts at the operational or working level. The CSCs were responsible for ensuring that DDS products were being used properly, along with trouble-shooting any problems clients might be experiencing. CSCs also put together most of the internal reports at DDS such as sales figures, forecasting, and risk analyses. The company believed in promoting from within and a typical career path was to be hired into DDS as a junior CSC. Service consultants were then ranked during annual branch reviews and the best of them were eventually given the chance to become sales executives.

DDS had a highly competitive work environment; top salespeople could earn up to one-and-a-half times their salary in bonuses and, as a result, the company had given out above average compensation every year for 15 years, even during the great recession of 2008–2009. Shortly after the ERM each month, bonuses were awarded on a monthly basis based on a combination of individual and branch results. However, DDS also had an unofficial policy of firing the bottom 10% of staff each year – motivated by the rank-and-yank philosophy articulated by Jack Welch, CEO of General Electric from 1981 to 2001. Branch vice presidents were similarly at risk; the Senior VP of Sales and Marketing was known to have a short fuse and did not tolerate underperforming branches for long.

The Mistake

The format of the monthly ERM was a videoconference, where each branch office filled their boardroom with the Branch Vice President, all of the sales executives, and a few of their top-ranked CSCs.

Michelle, a service consultant, was attending her first executive review. She had joined DDS three years ago, recruited straight from university where her marks, leadership capability, and community service had placed her among the top tier of talented graduates. Since then she had not disappointed. Michelle was recognized as high potential; she worked hard and smart and deftly handled even the most demanding client.

Pumped up for this opportunity, Michelle stayed late every night the week before the ERM to prepare. In the final night before the ERM, while drilling down into the sales details, she discovered an error in her branch's figures; they had overestimated sales by $30 million because of double-counting one transaction. She sent a number of urgent messages to Joe Cooper, her sales team leader, and the branch's top sales executive, titled "Urgent, Please Read" but he had not responded by the morning of the executive meeting. This was highly atypical, so Michelle arrived early for the meeting in hopes of informing Joe of the issue before the meeting started. Unfortunately, the presentation with the error in it had already been submitted to head office by the deadline of noon on the previous day; there was nothing Michelle would be able to do about the erroneous submission.

By 9:00 a.m., Joe had not arrived but everyone else had. The Branch VP came in and sat down next to Michelle in the seat she had been saving for Joe. The meeting started, and Joe snuck in at 9:15 a.m. on the other side of the room, just in time to speak to everyone across the country about his team's record-breaking sales month. "Not quite record-breaking," thought Michelle anxiously, as she pondered what to do. A number of possibilities came to mind, each with its pros and cons.

Michelle's Options

Her first thought was that she should speak up and give the correct numbers before Joe started speaking. If she admitted to having made the mistake, it would enable Joe to save face. On the other hand, it was Joe's job and his management responsibility to review the report carefully. What would Michelle say if the SVP of Sales asked her *when* she spotted the error? If she answered honestly by saying it was the night before, then the next logical question might be, "Why didn't you make sure Joe knew?" There would be no good answer to this from Joe's or the SVP's perspective. Also, should she let both Joe's boss (the Branch VP) and his boss's boss (the SVP Sales) know without having warned Joe?

Having quickly dismissed her first impulse to speak up, Michelle next thought that perhaps the best strategy would be to remain quiet during the meeting, then inform Joe immediately afterward. This would allow Joe to position it with his boss, who could then figure out how to tell the SVP. Michelle had no idea what might happen if the SVP found out in the middle of the sales meeting.

At the same time, Michelle realized that sitting next to the Branch VP was helpful, as she could whisper her mistake to him when she got a chance. Surely the Branch VP would have the authority to speak up if he felt it was needed? Similarly, Michelle could go over to Joe and whisper in his ear, or at least signal him to look at his phone. Although a little disruptive to the people in the boardroom at her sales office, it might be better to let Joe decide what to do.

Finally, Michelle realized she could say nothing. After all, this incident could seriously jeopardize her career if it became generally known. She knew that the mistake was not material to the company as a whole, nor damaging to any of the clients, nor her fault. It might affect bonuses in the short term, but Joe should have responded to her e-mail earlier. It was always his accountability and he needs to take the lead in deciding what to do from here on.

Scholarly Commentary

The case touches on two aspects of followership: (1) how do followers make "good" decisions and (2) what are the ethical responsibilities of followers? Both of these questions are much studied and discussed in leadership. Every major textbook on the subject (e.g., Northouse, 2013; Yukl, 2013) has a chapter on ethical leadership, authentic leadership, or values-based leadership. Similarly, although decision-making is much broader than leadership, it is often framed in a leadership context. The rest of this commentary provides a brief summary of some relevant aspects of decision-making and ethics from a leadership perspective and then suggests followership ideas that could be used as a starting point for discussing Michelle's quandary. There is a significant lack of research on followership in decision-making or ethics.

DECISION-MAKING

Vroom and Jago (2007) describe leadership as a process of intentional influence that is effective, that is, leadership produces an *intended* change in the behavior of another person. In this context, it is clear that making a decision is an act of leadership. Vroom and Jago go on to describe a normative model of decision-making – the Vroom-Jago-Yetton process – that matches situational variables, such as the need for commitment from followers, with the way in which a decision should be made. Their original model proposed that binary evaluations of specific situational variables lead to one of five ways to make the decision including (a) being democratic and allowing the group to discuss the solutions and then vote on the best one, (b) being consultative and getting feedback from the group but not putting the solution to a vote, or (c) autocratically making the decision with minimal to no consultation. For example, if it is not important that followers are highly committed to the decision, and if the leader has enough information to make a high-quality decision, then the best approach is to act without asking, that is, autocratically.

The Vroom-Jago-Yetton model is about the act of making a decision and, as such only represents part of a full process. Yukl (2013, p. 269), for example, suggests that there are an additional 11 steps in running a decision group meeting including:

Step 1: *Informing people about necessary preparation for a meeting*
Step 2: *Sharing essential information with group members*
Step 3–10: *etc.*
Step 11: *Clarifying responsibilities for implementation*

Both Yukl (2013) and Vroom-Jago-Yetton reduce decisions to the act of making it. A more comprehensive perspective, such as the incremental decision process (IDP) model (Mintzberg, Raisinghani, & Theoret, 1976), adds in preparatory elements.

The IDP model consists of three phases, the first of which involves finding solutions that are incremental changes from the existing state of affairs (the antecedent or *identification* phase). In the second phase – *development* – the consequences of a few select solutions are identified. And then, in the final *selection* phase, one of the alternatives is selected.

In all three models, followers are only important for how they will react or if their expertise needs to be solicited, as they are not full partners in the process. And none of these models apply if a follower is making the decision.

Hurwitz and Hurwitz (2015), by contrast, suggest a normative decision process – *the decision lifecycle* – that includes both leadership and followership as complementary roles. Leadership, in the decision lifecycle, simply refers to the person who has the responsibility to manage the process, rather than being a formal role in the organization or on the team. The lifecycle involves four stages, each of which requires specific tasks of the leadership and followership roles: (1) bringing the right people to the table; (2) gathering data; (3) making choices; and (4) implementation. The inclusion of implementation as a stage in the decision process is unique to this model; it acknowledges that implementing a solution often incorporates a series of new decisions that can change the outcome from what was originally decided.

The decision lifecycle also imputes agency to followers. For example, the role of followers in the second stage – gathering data – is to bring all the relevant information to the table, while the leader's responsibility is to manage and be the caretaker of the process. In the final stage, implementation, followers have a responsibility to understand the decision, know the intent behind it, and create a solution to the best of their ability.

None of these models, however, speaks to the other central issue of the case: What is Michelle's ethical duty?

ETHICS

Ethics is the focus of increased scrutiny by leadership scholars and practitioners. This recent prominence has been attributed to *failures* of ethical behavior at companies such as Enron, and to scandal-racked organizations such as FIFA. It is more likely, however, that the spotlight is due to social media channels that have made failures far more prominent, reactions swifter, and the scale of the reaction global. Another factor may be the realization that ethics has a direct impact on managerial effectiveness and interpersonal relationships (Yukl, Mahsud, Hassan, & Prussia, 2013).

Ethical leadership consists of a number of components. While there is no precise definition, it usually includes honesty, fairness, compassion, and values. Ethics are integral to beliefs about effective leadership. In surveys conducted over a period of 15 years, Kouzes and Posner (2002) found that the most admired leadership trait was honesty. It dominated the second place trait by a wide margin in every survey as well over 80% of people believe honesty is integral to their conception of a good leader. Is this unique to leadership? Interestingly, a survey by Agho (2009) of approximately 300 senior executives in the healthcare industry found that independent of a worker's relative position, honesty was also the highest rated trait for followership.

Ethics have always held a prominent place in most "new" leadership theories such as transformational leadership (Burns, 1978), servant leadership (Greenleaf, 1977), and authentic leadership (George, 2003). Gardner, Cogliser, Davis, and Dickens (2011), for example, describe how the definition of authentic leadership shifted over time, but usually included ethical components such as values, beliefs, and the alignment between those and action. Authentic leadership is also associated with positive impacts on followers such as organizational commitment, greater trust (in the leader), increased engagement, work happiness, and psychological well-being. A flipside to authentic leadership – authentic followership – has been proposed, but only in the context of follower motivation and performance (Leroy, Anseel, Gardner, & Sels, 2015) and not as a separate construct.

Only Chaleff's model of courageous followership (2003) directly speaks to followership ethics. His *courage to take moral action* suggests how followers should respond to unethical decision by leaders (but not by followers), while other elements of Chaleff's followership model such as *the courage to challenge* and *the courage to serve* implicitly include ethics.

There have been no studies on the extent to which followership ethics affects leaders, a follower's chances for promotion, or other organizational outcomes. In other words, when it comes to followership, we cannot say for certain whether "honesty is the best policy" or even what *best* means. What, then, can followers use as a compass for their ethical choices? Should it be the same or different as for leaders? As one example, it could be argued that utilitarianism, that is, the greatest good for the greatest number, is a primary responsibility for a leader when dealing with their team. But does a follower have the same duty? Does it make a difference if the leader has a tendency to "shoot the messenger?" And if a leader makes an error, is it more ethical for her follower to expose it in public fashion, or should it be done in private? These are all issues specific to followership ethics.

DISCUSSION QUESTIONS

1. Michelle is conflicted about what to do. Part of the conflict is about where her loyalty lies and to whom she is most accountable? Is it to her line manager, her manager's manager, the most senior person in the room, or no-one at all since her only real obligation is to respond to questions, not interrupt a meeting where she is effectively a guest?
2. To what extent should situational elements such as materiality, urgency, culture, and morality affect Michelle's decision?
3. What criteria should Michelle consider in making her decision? How should she rank these criteria (if at all)?
4. To what extent does Michelle have the ethical responsibility to act? If not an ethical duty, are there other considerations such as loyalty, legal responsibilities and liabilities, or duties of an employee that she should consider?
5. What do you think are the most likely outcomes for each of Michelle's options? Think about it for short-term as well as long-term outcomes. To what extent should these consequences be part of Michelle's decision-making process?
6. What would you do in Michelle's case, and why?
7. Have you encountered a similar situation? If so, what did you do?

References

Agho, A. O. (2009). Perspectives of senior-level executives on effective followership and leadership. *Journal of Leadership & Organizational Studies*, *16*(2), 159–166. doi:10.1177/1548051809335360

Burns, J. M. (1978). *Leadership*. New York, NY: Harper & Row.

Chaleff, I. (2003). *The courageous follower: Standing up to & for our leaders*. San Francisco, CA: Berrett-Koehler.

Gardner, W. L., Cogliser, C. C., Davis, K. M., & Dickens, M. P. (2011). Authentic leadership: A review of the literature and research agenda. *The Leadership Quarterly*, *22*, 1120–1145. doi:10.1016/j.leaqua.2011.09.007

George, W. (2003). *Authentic leadership: Rediscovering the secrets to creating lasting value*. San Francisco, CA: Jossey-Bass.

Greenleaf, R. K. (1977). *Servant leadership: A journey into the nature of legitimate power and greatness*. Mahwah, NJ: Paulist Press.

Hurwitz, M., & Hurwitz, S. (2015). *Leadership is half the story: A fresh look at followership, leadership, and collaboration*. Toronto: Rotman-UTP.

Kouzes, J. M., & Posner, B. Z. (2002). *The leadership challenge* (3rd ed.). San Francisco, CA: Jossey-Bass.

Leroy, H., Anseel, F., Gardner, W. L., & Sels, L. (2015). Authentic leadership, authentic followership, basic need satisfaction, and work-level performance: A cross-level study. *Journal of Management*, *41*(6), 1677–1697. doi:10.1177/0149206312457822

Mintzberg, H., Raisinghani, D., & Theoret, A. (1976). The structure of unstructured decision processes. *Administrative Science Quarterly*, *21*(2), 246–275. doi:10.2307/2392045

Northouse, P. G. (2013). *Leadership: Theory and practice* (6th ed.). Thousand Oaks, CA: Sage.

Vroom, V. H., & Jago, A. G. (2007). The role of the situation in leadership. *American Psychologist*, *62*(1), 17–24. doi:10.1037/0003-066x.62.1.17

Yukl, G. (2013). *Leadership in organizations* (8th ed.). Boston, MA: Pearson.

Yukl, G., Mahsud, R., Hassan, S., & Prussia, G. E. (2013). An improved measure of ethical leadership. *Journal of Leadership & Organizational Studies*, *20*(1), 38–48. doi:10.1177/1548051811429352

CHAPTER

23 Responding to Perceptions of Electoral Fraud: Followership, Emotions, and Collective Action from Malaysia's 13th General Election

Eugene Y. J. Tee, Douglas S. E. Teoh and TamilSelvan Ramis

Malaysia's 13th General Elections (GE13) is remembered among citizens as an event rife with controversies and allegations of electoral fraud. Central to public opinion and among voters was the belief that the ruling coalition, Barisan Nasional (National Front), resorted to fraudulent practices to garner an electoral victory. Although the opposing coalition, Pakatan Rakyat (People's Alliance[1]), obtained the majority in terms of votes,

[1]The National Front adopts a conservative ideological orientation, while the People's Alliance party's views are more reflective of social liberalism and social democracy. The National Front is comprised of three major parties, each representing a major ethnic group in Malaysia – UMNO (United Malays National Organization) for the Malays, Malaysian Chinese Association (MCA) representing the Chinese, and the Malaysian Indian Congress (MIC), which represents the Indians. The majority of seats in the National Front, however, are held by Malays.

it failed to form the majority government. The National Front secured 47.38% of all votes (5,237,699 votes) – its worst performance in the general election since its formation in 1973, while the People's Alliance managed to secure 50.87% of votes (5,623,984 votes). Political analysts state that the outcome was inevitable, due to widespread gerrymandering of constituencies by the National Front, which resulted in votes from certain constituencies being worth comparatively more than others (Chin, 2013; Ostwald, 2013).

In addition to allegations of gerrymandering, there were also accusations of dishonest and corrupt practices marring the fairness of GE13. Members of the public accused the National Front of manipulating both voters and the electoral policies to ensure that the results would turn out in their favor. Members of the public also raised concerns regarding the capacity of the Election Commission to ensure free and fair elections, and throughout the entire event observed that the National Front were flouting or manipulating electoral polices in order to retain majority governance. Members of the general public took it upon themselves to counter the National Front's fraudulent practices by forming informal coalitions during the lead-up to, during, and after the elections. Following the election, one notable mass movement that took place was the "505 Blackout Rallies," held to protest and reject the election results.

The Lead-Up to GE13 and Formation of Informal Coalitions

A few days prior to GE13, reports surfaced that the National Front was planning to allow migrant workers to vote. These migrant workers consisted of individuals who were not Malaysian citizens but resided in the country for employment purposes, usually on a work visa. News of such allegations spread quickly over social media. These migrant workers were allegedly provided Malaysian identification cards that would legally enable them to cast their vote for the National Front, and their votes would be recognized as those of legitimate voters. There were also allegations that the National Front used phantom voters. One report was of a supposedly "empty" local aircraft, MH8611, seen carrying Nepalese nationals arriving at the Kuala Lumpur International Airport. These individuals were also seen being ushered into vans bearing logos of the Ministry of Rural and Regional Development (Ding et al., 2013). Such incidents were video-recorded and uploaded onto social media sharing sites; this contributed to the general public's suspicions that the National Front was taking measures to ensure an electoral outcome that favored their political interests.

The circulation of such reports via social media had an unprecedented effect; members of the public began forming informal coalitions and making preparations to counter the possibility of illegal voters influencing the upcoming general elections (Augustin, 2013). Primary opposition came from an informal coalition called "Asalkan Bukan UMNO" (Anything but United Malays National Organization [UMNO]). This informal coalition was acting in direct opposition to the UMNO, the largest and most influential founding party of the National Front which champions Malay supremacy (Ketuanan Melayu) and conservative Islamic values. Initially formed in 2011, the Anything but UMNO coalition took steps to ensure that polling and counting agents were assigned in every polling center and also used social media to encourage fellow citizens to curb the entry of migrant workers into polling centers. Representatives from this informal coalition were asked to stop and question anyone suspected of being a migrant worker entering the premises to vote. Anyone stopped was asked about his or her place of birth and schooling, ability to converse in the national language (Bahasa Malaysia), and tested on the ability to sing the Malaysian national anthem and/or recite the National Principles. Should they fail to provide sufficient "proof" of their citizenship, they were unofficially detained in the form of a citizen's arrest. Many such arrests were documented and shared through Malaysian social media (Augustin, 2013).

Online reports were also abuzz with at least two alleged forms of cheating by the National Front in various constituencies. The first form included reports of blackouts and power failures at some counting stations during the vote counting. There were allegations that additional ballot boxes were brought in during these blackouts amidst the panic and confusion, resulting in some dramatic reversals in the electoral count. The second were reports of vehicles attempting to enter polling centers to deliver additional ballot boxes. These vehicles were suspected of bringing in additional votes from other constituencies. In the Lembah Pantai constituency, for example, voters formed a human barricade, linking arms to prevent a vehicle suspected of carrying additional ballot boxes to the polling center (Vinod, 2013a, 2013b). In another constituency, members of the public filmed what appeared to be a helicopter dropping bags of completed ballot forms onto a field, awaiting pickup from vans. There were also accusations that the Electoral Commission authorities were allowing voting to be done in advance for certain constituencies, were bribing voters, and were deliberately falsifying vote counting forms. These allegations further created the perception that the Electoral Commission was not fully independent or impartial from the National Front.

Electoral Results and Post-GE13 Sentiment

Despite the efforts of these informal coalitions, the National Front won 133 seats out of 222 in the Dewan Rakyat (House of Representatives), successfully forming the government. Public reaction to this outcome was mostly negative, with dissatisfaction and disappointment at the result being voiced online. Many changed their social media profile pictures to a pure black display upon hearing the results. The People's Alliance subsequently organized a series of mass protests to reject the election results. An estimated 120,000 individuals showed up for the first protest, expressing their opposition of the election results. During this protest, opposition leader Anwar Ibrahim described the incident as the "worst electoral fraud in our history." He invited Malaysians to "join hands and express [their] rejection and disgust at the unprecedented electoral fraud committed by Prime Minister and National Front Leader Najib Razak and the Electoral Commission."

Voicing the frustration and injustice felt by the Malaysian public, Anwar Ibrahim further asserted, "A fight for clean and fair election remains the single most important fight that any Malaysian should relate to." Public sentiment reflected the sustained feelings of discontent several days after these rallies. Protestors dressed in black every Saturday after GE13, symbolizing a sense of mourning over the "death of democracy" and expressing contempt over the tactics employed by the National Front to maintain political dominance in the country. Some opposition leaders opted to legally dispute the election results. The Coalition for Free and Fair Elections, for instance, went on to organize the People's Tribunal to examine allegations of the National Front's electoral fraud. From this hearing, the tribunal gave the following verdict: "The inescapable conclusion must be that GE13 fell short in every one of those seven parameters for democratic election" (BERSIH 2.0., 2014).

Scholarly Commentary

The GE13 event provides several points for discussion about the psychological processes that underlie Malaysian citizens' responses to allegations of unfair and ineffectual governance. Utilizing a follower-centric model of leadership, this case sheds some light on (a) the role of intergroup emotions in consolidating social identities and (b) how followers' emotions translate to collective action against leaders.

The events of GE13 can be analyzed and understood from a follower-centric perspective of leadership. Followership comprises the important roles and behaviors that followers play in the leadership process (Collinson, 2006; Meindl, 1995). Indeed, the call for understanding the importance of followership to the leadership process has been reiterated by other research scholars (Bligh, Kohles, & Pillai, 2011). In the GE13 case, followers (Malaysian citizens) formed loose, informal collaborations and coalitions in response to leaders (National Front leaders and Electoral Commission authorities) perceived as ineffectual or corrupt. The GE13 case is an opportunity to examine how informal, collaborative groups of followers who are bound by shared emotion and identity can form and engage in collective action toward leaders. More broadly, the case also reflects one instance in which followers took active steps to engage in behaviors and actions intended to directly influence leadership outcomes.

To understand the psychological processes involved in the event, we base our analysis on Tee, Paulsen, and Ashkanasy's (2013) model of followership, comprising both the emotion and social identity processes which give rise to the events described in the case. Tee and colleagues (2013) propose that shared identity and emotion can motivate follower action toward their leaders. The authors suggest that follower actions against leaders can be prompted by at least one of three key perceptions – leader self-serving behavior, perceptions of procedural unfairness, and/or expressions of inappropriate emotions. These emotions, felt by the Malaysian public, form the basis for group-level emotion and may, in turn, translate to collective action toward leaders. The extent to which these individual and group-level emotions translate to collective emotion is influenced by the degree of individual and group identification with their social identities.

From the case, followers appear to have been motivated by the second reason, that is, perceptions of the unfair and manipulative practices of the National Front and the Electoral Commission. These perceptions prompted the formation of informal coalitions to instigate direct action and take countermeasures to ensure that the election process was fair. These perceptions were essentially of procedural unfairness concerning the processes by which a decision was reached, as opposed to perceived unfairness as a result of a decision-making outcome (De Cremer, van Dijke, & Mayer, 2010; Van Dijke & De Cremer, 2010). During the lead-up to GE13, sentiments of suspicion and mistrust were evident among the public, and it was these shared emotions that first motivated members of the public to take precautionary steps toward ensuring that the elections would be conducted as fairly as possible. Reports shared via social media fueled such suspicions, with allegations of possible fraud in the forthcoming elections fueling the formation of these informal coalitions before the election event itself. While allegations were felt by prospective voters, social media channels facilitated the creation of group-level emotions more rapidly. Whether the allegations were accurate, or merely exaggerated and unfounded claims made by individual eyewitness reports, mattered little to the Malaysian public. They were sufficient to trigger unpleasant, reactionary emotions that were essential in the formation of informal coalitions in the days leading up to the election.

The formation of these informal coalitions was also instigated by Malaysians' sense of identification with their country rather than its formal leaders. This is evident from actions taken to prevent migrant workers from casting their votes at polling stations. At this level, Malaysians' social identity was based more heavily on their nationality than by race, ethnicity, or other demographic factors. The negative sentiment sown by allegations of corrupt electoral practices contributed toward the formation of distinct social identities, one that distinguishes Malaysian nationals from non-Malaysian nationals. The emotions felt and expressed toward non-Malaysian nationals (most of whom were migrant workers) can also be understood via Intergroup Emotions Theory (IET) (Mackie, Devos, & Smith, 2000). According to IET, the salience of social identities promotes group-level appraisals and emotions toward out-groups. Group-level appraisals toward out-groups may then motivate action toward out-groups; feelings of anger motivate such actions. Such processes may, in part, explain why Malaysians, who felt like they were part of the in-group, took assertive, forceful action toward out-group members and made citizens' arrests of migrant workers entering the polling centers.

This shared sense of identity was also reflected in Malaysians' actions toward both the National Front and Electoral Commission. Perceiving the National Front and Electoral Commission, as well as any individuals who supported these parties, as members of the out-group also explains the collective action taken against them after the elections. The rallies held after the election and collective show of force were effective expressions of a shared identity, bound by the collective emotions felt toward these out-group individuals and parties. The organization of the People's Tribunal by the Coalition for Free and Fair Elections reflects how the shared identity of "the people" united them in a collective expression of dissatisfaction and intention to challenge the election results. The shared identity and emotions were also reflected in shared expressions – wearing black in protest of the election result and utilizing the same profile picture in protest of the election results.

While effective in garnering the popular vote for the People's Alliance, the informal coalitions did not appear to sustain itself beyond the GE13 event itself. Public responses were evident a few days after the election, but continuing actions against the unfair electoral policies and challenges to the election results were sustained by members of the opposing parties. While many Malaysians recall the emotions felt during the GE13 event, most retain their sentiments of unfairness without necessarily engaging in actions to directly challenge the National Front or Electoral Commission further. As such, it would appear that the informal coalitions formed by the public were context-specific, motivated by the shared sense of identity and emotions surrounding GE13, but were not sustained beyond the event.

The GE13 event highlights one instance in which followers took collective action to challenge leaders and influence leadership outcomes. From this case, it can be observed that a combination of both shared emotion and identity are key psychological processes that motivate actions both toward, and against, the country's current governance. Integral to the formation of a collective identity, the Malaysian public's perceptions of unfairness served to trigger these shared emotions and were subsequently used to translate those emotions to actions taken in response to these perceptions.

DISCUSSION QUESTIONS

1. Discuss how electronic forms of communication may facilitate the creation and sustainment of informal coalitions in organizations. What other examples of social media prompting informal coalitions are you aware of? In what ways are those examples similar to, or different from, the case?
2. Were both shared social identity and collective emotion necessary in prompting collective action among the Malaysian public? Could informal coalitions be formed from just the sense of shared identity or from collective emotion alone?
3. Consider the statements made by opposition leader Anwar Ibrahim in response to the outcomes of GE13. What are some of the roles that leaders play in managing followers' collective identity and emotions?
4. Were the actions taken by the Malaysian public in response to the allegations of electoral fraud appropriate? Why or why not?
5. Provide some analysis and explanations for why the informal coalitions were not sustained beyond the GE13 event.

(*continued*)

6. Research on followership is scarce compared with studies that focus on the role of leaders in the leadership process. Provide some suggestions for how research in this domain can be advanced.
7. This case highlights collective followership action. How is that the same, or different, from individual action such as whistle-blowing?

References

Augustin, S. (2013, May 11). *ABU defends action to stop foreigners from voting.* Retrieved from http://www.fz.com/content/abu-defends-action-stop-foreigners-voting

BERSIH 2.0. (2014, April 8). *The people's tribunal on Malaysia's 13th general elections: Summary of the report.* Retrieved from https://www.globalbersih.org/2014/04/08/the-peoples-tribunal-on-malaysias-13th-general-elections-summary-of-the-report/

Bligh, M. C., Kohles, J. C., & Pillai, R. (2011). Romancing leadership: Past, present, and future. *The Leadership Quarterly*, *22*(6), 1058–1077. doi:10.1016/j.leaqua.2011.09.003

Chin, J. (2013). So close and yet so far: Strategies in the 13th Malaysian elections. *Round Table*, *102*(6), 533. doi:10.1080/00358533.2013.857145

Collinson, D. (2006). Rethinking followership: A post-structuralist analysis of follower identities. *The Leadership Quarterly*, *17*(2), 179–189. doi:10.1016/j.leaqua.2005.12.005

De Cremer, D., van Dijke, M., & Mayer, D. M. (2010). Cooperating when "you" and "I" are treated fairly: The moderating role of leader prototypicality. *Journal of Applied Psychology*, *95*(6), 1121–1133. Retrieved from http://www.apa.org

Ding, J., Koh, L., Surin, J. A., Dragomir, M., Thompson, M., Watts, G., ... Starks, M. (2013). *Mapping digital media: Malaysia.* London: Open Society Media Program.

Mackie, D. M., Devos, T., & Smith, E. R. (2000). Intergroup emotions: Explaining offensive action tendencies in an intergroup context. *Journal of Personality and Social Psychology*, *79*(4), 602–616. Retrieved from http://www.apa.org

Meindl, J. R. (1995). The romance of leadership as a follower-centric theory: A social constructionist approach. *The Leadership Quarterly*, *6*(3), 329–341. doi:10.1016/1048-9843(95)90012-8

Ostwald, K. (2013). How to win a lost election: Malapportionment and Malaysia's 2013 general election. *Round Table*, *102*(6), 521. doi:10.1080/00358533.2013.857146

Tee, E. Y. J., Paulsen, N., & Ashkanasy, N. M. (2013). Revisiting followership through a social identity perspective: The role of collective follower emotion and action. *The Leadership Quarterly*, *24*(6), 902–918. doi:10.1016/j.leaqua.2013.10.002

Van Dijke, M., & De Cremer, D. (2010). Procedural fairness and endorsement of prototypical leaders: Leader benevolence or follower control? *Journal of Experimental Social Psychology*, *46*(1), 85–96. doi:10.1016/j.jesp.2009.10.004

Vinod, G. (2013a). Pakatan rejects GE13 results, cries fraud. *Free Malaysia Today*, May 6. Retrieved from http://www.freemalaysiatoday.com/category/nation/2013/05/06/pakatan-rejects-ge13-results-cries-fraud/

Vinod, G. (2013b). PKR shows new proof of electoral fraud. *Free Malaysia Today*, May 27. Retrieved from http://www.freemalaysiatoday.com/category/nation/2013/05/27/pkr-provides-proof-of-phantom-voters-blackouts/

CHAPTER

24 Leading from the Middle: Effective Followership

Ted Thomas and Paul Berg

Going to a New Job

Major Jack Eric moved to his job at Fort Bliss, Texas, to work in a temporary position in the operations staff until a career enhancing job opened up. This unit was scheduled to deploy to Afghanistan four months after he took the position.

After two months on the job, Jack was reassigned to 1st Brigade Combat Team (1BCT). The 1BCT Brigade Commander, Colonel (COL) Nathan Brown, had just fired four majors after his brigade performed poorly in a pre-deployment exercise rotation at Fort Polk. COL Brown was a tough, no-nonsense, aggressive leader with a quick temper. He commanded units during Operation Desert Storm in 1990, during the invasion of Iraq in support of Operation Iraqi Freedom in 2003, and just finished a 15-month combat tour in Afghanistan on a general's staff. Leading the brigade for the last five months, many expected him to be a general officer someday.

While Jack waited outside his office, COL Brown said, "Who the hell are you? Why are you waiting to see me?" Jack explained that he was sent to the brigade to replace a recently relieved major. Unaware that Jack was assigned to him, Brown vented his displeasure. As Brown started his emotional rant, Lieutenant Colonel (LTC) Jeff Allen, the operations officer, came up the stairs and noticed the situation. LTC Allen quickly intervened and calmed COL Brown down by explaining he needed an additional major in his shop and mentioned that Jack was the new plans officer. This seemed to satisfy COL Brown and he quickly disappeared into his office. Jack gained his first glimpse of the brigade's organizational climate.

New Job; New Boss

After the office call, Jack visited LTC Allen, his new boss, for his initial welcome and orientation. LTC Allen explained his expectations and discussed Jack's responsibilities. He described how COL Brown operated his unique personality and his interpersonal tact. He explained there would be times when COL Brown made hasty, emotional decisions and did not always use his better judgment.

COL Brown had difficulty explaining his vision and intent to the staff and organizational leaders. LTC Allen described the staff's major challenge as adapting and improvising to stay on course with COL Brown's vision and never let the boss or the organization fail. LTC Allen was a motivated professional and reiterated his major leadership theme that the overall purpose of the staff was, "To ensure the success of the organization, its subordinates, and leaders, always."

As he settled into his new job, Jack began to develop his initial impressions of the other officers that formed the brigade staff, as well as the organization's culture and climate while envisioning what the next year held for him. The staff included officers that performed required roles in personnel, intelligence, operations, and logistics that contributed to the organization's mission success. The four officers who worked closest with MAJ Eric were LTC Allen who was responsible for the coordination and synchronization of all training and operations in the brigade and was MAJ Eric's immediate boss, LTC Lock who was the second in command of the brigade, LTC Franklin who was third in line of seniority and supervised the staff, and MAJ Casey who was the director for human relations.

LTC Allen was a highly educated infantryman and excellent staff officer. He was an articulate writer, dynamic presenter, and had been in the organization for four years. He was always reading to expand his knowledge and improve himself. He developed subordinates deliberately and demanded performance from them. He treated everyone with respect and had a reputation of being tough but fair. Jack observed, "If staff officers did their jobs and were team players, LTC Allen never had an issue. Overall, the office ran smoothly and everyone in the shop seemed to carry their work load."

LTC Pete Lock was the Deputy Commander and spent most of his military career in the Army Reserves. He attempted to get involved in current operations, but became an obstacle to the staff. The other staff officers described him as a "yes-man," blindly following the commander's guidance without any questions. He displayed little critical thinking and did not play a constructive role on the staff. When he tried to argue operations or policy, he did not have the intellectual base to make his case or defend his argument. He was an ineffective staff officer and this job would be his last active duty assignment.

LTC Jeff Franklin was the Brigade Executive Officer (XO) who was recently promoted to LTC and was anxiously waiting to see if he would be selected to become a battalion commander. He frequently reported to the brigade commander any rumors or anything that might upset the commander. He routinely solidified his position by being the ultimate informant. He publicly announced he had the brigade commander's back. The staff realized they could not trust LTC Franklin because every insignificant comment got back to COL Brown. The staff knew he sent blind copy e-mails to COL Brown with every reply e-mail he received from the staff and commanders. Overly concerned with guarding his reputation, he showed little initiative except to show his importance to COL Brown.

Major Melinda Casey was the brigade adjutant. She was an efficient staff officer. She worked for COL Brown on her last deployment and personally requested the position. She knew him well but also needed the position to enhance her career. She ran a well-organized office and took care of the soldiers with timely administrative actions. She dedicated herself to her job despite the tough command climate. Jack noted he never saw COL Brown yell or scream at Melinda. She knew how to manage him and ensured she met his requirements without alienating the other key leaders on staff.

Deploying to Afghanistan

The process of planning a military logistical movement to deploy over 2,000 people, their assigned equipment and vehicles to Afghanistan was extremely difficult, as well as finding the time to prepare training for the future diverse combat missions they would conduct in the austere environment of the mountainous terrain of Afghanistan. Each staff officer was required to be exact in the planning estimates to move by rail, ship, and air through six countries and plan the future combat requirements under the continuously changing national strategy for operations in Afghanistan.

The commander's initial planning guidance drove the operations process. The staff desperately needed guidance to prioritize what the commander deemed the most important activities and to ensure they were not leaving anything out. They also needed help in resolving disputes between staff officers who tried to get their agendas put first. However, receiving guidance from COL Brown became close to impossible.

During the early planning briefs, COL Brown procrastinated and continued to resist making important decisions. He routinely sent his staff back to redo analysis and planning for no logical reason. In the last brief, COL Brown made no decision on the critical recommended courses of action by the staff on training and logistical movements, which forced the staff to move forward with the planning process hoping to meet their commander's wishes and not have to redo and delay the movement. The brigade staff was concerned about the deployment and vented their frustrations to LTC Allen. He told the staff, "Look, I understand your frustrations. However, we must continue to plan, work through this, and make it happen. We have a duty to this unit and we owe it to the organization to do our job. No one promised this would be easy." The staff felt confused that the boss was making it much harder than it needed to be, feeling the problem was not about his leadership behavior but his lack of decisiveness. The organizational climate made it easy for the staff to just simply comply and say what the boss wanted to hear, but their duty to their military service demanded that the staff work through these challenges.

When the staff finally briefed COL Brown, he responded, "That is exactly what I wanted you to do in the first place." COL Brown's complex communication style revealed it was going to be a long deployment. Often frustrated with COL Brown, LTC Allen repeatedly used tact when advising him behind closed doors about the brigade operations. He reminded the staff that it took art and science to manage the boss.

Scholarly Commentary

Many leaders believe good followers make good leaders and leaders must learn to follow before they can learn to lead. This is an Army paradigm. However, many leaders are not effective followers and many followers are not effective leaders. There are individuals who are satisfied with following in a passive manner, but do not understand or accept the responsibilities of effective followership. This is understandable since leader development programs focus on developing leaders, not followers.

Individuals often misinterpret followership as simply following orders, thereby abdicating any responsibility for critical thinking other than to execute the task. However, people cannot be effective followers by simply following orders. While the senior military leader shoulders the ultimate responsibility for success of the organization, subordinate leaders or followers also share in this responsibility. This lesson provides the opportunity to discuss the importance of followership in the leader's duties and responsibilities making followership an integral part of leadership. The multitude of senior officer firings and investigations over the past few years bring to the forefront the responsibility of subordinates in preventing their boss and their organization from failing. What is the role of a follower in ensuring the success of the organization and the boss? Leaders need to understand the dynamics of the leader-follower relationship to fully answer this question. Leaders need to understand when they need to lead and when they need to follow. LTC Allen provides a perfect example of a follower who led when needed and acted courageously in leading up to prevent his boss from failing.

This case study provides an opportunity to identify followership styles in a brigade staff and the influence these styles have on the organization and its leaders. Kelley (2008) declares followers deserve more attention because of their importance to the organization's success and because of their importance to effective leadership. According to Kelley who is one of the most authoritative and quoted authors in followership literature (Crossman & Crossman, 2011), any conversation about leadership must include followership because by definition a leader needs to lead someone. This case study provides an opportunity to explore Kelley's premise.

After defining and assessing followership, the students should see connections to followership characteristics and traits in their organizations. In the book *Military Leadership: In Pursuit of Excellence*, Kelley (1992) wrote an article "In Praise of Followers," in which he states the difference between effective and ineffective followers is enthusiasm, self-reliance, and intelligent decision making in accomplishing organizational goals. Kelley further emphasizes that just understanding what motivates a follower is not sufficient to know how to fully develop them. Kelley argues that effective followers participate in the leadership process and lend their critical thinking skills to solving problems. They dissent when necessary and exercise judgment and humility in doing so (Kelley, 1992, p. 100).

He explains effective or exemplary followers have essential qualities such as: self-management, commitment, competence and focus, and courage. In this case study, LTC Allen constantly balanced between being a subordinate follower for COL Brown and a leader of his section and the brigade to ensure organizational success. There is a close linkage between the leadership characteristics of an effective organizational leader and an effective follower. Without the proper dynamics between leaders and followers, it is difficult to build a team and accomplish the difficult combat mission, as did LTC Allen. An effective follower usually makes the transition to an effective leader easier than do ineffective followers.

Kelley (1992) lists four other followership patterns: *sheep* who lack initiative and only do what they are told (MAJ Casey could possibly fall into this category), *alienated followers* who do not openly criticize but can be a cancer in an organization (there were many in this brigade, but not among the key leadership), *yes people* who enthusiastically do what the boss wants trying to ingratiate themselves (LTC Lock fits this category), and *survivors* who act like a chameleon to drift into whatever category will allow them to do enough to get by (LTC Franklin might fit into this category). There is not enough information about MAJ Eric to determine where he might fit, but it would be well to ask the students to imagine they were MAJ Eric and what they would do.

Ira Chaleff is another author in the research and academic writings of the field of followership whose publication became one of the primary works upon which followership discussions are based (Baker, 2007). He wrote *The Courageous Follower: Standing Up to and For Our Leaders* in 1995. Chaleff defines courageous followers as those who have the character and commitment to proactively seek to accomplish the mission of the team. Chaleff describes five dimensions of courageous followership in his book. Each dimension works in tension and in balance with the others.

The Courage to Assume Responsibility: Courageous followers feel responsible for the success of the organization and its mission. When they are in charge, they take charge and proactively work to accomplish the mission and improve the organization while it is operating (p. 6). LTC Allen followed his commander's intent as best he could understand it and used his own judgment when he had to. He assumed responsibility for the success of the organization.

The Courage to Serve: Courageous followers recognize that serving is hard work and serve with passion in accomplishing the mission and supporting the leader (p. 7). Many of the officers in this unit served with passion to accomplish the mission and in effect support their leader, even in an environment which was not conducive to teamwork and collaboration. LTC Allen could have easily fallen into a compliance mode of only doing what the boss wants, but his responsibility and duty to the organization kept him serving honorably to assist in mission accomplishment.

The Courage to Challenge: Courageous followers know when to challenge unethical, immoral, or illegal policies. They are willing to risk rejection and harmony for the common purpose and to maintain their integrity (p. 7). In this case study, few of the officers seemed willing to challenge COL Brown. His firing of four Majors had a significant impact on the willingness of the followers to confront their boss. LTC Allen seemed an exception, albeit he challenged his boss behind closed doors. LTC Allen used interpersonal tact in his relationship with his superior and in doing so learned the best approach to discuss critical challenges that the organization needed to accomplish to be successful.

The Courage to Participate in Transformation: Courageous followers champion the need for change when change is needed. They become full participants in the change process by working with the leader and others to accomplish the desired goals and objectives (p. 7). Few stepped forward to try to change the operations within the brigade, even though change was needed.

The Courage to Take Moral Action: Courageous followers are willing to risk their future with the organization if attempts to resolve morally corrupt situations fail. In doing so they understand that if they cannot prevent the organization from going down the wrong path, it is probably not an organization they want to be a part of (p. 7). None of the officers were willing to take this drastic a step and perhaps it was not needed in this case. The organization was not morally corrupt, just poorly run.

DISCUSSION QUESTIONS

1. Why is followership important in this case study?
   Do the officers in this case study act as both leaders and followers? Being a responsible military subordinate implies supporting the commander and making sure that the team supports the larger organization unit and its purpose. Can LTC Allen and COL Brown succeed without building an effective team?
2. What kinds of followers are the characters in this case study?
   Why is it important for LTC Allen to conduct a self-assessment of the relationship between his leadership and his followership? Properly answering this question requires self-reflection and a dialogue or discussion with the leader and peers as well as subordinates. Is it important to assess the other officers' level of followership?

(*continued*)

3. How did the command climate influence followership at the brigade?
   Did the climate of the brigade encourage certain officers to be "yes men" and to be rewarded for their loyalty? Were survivors encouraged in this unit who then did minimal work but enough to not get fired or removed from their jobs. What happens when a few dedicated effective followers carry the load of the organization and carry the brigade through the deployment?
4. How would you describe the brigade's paradigms?
   Was there a belief that rank and position equate to competence and ability to lead? The established cultural paradigm in the Army is that all field grade officers (promotion and 10+ years of service) are capable officers and effective followers on a brigade staff. Do rank and position always translate to an effective and capable staff officer?
5. From a followership perspective, what were some ramifications of the social environment in the brigade?
   Does the leadership in the staff determine the effectiveness of the followership within the staff? In a followership environment with no support from the boss, who is the ultimate bill payer? How can the alienated followers be encouraged to contribute to the staff? Is it worth the effort to get the sheep and yes people to contribute effectively?
6. What is the major problem or dilemma facing this organization's followers?
   How can a leader in this organization use the different follower styles to improve their organization?
7. Does the commander of this unit want each type of follower? Why or why not?
   How do you move MAJ Erik or LTC Lock or LTC Franklin as a follower to a more desired style?
8. Does this situation require courageous followers?
9. Does LTC Allen have to develop an effective follower relationship with his boss to succeed in his job?
10. Is the relationship with LTC Allen's superior dependent on LTC Allen's follower type?
    Which of the dimensions of courageous followership did the members of the staff employ?
11. Would LTC Allen need to be a courageous follower if the climate freely allowed for dissent in this case study?

References

Baker, S. D. (2007). Followership: Theoretical foundation of a contemporary construct. *Journal of Leadership and Organizational Studies*, *14*(1), 50–60. doi:10.1177/0002831207304343

Crossman, B., & Crossman, J. (2011). Conceptualizing followership: A review of the literature. *Leadership*, *7*(4), 481–497. doi:10.1177/1742715011416891

Kelley, R. (1992). In praise of followers. In R. L. Taylor & W. E. Rosenbach (Eds.), *Military leadership: In pursuit of excellence*. Boulder, CO: Westview Press.

Kelley, R. (2008). Rethinking followership. In R. E. Riggio, I. Chaleff, & J. Lipman-Blumen (Eds.), *The art of followership: How great followers create great leaders and organizations*. San Francisco, CA: Jossey-Bass. Retrieved from http://media.johnwiley.com.au/product_data/excerpt/53/07879966/0787996653.pdf

CHAPTER

25 Bernie Madoff's Inner Circle

Rodger Adair

As Stew Cross sipped his morning coffee at a small outdoor café in southern California, he received an e-mail alert regarding the latest verdict. The last of Bernie Madoff's co-conspirators, Joan Crupi, had been sentenced to six years in prison. Cross' morning caffeine jolt tasted all the better as he remembered the day that he lost $20 million to Bernie Madoff's Ponzi scheme.

Bernie Madoff Investment Securities, LLC, was established in 1960 and seemed to do very well for 48 years. In fact, it did better than anyone imagined prior to the arrest of Bernie Madoff himself on December 11, 2008. His list of clients included celebrities and top-level executives. Although he admitted that his fraud began in the 1990s, federal investigators suggest that he began his Ponzi scheme in the 1980s. In 2009, Madoff was sentenced to 150 years in prison for the largest Ponzi scheme in history. This criminal act rocked Wall Street.

The media talked about Bernie Madoff as if his Ponzi scheme had been created by him and him alone. Stew could only think of Bernie Madoff's team of loyal employees who ripped off innocent people. Stew thought, "He couldn't have done this alone. He started his company way back in the 1960s, but he wasn't arrested until 2008. That's a long time." No one knows exactly how long his Ponzi scheme ran, but Bernie insisted that he started out as a legitimate business man.

In reality, Madoff had five key employees who helped him in his fraud. His prison sentence was for 150 years, while his inner circle of loyal employees received much shorter ones. First on the list was Daniel Bonventure, the director of Madoff's broker-dealer unit. He ran the brokerage for over 40 years. Second was Annette

Bongiorno, Madoff's personal secretary who ran the investment advisory unit. Third, Joan Crupi, the large accounts manager, and fourth and fifth, Jerome O'Hara and George Perez. Both were computer programmers. Each of them played an active part in keeping the fraud alive.

Some might say that they were just following orders, that they would have never broken the law if Bernie Madoff hadn't put them up to it, but former clients like Stew Cross would scoff at that thought. Bernie Madoff was the face of his organization, but his inner circle was the engine. His inner circle ran the mechanics of the multi-billion dollar Ponzi scheme where they simply would deposit client investments into a bank account rather than actually invest the funds into the market. He told his clients that his firm had grown steady returns regardless of economic performance, but the performance of his firm was a statistically impossible accomplishment that made many regulators suspicious. The Federal Trade Commission (FTC) got complaints and warnings from analysts and competitors, but not from his employees and clients.

From the 1990 to 2008, the FTC made several trips to audit Madoff Investments. Each time, Bernie Madoff and his staff would lie, hide evidence, and produce false documentation. Each time, the FTC gave Madoff's investment company a passing grade. Stew believed that Madoff's staff did as much as their boss in stealing money from clients. Daniel Bonventure, Annette Bongiorno, and Joan Crupi all created false documents such as trade reports and investment statements reflecting fake returns and earnings. These employees entered fraudulent trades from prior dates and then recorded fake closing trades that matched amounts of growth Madoff himself had promised clients. Jerome O'Hara and George Perez both made sure that transactions looked legitimate to both clients and federal auditors. They did this by creating documents and forms that looked real, providing a growth history for each client's *investment*.

Some people also ask why none of Madoff's five core employees ever turned their boss into the FBI. Cross thought, "Seems a bit fishy when you really think about it. They stuck with Bernie Madoff until the bitter end and the scheme unraveled only when too many investors began to withdraw earnings of $7 billion dollars from Madoff's firm."

In the end, Annette Bongiorno and Joan Crupi each received six-year prison terms. Daniel Bonventure was sentenced to 10 years, while both Jerome O'Hara and George Perez each ended up with terms of only two and a half years. These sentences seemed rather pale when compared to Bernie Madoff who received 150 years.

It seemed that the courts and juries all agreed. As the ring leader, Bernie Madoff carried the greatest weight of responsibility.

A looming question is whether the followers within Madoff's inner circle carry the same burden of culpability for their own crimes as committed?[1]

Scholarly Commentary

This case study discusses the roles played by the five key employees in Bernie Madoff's inner circle, and how each of them contributed to Madoff's Ponzi scheme. If we assume that leadership is relational, as do Ahlquist and Levi (2011), it seems reasonable to also assume that a person cannot be a leader without one or more followers. This leads to another important question: In a discussion on ethical followership, Carsten and Uhl-Bien (2013) allude to this point in drawing attention to the role of the leader in modeling, promoting, and reinforcing specific behaviors for followers to emulate. As noted by Trevino, Brown, and Hartman (2003), the assumption is that a leader portrays the example, while followers simply mimic leader behaviors. By contrast, Hollander (1995) proposes that leaders and followers are unified in an interdependent relationship. Hollander's definition suggests that leaders and followers influence each other. Perhaps Bernie Madoff was as influenced by his employees' behaviors as much as his employees were influenced by his own behavior. Bernie Madoff's key five employees may have felt a sense of affection or trust that translated the leader-follower relationship into a cohesive, group of loyal employees (Zhu, Newman, Miao, & Hooke, 2013). Zhu, Riggio, Avolio, and Sosik (2011) suggest that leaders can influence employee moral behaviors.

Colbry, Hurwitz, and Adair (2014) suggest that some employees carry the attitude of *Me First* or *Individual First*. Individual First employees take from their work that which builds their careers. This means they may take from the team to gain personally. Other employees, however, have a *Team First* attitude, or an attitude that strengthens the dynamics of the team (Colbry et al., 2014) before the career. Bernie Madoff's demise may have been influenced by a Team First dynamic in which his employees naturally protected their boss while looking out for each other as members of the team.

In 2009, Bernie Madoff was convicted for defrauding investors out of billions of dollars over a 20 plus year span (Frizell, 2014; Lensner, 2008). During that extended period, he could not have

---

[1]*The following articles were used to organize the material for the case titled Bernie Madoff's Inner Circle.* Caitman and Gotthoffer (2014), Frizell (2014), Lensner (2008), Raymond (2014), and Weidner (2014).

acted alone (Caitman & Gotthoffer, 2014). Those who followed Bernie Madoff down the road of high dollar crime committed many of the same crimes as their boss. At what point did Bernie Madoff's employees consciously decide to break the law and obstruct justice to protect their boss from criminal prosecution? Can followers be as culpable as their leaders when violating an ethical norm or committing a crime? Bernie Madoff received a 150 year prison term. The sentences for his inner circle have been far more lenient with the longest prison terms at 10 years and the shortest only two and a half years. These primary operants played key roles in defrauding clients by lying, falsifying documents, hiding evidence from regulators, and back dating transactions so clients believed they were making huge profits where none existed. But, did they perform these illegal acts fully aware, or were they somehow duped and less capable of making ethical decisions when confronted with Bernie Madoff's presence and leadership?

THE TWO ARGUMENTS

In this scholarly summary, the reader will be asked to consider two arguments and the evidence presented. The first argument states that Bernie Madoff's employees were less culpable, though not innocent. Therefore, all five of his employees deserved the shorter sentences they had received. The second argument states that all of Madoff's employees were equally culpable of the crimes committed, and that they should have each received much harsher sentences.

Argument One: Followers are Less Culpable than Their Leaders

Liu, Lin, and Hu (2013) suggest that an employee's in-group or out-group status is an indicator of potential ethical and unethical work behaviors. According to Leader-Member Exchange (LMX) theory, leaders segregate employees into two categories, in-group and out-group. In-group employees receive more positive attention from their supervisors, obtain relevant work-related information, have more privileges, and enjoy higher job security and career advancement, as well as experience greater compassion when things go wrong. This in-group dynamic is based on trust. When leaders act unethically, in-group members have also been found guilty of acting unethically (Gino, Ayal, & Ariely, 2009). There are many reasons for behaving in an unethical manner; one such reason includes workplace peer pressure, especially when this pressure comes from management (Liu et al., 2013).

Carsten and Uhl-Bien (2013) introduced the basic assumption that leader behaviors, and their effects on the leader-follower dynamic, are strong predictors of ethical behavior in organizations.

While some employees find it within themselves to rise above their unethical environment, other employees end up engaging in crimes of obedience, or obeying their leaders in performing unethical acts even though they know that they should not. Those engaged in crimes of obedience are likely able to act this way because they displace responsibility for their unethical acts onto their leader. These employees possibly believe that they can avoid punishment simply by blaming the authority figure for their unethical behavior.

According to Lipman-Blumen (2005), many employees also rationalize their relationships with toxic leaders as something that fulfills their basic needs such as a pay check, advancement opportunities, or even a sense of belonging. These dangerous rationalizations bind employees to toxic leaders. Ironically, the world readily identifies this destructive dynamic, while the leader, nor follower, does not often see the same until it is too late. In a toxic relationship, the leader seems to have control over the employee. Lipman-Blumen (2005) calls this control phenomenon a myth, suggesting that these myths are unfulfilled needs within a follower's psyche. While some feel inferior to leaders, others fear what repercussions leaders might wield. Some followers gravitate easily to leaders who control resources, as many other followers like leaders who protect the *status quo*. Some feel leaders are there to shield them from real consequences. Finally, some followers suffer from hero-worship, opening them to manipulation.

Regardless of how a leader may seem to control a follower's actions, other factors need to play out to answer how a follower would act unethically, even break the law, for a leader. Wiltermuth (2012) found that leaders and followers involved in synchronous work often become attached to each other in ways deeper than just work expectations. Managers and employees sharing resources, performing similar process duties, even seeking to achieve similar goals and objectives engage in synchrony. Synchronized behaviors occur as coordinated actions in a sports team, a symphony, or a pair walking together. Synchrony requires anticipation of others' behaviors (Hove & Risen, 2009). Synchrony can also influence people to more easily engage in destructive obedience at the behest of authority figures (Wiltermuth, 2012), suggesting that people are more likely to comply with requests from those to whom they feel socially connected (Liu et al., 2013).

To summarize this argument, followers with in-group status may be more greatly influenced by unethical leaders than those in out-group status. If this is the case, unethical leaders can push loyal employees across ethical lines. Tools such as peer pressure can lead to crimes of obedience, motivating followers to rationalize responsibility to leaders because of the inferior status of followers.

Argument Two: Followers Are Just as Culpable as Their Leaders

According to Steger, Manners, and Zimmerer (1982), employees have one of two grand objectives in mind. These two objectives are self-enhancement and self-protection and they help to explain how employees engage at work. Followers who are focused on self-enhancement may seek to better themselves through training, education, and possibly networking. Followers may also set up self-protections to avoid being hurt, taken advantage of, or disciplined. Toxic leaders may be able to recognize and manipulate these employees (Lipman-Blumen, 2005), but employees still manifest free will in aligning or rejecting toxic leaders.

Hurwitz and Hurwitz (2015) identified that leaders and followers need to have shared goals to work well together. The fact that this Ponzi scheme lasted multiple decades suggest that Bernie Madoff and his team worked well together, which lends to the idea that they had shared goals to defraud clients and launder money into the company savings account. At any point in the process, during any board meeting, or at every FTC audit, his employees could have become a whistle-blower. Instead, they protected Bernie Madoff and upheld the lie. Bernie Madoff's employees faced an ethical dilemma each time he approached them with inappropriate requests. Even after years of compliance, they could still agree with or reject their boss's offer of unethical behavior (Carsten & Uhl-Bien, 2013).

The decision to accept or reject the leader's request comes from personal narratives or socially negotiated constructs to organize a person's thoughts and actions (Moore & Gino, 2015). Narratives constructed in the mind will later manifest as behavior. Employees who consider themselves moral individuals, then consciously engage in unethical behavior, will trigger cognitive dissonance. Cognitive dissonance is psychological tension that creates stress when a follower's beliefs are inconsistent with the individual's actions. According to Moore and Gino (2015), dissonance requires resolution either through changing the actions to better align with beliefs or in changing beliefs to align with actions.

Effelsberg, Solga, and Gurt (2014) coined the term *unethical pro-organizational behavior* (UPB). UPB denotes choices and actions in which followers engage that benefits their organization while violating ethical norms. Employees who strongly identify with their organization, or identify with a team first attitude (Colbry et al., 2014), would be more inclined to engage in UPB and more likely to engage in unethical and/or illegal behavior to increase organizational success (Effelsberg et al., 2014). Bernie Madoff's inner circle were committed to the company and Bernie himself. Each of their choices supported Bernie Madoff's success as a criminal while hiding his scheme from clients. Their relationship within the company, and their personal dispositions toward ethical or unethical behavior, led them to blind obedience and group think.

To summarize this last argument, followers have free will to cross, or not cross, ethical boundaries when working with unethical leaders. Employees can have shared goals with leaders, similar values, even aligned desires to take short cuts to accomplish goals. All this stems from an employee's personal narrative, not pressure from a leader. Those employees who do comply against their conscience will experience cognitive dissonance, but continued compliance is a choice. Sometimes employees choose to engage in UPB to benefit the organization, not the unethical boss.

Conclusion

This case study is about Bernie Madoff's inner circle of employees. The reader learned the history of Madoff Securities and how this financial giant fell, as well as the roles of each of the key players behind the scenes and how they each contributed to the Ponzi scheme. This case discussed the sentences handed out for each employee. The reader was introduced to the form of toxic followership Bernie Madoff's employees exhibited, and discussed whether followers are as culpable as their leaders for successes and failures within organizations. The scholarly summary presented two contrasting arguments for the reader to consider. Can followers be as culpable as their leaders when violating an ethical norm or committing a crime? This critical question deserves further consideration.

DISCUSSION QUESTIONS

1. Assume you joined the Bernie Madoff team six months ago. You were hired by Daniel Bonventure who became your immediate boss. Earlier today, Daniel presented a plan to increase returns at an investor's meeting. You realize the numbers he presented were not the same you have seen internally. You are unsure of the ethical nature of this discrepancy. What should you do?
2. Stew Cross was bothered by the disparity between prison terms for Bernie Madoff and his inner circle. Some may suggest that this disparity results from a higher standard to which society holds its leaders. Is it right to hold

(*continued*)

leaders more accountable than followers? Explain your answer.

3. Any one of Bernie Madoff's inner circle could have gone to the FTC or FBI, but all chose to support their boss. Assume that one of them was tempted to become a whistle-blower, but feared reprisals similar to other whistle-blowers in other industries. Why does society look down on employees who expose great wrongs within organizations? What could be done to change this negative perception?
4. According to Carsten and Uhl-Bien (2013), leader behaviors and their effects on the leader-follower dynamic are strong predictors of ethical behavior. Assume this premise was true, and Bernie Madoff was an honest financial broker. Would his standard of ethics have influenced his inner circle to be of a more ethical character? Do you support this premise? Do you disagree with this premise? Explain and support your response.
5. What opportunities did each of Bernie Madoff's inner circle have to become whistle-blowers? Why do you feel they instead chose to engage in *crimes of obedience*?
6. Which of Bernie Madoff's employees had the most to lose by exposing the truth to the FTC? Please elaborate on your response.
7. Which of the two arguments in this case, *less culpable or just as culpable*, hold the greatest validity? Why? Support your response.

References

Ahlquist, J. S., & Levi, M. (2011). Leadership: What it means, what it does, and what we want to know about it. *Annual Review of Political Science*, *14*, 1–24. doi:10.1146/annurev-polisci-042409-152654

Caitman, H. D., & Gotthoffer, L. (2014). *JPMadoff: The unholy alliance between America's biggest bank and America's biggest crook*. Retrieved from www.jpmadoff.com

Carsten, M. K., & Uhl-Bien, M. (2013). Ethical followership: An examination of followership beliefs and crimes of obedience. *Journal of Leadership & Organizational Studies*, *20*(1), 49–61. doi:10.1177/1548051812465890

Colbry, S., Hurwitz, M., & Adair, R. (2014). Collaboration theory. *Journal of Leadership Education*, *13*(4), 63–75. doi:10.12806/V13/I4/C8

Effelsberg, D., Solga, M., & Gurt, J. (2014). Transformational leadership and follower's unethical behavior for the benefit of the company: A two-study investigation. *Journal of Business Ethics*, *120*, 81–93. doi:10.1007/s10551-013-1644-z

Frizell, S. (2014). Where are Bernie Madoff and his inner circle now? *Time*, December 11. Retrieved from http/time.com/3626632/Madoff-where-are-they-now

Gino, F., Ayal, S., & Ariely, D. (2009). Contagion and differentiation in unethical behavior: The effect of one bad apple on the barrel. *Psychological Science*, *20*(3), 393–398. doi:10.1111/j.1467-9280.2009.02306.x

Hollander, E. P. (1995). Ethical challenges in the leader-follower relationship. *Business Ethics Quarterly*, *5*(1), 55–65. doi:10.2307/3857272

Hove, M. J., & Risen, J. L. (2009). It's all in the timing: Interpersonal synchrony increases affiliation. *Social Cognition*, *27*(6), 949–961. doi:10.1521/soco.2009.27.6.949

Hurwitz, M., & Hurwitz, S. (2015). *Leadership is half the story: A fresh look at followership, leadership, and collaboration.* Buffalo, NY: University of Toronto Press.

Lensner, R. (2008). Bernie Madoff's $50 billion Ponzi scheme. *Forbes*, December 12. Retrieved from http/www.forbes.com/2008/12/12/madoff-ponizi-hedge-pf-ii-in_rl_1212croesus_inl.hlml

Lipman-Blumen, J. (2005). *The allure of toxic leaders: Why we follow destructive bossed and corrupt politicians – and how we can survive them.* New York, NY: Oxford Press.

Liu, S., Lin, X., & Hu, W. (2013). How follower's unethical behavior is triggered by leader-member exchange: The mediating effect of job satisfaction. *Social Behavior and Personality*, *41*(3), 357–366. doi:10.2224/sbp.2013.41.3

Moore, C., & Gino, F. (2015). Approach, ability, aftermath: A psychological process framework of unethical behavior at work. *The Academy of Management Annals*, *9*(1), 235–289. doi:10.1080/1946520.2015.1011522

Raymond, N. (2014, December 15). *Former Bernie Madoff manager sentence to 6 years prison for fraud.* Retrieved from http/bangordailynews.com/2014/12/15/business/former-bernie-madoff-manager-sentences-to-6-years-prison-for-fraud

Steger, J. A., Manners, G. E., Jr., & Zimmerer, T. W. (1982). Following the leader: How to link management style to subordinate personalities. *Management Review*, *71*(10), 22–28, 49–51. Retrieved from http://www.ncbi.nlm.nih.gov/pubmed/10262397

Trevino, L. K., Brown, M., & Hartman, L. P. (2003). A qualitative investigation of perceived executive ethical leadership: Perceptions from inside and outside the executive suite. *Human Relations*, *55*, 5–37. doi:10.1177/0018726703056001448

Weidner, D. (2014). Who helped Bernie Madoff get away with his crimes? *Opinion*, October 30. Retrieved from www.marketwatch.com/story/who-helped-bernie-madoff-get-away-with-his-crimes-2014-10-30

Wiltermuth, S. (2012). Synchrony and destructive leadership. *Social Influence*, *7*(2), 78–89. doi:10.1080/15534510.2012.658653

Zhu, W., Newman, A., Miao, Q., & Hooke, A. (2013). Revisiting the mediating role of trust in transformational leadership effects: Do different types of trust make a difference? *The Leadership Quarterly*, *24*(1), 94–105. doi:10.1016/j.leaqua.2012.08.004

Zhu, W., Riggio, R., Avolio, B. J., & Sosik, J. J. (2011). The effect of leader and follower moral identity: Does transformational/transactional style make a difference? *Journal of Organizational Studies*, *18*(2), 150–163. doi:10.1177/1548051810396714

About the Editors

Lead Editor

Rob Koonce has published on subjects ranging from leadership to metabolic disease and has spent the past three decades working in business, education, medicine, and the legal profession. As a professor, social entrepreneur, and consultant, Rob now enjoys utilizing his life experiences to help others think more boldly about the world around them. Recognized as a leading voice in followership, Rob serves as the 2016 chair of the Leadership Development Member Interest Group (MIG) for the International Leadership Association (ILA). As the 2014–2015 chair of the ILA Followership Learning Community (FLC), he originated and co-developed the 2014 International Followership Symposium with Ira Chaleff and served as the guest editor for the symposium's published proceedings. He serves on the Editing Advisory Board of the *Journal of Leadership Education* and the Editorial Board of the *Creighton Journal of Interdisciplinary Leadership*. Rob obtained his doctorate in organizational leadership and holds a MBA in entrepreneurship and a master's degree in organizational learning.

Associate Editors

Michelle C. Bligh is Professor of organizational behavior and leadership at Neoma Business School in France. Published in over a dozen academic journals, and recognized by *The Leadership Quarterly* as one of the top 50 most cited authors of the last decade, she also serves on the Review Board of *The Leadership Quarterly* and as an associate editor of *Leadership*. Prior to joining Neoma, Michelle was a professor at the Drucker–Ito School of Management at Claremont Graduate University (USA), where she served as Associate Dean. She has taught leadership and change management around the globe, including Europe, Asia, North America, and Latin America. She regularly consults with organizations in the areas of leadership development, organizational culture, and change management in a variety of industries, including law enforcement, finance, healthcare, and real estate. Michelle received her doctorate in management and organizational behavior and her master's degree in organizational culture and communication.

Melissa K. Carsten is Associate Professor of management at Winthrop University in Rock Hill, South Carolina. Prior to joining the faculty at Winthrop, she was a post-doctoral fellow in leadership at the University of Nebraska. Her research seeks to understand how followers' role beliefs and behaviors affect leaders and leadership processes in organizations, and how followers can work with leaders to form effective partnerships. Melissa has written several book chapters on leadership and followership, and has published her research in refereed journals such as *The Leadership Quarterly*, *Journal of Organizational Behavior*, *Organization Management Journal*, *Journal of Leadership and Organizational Studies*, and *Organizational Dynamics*. Melissa serves on the Editorial Board of *Group and Organization Management* and is an active member of the *Network of Leadership Scholars*. She has also consulted for both public and private organizations to build leadership development programs and conduct culture change initiatives. Her doctorate is in organizational psychology and her master's degree is in industrial-organizational psychology.

Marc Hurwitz is Co-author of *Leadership is Half the Story: A Fresh Look at Followership, Leadership, and Collaboration* (University of Toronto Press, 2015), Marc is the Co-founder and Chief Insight Officer of FliPskills, a training and development company that focuses on Followership, leadership, innovation, and Partnerships (FliP). For over 10 years Marc was a consulting partner with Thinkx, one of the top creativity firms in North America. With its founder, Tim Hurson (*Think Better*, McGraw-Hill), Marc co-developed new techniques for creativity that have been adopted by companies and consultants across America, Mexico, Europe, and Africa. Recognized with numerous awards for teaching, academic achievement, speaking, professional training, acting, and poetry, he is on faculty at the Conrad Business, Entrepreneurship and Technology Centre, University of Waterloo where he teaches business and entrepreneurial skills to graduate and undergraduate students. He holds a doctorate in cognitive neuroscience, a MBA, and master's degrees in physics and mathematics and combines that with many years of corporate, executive, and entrepreneurial experience in diverse areas from Marketing to HR to Actuarial.

About the Authors

Rodger Adair is Assistant Professor in the Keller Graduate School of Management at Devry University, Rodger authored a chapter in *The Art of Followership* and co-authored an article that appeared in the published proceedings for the 2014 International Followership Symposium. He is the current Chair of Community for the Followership Learning Community and former Chair for the Scholarship Member Interest Group of the International Leadership Association. An Arizona state level Malcolm Baldrige Examiner, Rodger's career focuses on organizational development, industrial psychology, and corporate training. He holds a PhD in industrial/ organizational psychology, a master's degree in organizational management, a MBA in international management, and a bachelor's degree in adult/workforce education.

Tanuja Agarwala is a Professor of human resource management and organizational behaviour at Faculty of Management Studies, University of Delhi, India. With 26 years of teaching and research experience, she has also received national and international awards for her research. She has authored a book and published several book chapters, journal articles, and conference papers in journals such as the *International Journal of Human Resource Management*, *Career Development International*, *Indian Journal of Industrial Relations*, and *the Indian Journal of Training and Development*. She is currently on the Editorial Advisory Board of *Equal Opportunities International* and the Editorial Review Board of *Gender in Management*. She also served as the guest editor for a special issue of *Gender in Management* on the theme of "women in academia."

Sharon Armstead is a Clinical Assistant Professor at Texas State University where she currently lectures and provides didactic training for RC students. She is a registered respiratory therapist with more than 30 years of clinical experience. She recently completed the 2015 Multicultural Curriculum Transformation Institute, and was awarded the Multicultural Designation (MC) for her senior level leadership and management course. She is a strong supporter of the American Association of Respiratory Care, National Board of Respiratory Care, and Coalition for Baccalaureate and Graduate Respiratory Therapy Education (CoBGRTE). Sharon has an Executive MBA.

Paul Berg, U.S. Army, is currently a military leadership instructor in the Department of Command and Leadership and Team Leader at the U.S. Army Command and General Staff College. During his career, LTC Berg served with the 1st Cavalry Division, 101st Airborne Division (Air Assault), 25th Infantry Division (Light) to include four combat tours. He is currently a doctoral student at Kansas State University majoring in adult and continuing education. He has master's degrees in marketing and adult and continuing education. His bachelor's degree is also in marketing.

Thomas Bisschoff is Senior Lecturer at the University of Birmingham in the School of Education and Emeritus Professor of the University of Johannesburg, South Africa, Tom is the former deputy president of the Commonwealth Council for Educational Administration and Management (CCEAM) and co-editor of the academic journal, *International Studies in Educational Administration* (ISEA). Author of several books and contributed chapters to books in the field of Educational Leadership, he has contributed over 30 research based papers to peer-reviewed journals. His latest book is on school finances, an increasingly important topic to schools in England and his latest paper is on the barriers that prevent deputy head teachers in England from moving into headship. Tom's research interests are around the establishment of academy schools in England, leaders and followership and educational leadership development in general.

B. Ariel Blair is a Doctoral Candidate in organizational behavior at Claremont Graduate University. In addition to studying followers in a global workforce, her research examines cross-cultural influences on team effectiveness, innovation, and minority dissent. She is currently conducting cross-national research comparing followership and follower dissent. Prior to returning to a doctoral program, Ariel spent more than 25 years in the business world focused on developing strong business strategy and the organizational capabilities needed to implement that strategy. During many years at Hewlett Packard Corporation, Ariel designed and led strategy and planning processes. Her education includes a bachelor's degree in development studies from Brown University, as well as a MBA from the Amos Tuck School at Dartmouth College.

Sandra Corlett is a Principal Lecturer in organization and human resource management at Newcastle Business School, Northumbria University. Her work has been published in *Gender in Management: An International Journal*, the *Journal of Business Ethics, Management*

Learning, and the *Scandinavian Journal of Management*. Her research interests broadly focus on identity and manager learning, and processes of identity work and becoming for managers and professionals. Sandra is currently Chair of the Identity Special Interest Group within the British Academy of Management.

Eric Downing is the Director of Organizational Development for Pioneer Investments, Inc., a global asset management corporation. A Registered Corporate Coach© (RCC©) and Six Sigma Black Belt practitioner, he has held various positions associated with organizational development within a Fortune 100 global asset management company for over 25 years. Eric has also conducted academic research in areas of individual inherent motivation and leadership style preferences. He holds a doctoral degree in interdisciplinary leadership, a master's degree in management and leadership, and a bachelor's degree in aeronautics.

Debra Finlayson is a human resources consultant specializing in organizational development for Vertical Bridge Corporate Consulting Inc. in Vancouver, Canada. She is the former manager of member relations for the Human Resources Management Association where she oversaw over 70 volunteers and delivered the professional development and regional services for over 2000 human resources members. Her 2014 MA dissertation focused on linking followership and professional reputation. She now plans to focus her PhD work on advancing research and understanding the cultural and global impacts of followership. Debra also serves as the current Chair of the Human Resources Advocacy Team for the Surrey Board of Trade.

Andrew Francis is Head of the Department of Marketing & Enterprise at Hertfordshire Business School in the UK. Andrew is currently a doctoral student in the School of Education at the University of Birmingham and is soon to complete his thesis on the followership of school teachers. His paper for the 2014 International Followership Symposium entitled Followership among UK Secondary School Teachers was published in the Journal of Leadership Education. Andrew previously worked as a Helicopter Engineer in the British Armed Forces and is a fellow of the Chartered Institute of Personnel & Development and of the Chartered Management Institute.

Heather Getha-Taylor is Associate Professor in the School of Public Affairs and Administration at the University of Kansas, Heather's research and teaching interests include public management, human resource management, public sector leadership, and collaborative governance. Her research has appeared in peer-reviewed journals and edited volumes. Prior to joining the faculty at the University of Kansas, Heather was a faculty member at the University of South Carolina. She is a member of the editorial boards of *Public Personnel Management* and *Review of Public Personnel Administration*. Her doctoral degree and master's degree are in public administration and her bachelor's degree is in communication.

William S. Harvey is Research Director and Senior Lecturer at the University of Exeter Business School, William has published in a range of journals in business and management, sociology, geography and industrial relations including: *Work, Employment and Society*, *Journal of Management Development*, *Work and Occupations*, *Employee Relations, Population, Space and Place*, *Qualitative Research*, *Global Networks*, *Asian Population Studies* and *Geoforum*. He has co-edited a book with Cambridge University Press on *International Human Resource Management* and has a co-authored book on leadership forthcoming with Cambridge University Press.

Eric K. Kaufman is "Faculty Principal" for the Honors Residential College at Virginia Tech. Eric also serves as an associate professor and Extension specialist in the Department of Agricultural, Leadership, and Community Education at Virginia Tech, where he teaches leadership courses for students in all disciplines at the graduate and undergraduate levels. He coordinates the graduate certificate program in Collaborative Community Leadership and supports the undergraduate minor in Leadership and Social Change. Eric is a past president of the Association of Leadership Educators. Eric's research interests include collegiate leadership education and leadership development with adults in community and volunteer settings. He holds a doctoral degree and master's degree in agricultural education and communication and a bachelor's degree in agricultural education.

Susan Keim is Director of Organizational Leadership at Donnelly College, Susan's areas of expertize are leadership, followership, organizational theory and behavior, citizen engagement, and local government. In addition, she facilitates strategic planning, community leadership and development, and team building for governments, businesses, and not-for-profits throughout the country. Susan's past leadership accomplishments include chairing the All-America City Steering Committee, which won the coveted All-America City Award for Kansas City, Kansas/Wyandotte County. She is also the founding chairperson of the Community Foundation of Wyandotte County. She has won the Preceptor Award and the Distinguished Leader Award from the Community Leadership Association and the Distinguished Leadership Award from the Kansas Leadership Forum.

Susan has a doctoral degree and a master's degree in public administration, as well as a bachelor's degree in political science.

Kimberley A. Koonce is the President of Can We Communicate, an agency committed to teaching, research, writing, and improving leader-follower relations in a wide variety of organizational contexts around the globe. Her research interests include understanding how visual art and artists can be used to positively impact follower and leader development. Kimberley holds an Executive MBA and is a recipient of the Ken Blanchard Servant Leadership Award. She is a part-time adjunct professor of organizational leadership.

Karlijn Kouwenhoven worked as an organizational change and leadership consultant at Deloitte's Human Capital Consulting practice in the Netherlands. She is specialized in personal development, leadership, and change management. As a facilitator for organizations, groups, and individuals, Karlijn combines a down to earth mindset with far eastern insights (e.g., deep democracy). She has a master's degree in social and organizational psychology.

Suzanne Martin is Senior Principal of transform, an organizational leadership coaching and consulting firm based in Birmingham, AL (USA), Suzanne spent 20 years in academia, teaching and providing leadership programs. For twelve years, she served as advisor, program director, and executive director for the Leading Edge Institute (LEI), a statewide leadership development program for college women with the mission of changing the face of leadership in Alabama. An avid volunteer, she is the volunteer district organizer for Bread for the World, a faith-based advocacy group seeking to end hunger and poverty. Suzanne also serves on the leadership team for the Alliance for Responsible Lending in Alabama (ARLA) and the Homewood Environmental Commission. She has a doctorate in organizational leadership and a master's of divinity. Her research interests include Mary Parker Follett, followership, conflict, dialogue, presence, women's leadership, and invisible leadership.

Rachael Morris is graduate tutor and PhD candidate at Newcastle Business School, Northumbria University, Rachael was selected by an international panel of judges as the winner of the Student Competition for the 2014 International Followership Symposium. Her work has been published in the *Journal of Leadership Education* and the *Journal of Business Ethics*. Her current research on followership adopts qualitative and visual research methodologies.

Jennifer Moss Breen is Director of the Interdisciplinary Leadership EdD Program and an associate professor at Creighton University. She also serves as the 2015–2016 President of the Association for

Leadership Educators (ALE). Prior to joining Creighton University, Jennifer was the founding director of Bellevue University's PhD in Human Capital Management. She earned her doctorate in leadership studies and a master's degree in qualitative and quantitative psychometric measures. She is currently conducting research on leadership humility, leadership resilience, interdisciplinary education, and leadership education in medical school.

TamilSelvan Ramis is a former columnist for Free Malaysia Today where he primarily covered social issues in Malaysia, Tamilselvan is currently serving as a tutor in the Department of Psychology at HELP University in Kuala Lumpur, Malaysia. He completed his bachelor's degree in psychology at the University of British Columbia, Canada with a Wesbrook Scholar designation, the university's most prestigious designation awarded on the basis of outstanding academic performance, leadership, and involvement in student and community activities. His research interests lie in the areas of social psychology and educational psychology.

Kae Reynolds is Senior Lecturer in the Department of People, Management and Organisations at the University of Huddersfield Business School and a Fellow of The Higher Education Academy in the United Kingdom. She is an international business communication expert having gained extensive professional experience in German multinational corporations. Kae received a Greenleaf Scholar Award for her dissertation research on servant leadership. She serves on the Editorial Board for the *Journal of Leadership Education* and as a referee for other peer-reviewed leadership journals and conferences. Her research interests include ethical leadership and followership, servant leadership, feminist ethics, leadership education, women and leadership, as well as the application of content analysis and critical research perspectives.

Rushton 'Rusty' Ricketson Sr is Professor of leadership for Luther Rice College and Seminary. He is the author of *Followerfirst: Rethinking Leading in the Church* (Heartworks Publications) now in its second edition. His research interests include followership, as well as leader and follower roles and responsibilities within church and for profit organizations. His doctorate is in organizational leadership with a major in human resource development. He also has a master's of divinity degree and a bachelor's degree in social science education.

Rhonda K. Rodgers is an organizational psychologist and founding partner at Way of Well-Being, a Los Angeles based consulting firm that specializes in self-management training and well-being mentorship for individuals and groups. Her management experience spans industries from industrial supply to international logistics.

Rhonda's passion of pursuing authenticity in one's work and life inspired an article co-authored by Michelle Bligh entitled *Exploring the "Flip Side" of the Coin: Do Authentic Leaders Need Authentic Followers?* The article appeared in Lapierre and Carsten's (2014) edited volume of *Followership: What is it and why do people follow?* (Emerald Group Publishing Limited). She has a MBA in entrepreneurship and a master's degree in organizational behavior.

Sonya Rogers is Lead Professor for the College of Business at Columbia Southern University, Sonja's passion for leadership includes team building, communication, professionalism, followership, inclusion, and career development. She has received a Spotlight on Excellence Award for her many writings and public relation's submissions as an educational columnist. Her doctorate is in organizational leadership. She also has a master's degree in elementary education and a bachelor's degree in psychology and human services.

James H. Schindler is Author of *Followership: What It Takes to Lead* (Business Experts Press, 2014), James is a professor of Business Administration at Columbia Southern University where he teaches graduate leadership, strategic management, and research methods courses. His doctorate is in business administration with a concentration in leadership. He also has a master's degree in personnel management and an undergraduate degree in biology and chemistry.

Steven Lee Smith is a retired naval officer, working in academia as an Associate Professor and in university administration, Steve is the recipient of the William P. Foster Dissertation of the Year Award, University of San Diego, as well as numerous military awards to include the Nippon Zenkokai Award for humanitarian orphanage work on Okinawa and the Meritorious Service Award from Po Wha Bo Yook Won Orphanage, Korea. His recent publication, *The Uprising of POW/MIA Wives: How Determined Women Forced America, Hanoi, and the World to Change* appeared in the proceedings for the 2014 International Followership Symposium. His research interests are in the areas of powerless people influencing change, leader-follower exchange, applied ethics and morality, goodness, and spirituality. He holds a doctoral degree in education and leadership science and a master's degree in divinity.

Eugene Y. J. Tee is presently a Senior Lecturer in the Department of Psychology at HELP University in Kuala Lumpur, Malaysia. His work on emotions in leader-follower interactions has appeared in the Leadership Quarterly, Advancing Relational Leadership Theory, and Research on Emotions in Organizations. Eugene continues to collaborate with international researchers and research students on topics such as emotional contagion, emotional intelligence, and emotional labor. He is a member of the International Society for Research on Emotion (ISRE), Asian Association for Social Psychology (AASP), International Association of Applied Psychology, Academy of Management (AoM), and the Australian and New Zealand Academy of Management (ANZAM). Eugene's doctorate is in management.

Douglas S. E. Teoh is currently pursuing a master's degree in cultural studies at the University of Nottingham, Malaysia Campus. After serving at HELP University as a Psychology Tutor, he worked with Institut Rakyat, a think-tank whose role is to advise parliamentarians and policy makers as well as contribute to public debates on current socio-political issues. He is also active as a socio-political commentator for Aliran Kesedaran Negara, the oldest human rights group in Malaysia. His current research interests lie in the areas of critical psychology and qualitative research.

Ted Thomas (ret) is the Director of the Department of Command and Leadership in the U.S. Army Command and General Staff College (CGSC) at Ft. Leavenworth, Kansas. He joined the faculty at CGSC in 2005 before becoming the director in 2007. Ted served 20 years in various command and staff positions before retiring as a Battalion Commander of the 554th Engineer Battalion. His doctorate is in engineering management and his master's degree is in civil engineering.

Rens van Loon is Professor of Dialogical Leadership at the School of Humanities, Tilburg University, and a director at Deloitte Consulting. He is specialized in leadership and organizational change and transformation. A consultant for more than 25 years, Rens has developed global leadership programs and worked closely with leaders in both the private and public sectors. He is a board member of the International Leadership Association (ILA), member of TAOS, and active in the International Society for Dialogical Science (ISDS). He completed his doctorate in social sciences and psychology and a master's degree in philosophy with a minor in psychology.

W. David Winner is the recipient of the 2012 Bentley Brittingham Award for Academic Achievement and Contribution to Learning. He is a professor at Northampton Community College where he has been a past nominee for the Adjunct Excellence in Teaching Award. He holds a doctorate in organizational leadership with a major in human resource development and a master's of divinity degree. His research interests include leadership sternness and self-directed learning.

Case Matrix

	CASE											
	1	2	3	4	5	6	7	8	9	10	11	12
	The Fam	**Mission**	**Alert**	**Exec**	**MPFoll**	**Corp Pres**	**Invest**	**Paradox**	**JIT**	**Diversity**	**Reput**	**Dancing**
Primary Topics												
Business	X	X	X	X	X	X	X	X	X	X	X	
Education / The Arts												X
Ethics												
Government												
Military												
Sub-Topics												
Board Relations		X										
Conflict Resolution					X					X		
Consulting						X					X	
Corporate / For-profit	X					X					X	
Culture				X								
Cybersecurity												
Decision Making												
Dialogue	X											X
Diversity										X		
Franchising	X											
Hierarchy	X											X
Human Resources												
Identity									X		X	
Mergers / Acquisitions				X								
Mindset	X											
Mutuality				X								
Non-profit		X										
Organizational/Work Climate					X							
Performance				X				X	X			
Power					X							
Promotion								X	X	X		
Reputation											X	
Self Discovery												
Team Relations			X		X					X		
Training and Development							X	X	X			

	CASE												
	13	14	15	16	17	18	19	20	21	22	23	24	25
	U Prof	Artist	CyberSec	Resident	Sec School	Wave	VHA	Tale/Power	Pub Sector	Mistake	Electoral	Mid Gov	Madoff
Primary Topics													
Business													
Education / The Arts	X	X	X	X	X								
Ethics						X		X		X	X		X
Government							X				X		
Military												X	
Sub-Topics													
Board Relations			X							X			
Conflict Resolution									X				
Consulting										X			
Corporate / For-profit								X					X
Culture													
Cybersecurity			X										
Decision Making			X	X		X	X			X			
Dialogue				X									
Diversity													
Franchising													
Hierarchy	X				X	X	X	X	X				
Human Resources													
Identity	X					X					X		
Mergers / Acquisitions													
Mindset													
Mutuality	X								X				
Non-profit													
Organizational/Work Climate							X					X	
Performance					X		X						
Power				X		X	X	X	X		X		
Promotion													
Reputation													
Self Discovery		X											
Team Relations	X			X		X						X	X
Training and Development													